An Ethiopian Odyssey

A return to the past to discover my destiny

Annette Allen

AuthorHouse™ UK Ltd.
500 Avebury Boulevard
Central Milton Keynes, MK9 2BE
www.authorhouse.co.uk
Phone: 08001974150

First published by AuthorHouse 7/31/2009

ISBN: 978-1-4343-5704-5 (sc)

Library of Congress Control Number: 2007909749

Printed in the United States of America
Bloomington, Indiana

This book is printed on acid-free paper.

Half of the royalties will be helping to provide water and a future for the very poor in Ethiopia, and hope in the Middle East.

Dedication

To my father, Ben Allen, the globe-trotting engineer
Thank you for your risk-taking nature;
To my mother, Halldis, the extrovert
Thank you for teaching me to care for others;
And to Marta Asrat, my classmate
Thank you for finding the names which enabled my odyssey.
May you all rest in peace.

Freedom

Whoever I am
I am no different from you,
Whatever I have
I am no better than you,
However deep my knowledge,
It is no greater than your faith.

So knowing that, you and I
Have nothing to fear from each other,
Just the freedom to give
All that we each are.

Contents

IV: Europe

V: USA

VI: Conclusion

Index

Acknowledgements:

Thanks are due to so many people, because without them this journey – and book – would never have been possible. A huge hug to Rob and James for listening patiently to my stories and letting me travel 25,000 miles! I am also very grateful to Ethiopian Airlines, my father's former employer, for being the first to step forward and help me, with a discount ticket.

Theodros Abraham; Wolde Absa, Ethiopian Airlines; Eshetu Aredo, AGOHELD; Evelyn Albrecht; Revd. Kevin and Alyson Ashby; Mary Asfaw Wossen; Freghenet Asseged; Mulugeta Kassa Asrate; Jack and Therese Atamian; John Bercow MP; The 'Buckingham Advertiser'; Michael Buerk; Kidist Dagnew; DPP Publicity; The Door magazine; Bernd Dreesmann; Tirlaye Gebre Medhin; Girma and Tiringo, Ras Amba Hotel; Ghennet Girma; Fedrelandsvennen newspaper, Kristiansand; Silva and Jack Hagopian; MediaVision; Ken Lee; Einar Lunde; Mary Nalbandian; Helen Pankhurst and the WaterAid team in Ethiopia; Paul Pavey; Louise Raimondo; SS Peter and Paul's Church, Buckingham; The Royal Collection; Fanaye Saifou; Rui Santos; Allen Scott; Odd Inge Skjaevesland; Abune Berhaneyesus Souraphiel; Roger Stotesbury; Liben and the Tadias team; Leikun Teferra; Abba Bogale Tiruneh; Atamenta Tsige; Archbishop Desmond Tutu; Jack Valero, Opus Dei; Voice of America Horn of Africa team; Myles Wickstead; Gill Williams – a great sister; President Girma Wolde-Giorgis and Linda Woolston.

And finally to Nicky Falkof, my editor, for working so hard with me in turning the initial manuscript into something I could be proud of.

Preface

April 2000

Heat scorched my scalp and trickles of sweat ran down my face. The fierce unrelenting sun illuminated the parched, red ochre soil on which I stood with an Ethiopian couple, friends of mine.

In the distance, smoke drifted from the thatched roofs of round tukuls (mud huts) while the tall eucalyptus trees whispered a soft melody as a breeze wove through their leaves. I realised with a start that I was back – back in the foothills of Addis Ababa, the capital of Ethiopia, which I'd last seen in July 1964.

As the dream continued, we talked about poverty and drought – the cause of so many famines in the country. The man leaned towards me, making a point and stabbing his finger at the ground. Suddenly I knelt down and began to rub the dry soil between my fingers. At that moment, an overwhelming feeling engulfed me: I knew beyond all doubt that I was there to help provide permanent clean water for Ethiopia's poor. With that intuition, the dream faded.

Waking with a start, I reached for the bedside light. It was 3.30am and the sky outside was still a deep blue, waiting for the sunrise. Why had I had that dream? Why now? I didn't even have any Ethiopian friends: I'd lost contact many years ago with my friends from Nazareth School, a Catholic girls' school in Addis.

I'd been horrified by the stories of mass killings during Colonel Mengistu's Marxist regime in the late 1970s and 1980s, known as the Red Terror. I'd watched Michael Buerk's 1984 report about the famine caused by drought in northern Ethiopia with tears running down my cheeks. I'd given money during LiveAid. Then Ethiopia had become a dim and distant memory once more.

But somewhere inside me, I knew that this dream was just as important as the others I'd had since 1970. These lay locked in my mind's treasure chest, waiting for me to open it one day.

Two years after the dream, I was made redundant. I was sick of it – the third time in a decade. It didn't matter how hard I worked or how successful my projects were, politics were politics. After my boss told me the news I'd been expecting, I buried my head in my hands. What would Rob, my husband, say? It had been just three years since the last time. How about James, our eleven-year-old? We'd moved twice in two years because of my insecure jobs. But a comforting thought filled my mind: 'You're going to be alright,' it said.

I told my boss that I'd make the most of the opportunity to work part time so that I could become a writer, a calling I'd nurtured for seven years, and that some of the book's profits would be used to provide water in Ethiopia. I had no idea then how I'd achieve it, but I was absolutely determined to make my dream come true.

*****

This is the story of my journey to find nine former classmates from my school days in Addis Ababa, the tests I'd faced before that decision was finally made and the guides and amazing synchronicity I experienced along the way.

We'd lived in Ethiopia for two years when my father worked for Ethiopian Airlines as chief testbed engineer. Nazareth School was one of eight I attended in six years: my father was an itinerant traveller, and we trailed behind him with our suitcases and shattered dreams of a permanent home and loyal friends. We had lived all over the UK, and finally ended up in South Africa during the apartheid era: an unhappy time for us.

From 1972, I was finally free to make my own way in life. After that I'd done what was expected of me - worked hard, climbed the corporate ladder, met and married Rob and, amazingly, had James against all odds, after I was diagnosed with severe endometriosis in 1987.

Becoming pregnant in 1988 had made me really believe in miracles. I'd had two operations, but after I was given the diagnosis and debilitating medication, I suddenly woke up to a great longing for a child. On the phone to a friend one afternoon, tears welled up and starting coursing down my cheeks as I told her that I'd only just realised how much I'd love to become a mother. I decided to use my simple faith to pray for a child, and then forgot all about it. Within twelve months, the unbelievable had come true and the pregnancy test showed a clear blue line.

James was born in 1989, and as he grew up, I changed too. Being with him was magical: what I most appreciated was his spontaneity and sheer joy in being alive. I'd long forgotten those feelings in the planning and doing of work: I'd become boring, lifeless, and felt that life was too stressful and meaningless. In fact, the more I had, the less I felt I had.

Something was missing – could life really still be an adventure? How many more miracles were waiting to be uncovered, glinting there in the deep earth, shimmering beneath the water, hidden at the top of great mountains?

So when the opportunity arrived in 2002, I set off to find my destiny, and to discover all that I was meant to be. I decided to travel light – I would use just faith and prayers, and be led by my dreams and the kind guides whom I'd meet along the way. I had no idea how things would proceed, but I decided to abandon planning and live a freer life.

It was vital that I find some way to integrate my dream of writing with the covenant I'd made with God in 1995. I realised with hindsight that my constant failures thereafter had happened because I hadn't honoured it. Loosening the bonds of limited thinking, I just focused on being the peace I wanted to see in the world, providing water and helping the very poor in a pragmatic way.

As I travelled, I also learned that I had to give up all my assumptions and beliefs about life and people, and just enter the flow. My ego was very upset at times, but it learned to shut up and, over time, completely let go of the need to control people and events. I wanted every step to be sure, confirmed in the stars and my dreams – to let the true magnificence of my life unfold.

Every word in this book is true. I hope it will inspire you to listen to and live out the dreams that may be locked in your heart, and become all that you're capable of being. Most of all, I pray these pages help you appreciate that following your life's purpose lets you discover just how connected you are to every living thing on this planet.

Today I am still on the journey, and that is the most important thing of all.

Annette Allen

Buckingham
October 2006

For students and others interested in source material, I have included information at the end of each chapter, which is not intended to be exhaustive. All the interviews have been double-checked and approved by the people concerned.

I: ETHIOPIA 1962 – 1964

1 Eucalyptus, kisses and hot curries

It was at London's Heathrow airport in August 1962 when, with a heavy heart, I boarded the Ethiopian Airlines turbo prop with mum, my twin brother Roy and my younger brother Eric, bound for Addis Ababa.

Along with good friends and memories, we were leaving behind Jackie and Gill, our two half-sisters. Dad had been a young widower when he met Halldis, my mother, who was Norwegian. His first wife, Doreen, had died from TB when the girls were very young and they'd been farmed off to relatives and then to boarding school. He'd never spoken about Doreen, which made me feel sad for Jackie and Gill. But they were almost grown up now – Jackie was training to be a nurse, whilst Gill had moved into a bedsit, and was looking for a job after she'd completed her A levels.

Gazing out of the airplane window on the way to our new life, I hoped that this would be the last of our moves for a while. At nine years old, my next school was to be my fifth. Dad was an itinerant traveller, he never seemed to settle anywhere for long. He didn't get on with his father, and mum's relatives were all in Norway, so we had virtually no contact with our extended family. No point complaining, that's just the way it was.

Arriving in Addis Ababa was a huge shock to all my senses. Being so close to the equator, Ethiopia was incredibly hot in summer. Apart from the June to September rainy season, the heat was unrelenting.

In addition to the high temperatures, there was the dirt. Even walking along the street could be hazardous: litter was thrown down any convenient path or hillside, men would urinate wherever they wanted to and the smell from the open drains was unspeakable, full of rotting food and raw sewage. Pavements were located haphazardly, as the new city began to sprawl outwards. The most westernised areas were in the piazza where the better shops and cinemas were located, and around the two main palaces: Menelik at the top of the city and the Jubilee Palace, built in 1955, where Emperor Haile Selassie had his court and offices, at the bottom of Menelik II Avenue. But a trip on a gari – a horse and trap taxi, where I'd sit beside mum and the driver – would soon dispel the heat and odours.

We joined thousands of foreigners, or 'faranj' as the Ethiopians called us. Some nationalities had been there for centuries, others were more recent arrivals. There were Greeks, French and Italians who'd made their home in the country after Mussolini's army was ousted in 1941, along with Egyptians, Yemenis, Swiss, German, Portuguese, Israelis and efficient, hard-working Indians. There were also many Armenians, most of whose parents or grandparents were refugees from the genocide, when one and a half million were massacred between 1915 – 1923 by the Ottoman Turks and driven from their homeland forever.

And then there were the Americans. A few of them came to work for Ethiopian Airlines, at that time owned by Trans World Airlines, part of the multi-millionaire Howard Hughes's business empire. Out in the bush were the missionaries, intent on converting heathen tribes to Christianity. In 1962 more Americans arrived - the first Peace Corps volunteers to visit the country.

Ethiopia has a very special place in the heart of Africans and black people across the globe. It has never been colonised by Europeans apart from the brief Italian invasion, thus its culture is uniquely African. Its emperors claim direct descent from the Queen of Sheba who, according to Biblical tales, had a love affair with King Solomon during a visit to Jerusalem. She returned to Ethiopia, pregnant with King Menilek, and created the line called Judah, with emperors being granted divine rule.

Later in his life, Menilek went to visit the father he'd never seen. Legend has it that he returned to Ethiopia with the Ark of the Covenant, the beautifully decorated wooden cask which held the stone tablet containing the ten commandments handed down by God to Moses at Mount Sinai. Today a priest in Maryam Seyon (Mary of Zion), a small church in Aksum, northern Ethiopia, keeps this under careful guard. Ethiopia is also the reputed home of part of the cross on which Jesus Christ was crucified, but like the Ark, it remains unseen. [1]

Emperor Haile Selassie had been on the throne for 32 years when we arrived, and it was a golden time for his empire. Roads outside the city were being extended, hydroelectric dams constructed to provide electricity to the growing population, and work was well underway on the headquarters of the Organisation for African Unity (now the African Union) on Menelik II Avenue, right opposite the Jubilee Palace. With the increase in air travel, Ethiopia was becoming an exotic holiday destination for the more adventurous traveller, just ten hours from London.

Our first home in the capital was Hotel Villa Verde. A single storey, white-washed building with a green roof, window shutters and doors, it looked out onto the Addis – Djibouti railway line, the only one in Ethiopia and the country's link to the sea. Our footsteps would clatter on the cool, grey Italian marble passageway to the hotel's restaurant. A remnant of the Italian occupation, Villa Verde was run by the ample Italian owners, Senor Tiso and his wife Maria. I remember his good-natured laugh and the glinting gold teeth at the side of his mouth. Their Alsatian was equally rotund – good eating ran in the family! I developed a real passion for good food there: the three-course meals were mouth-watering, and my waistline soon thickened.

In the African heat, the flora and fauna were magnificent – the deep fragrance of the giant white angels' trumpets outside infused my bedroom. Bright pink bougainvillaea tumbled over pots by the entrance and the wind whispered and sighed through the slender leaves of the tall eucalyptus trees bordering the river at the far end of the grounds. They seemed to be everywhere, like giant slim fans cooling and perfuming the hot city air. I discovered how good they were at clearing blocked noses when I rubbed the leaves between my fingers and sniffed them.

Like the plants, insects and animals were much larger in the African heat. There were the red soldier ants with their large pincers for biting and killing: I found out just how painful a bite could be when I wandered into the path of an advancing army one afternoon. Butterflies came in iridescent colours – the pale blue ones with orange circles in the middle of their wings were my favourites. Vultures would circle the city each day, looking for wounded dogs or other animals, gradually flying closer and closer until they flopped ungainly to the ground. Their large hooked beaks would dive into the flesh and soon they'd be ripping it to pieces as they gorged themselves, flapping and squawking to keep their position. But above all, I was entranced by the little hummingbirds - the sun's rays broke up their breast feathers into shimmering rainbows of colour while wings whirred a thousand times a minute, enabling their long beaks to suck nectar from the open hibiscus flowers.

Soon after settling in to our new home, I accompanied mum to look at the local schools. We decided on the Nazareth School for Girls, my first all girls' establishment. It was to be a wrench, as it meant I wouldn't be in the same school as Roy. He and Eric were going to St. Joseph's, a Christian Brothers school not far from the Jubilee Palace.

Nazareth was the first Catholic school I'd attended, run by French Canadian Sisters. It was much bigger than my previous ones and taught girls aged from three (kindergarten) to 18, based on the American schooling system. The main building was T-shaped, with classrooms on two floors looking onto a broad street, iron railings and gates marking its perimeter. The dining room and small chapel were on the ground floor, at the rear of the classrooms.

I walked shyly through those open gates on my first day, my new red shoes gleaming. The girls stood up as Miss Bouchard introduced me. Scanning the faces, I was overwhelmed by the variety of skin colours, hairstyles, dress and ages. I learned later that students were placed in the class that suited their academic ability rather than their age.

The girls introduced themselves one by one. Miss Bouchard was enormously proud of the fact that we had two princesses in grade 5A, Princesses Mary and Sihin, Asfaw Wossen, granddaughters of the Emperor. I felt that it would take quite a while to get used to my new classmates and the stricter school regime – talking in class was strictly forbidden here.

But after that first day, I was greeted with a handshake from each of my classmates and, more often than not, a kiss on both cheeks, with a warm 'tanasterlign' – God give you health - every day. I was soon adopted as the baby of the class.

For the first month or so I had school lunches in the dining room, which was always cool, no matter what the weather. There was a selection of white bread sandwiches but the only hot food was injera, a pancake of unleavened, very sour bread made from tef grain, and watt, a spicy curry made with different types of meat – beef and lamb were popular, or sometimes shuro, made from vegetables. I managed to eat some, enjoying the pungency. From October onwards I took sandwiches from home and would swap them for my Armenian classmates' falafels, more injera and watt or the chips (crisps) the American girls would often bring with them.

Discipline at Nazareth School was much stricter, and for the first time I got detention when I talked in class. Religion, which had been confined to weekly school assemblies and Sunday school in England, was much more part of the school day, beginning with the Hail Mary every morning. Even now I can see my classmates holding their rosary beads, heads bowed, reciting after the teacher, "Hail Mary, full of grace, the Lord is with thee, blessed art thou amongst women..."

There were five nationalities in my class, a cross section of the different influences in Ethiopia. Kathy Miller and Penelope Heilman were American: Kathy was a lively, ginger haired girl with freckles scattered over every inch of her skin, while Penny, as she preferred to be called, was petite, with beautiful wavy auburn hair tumbling over her shoulders. There was Phoebe Khalil, a studious Egyptian with a mellow laugh and a plait of thick curly black hair; Celina Fernandes, a tall, graceful Indo-Portuguese girl from Goa; Sumitra Goyal, an Indian whose arms tinkled as she walked, with her gold bracelets and handkerchief always tucked in her cardigan: and four Armenians, most of whom seemed to be related.

I was closest in age and temperament to Kathy. Unlike many of the other American students, she wasn't inclined to show off her many clothes or a large sandwich box stuffed with treats from the PX, the tax-free store where Americans could buy US products. We would often sit and have a chat at break time. Penny left the school not long after I arrived – her mother had died from carbon monoxide poisoning whilst she'd been taking a bath. Her father took Penny home after that – their memories of the country forever tainted.

I also liked Fanaye Saifou a great deal, a small, slight Ethiopian who wore her long plaited hair pinned to the top of her head. Fanaye was a solitary person and I learned that she lived with her grandparents, who were quite strict. She also told me that she rarely saw her mother, which must have been very lonely for her. Perhaps that was why she recognised my loneliness and would do her best to cheer me up – her scratchy laugh was very unusual and she often succeeded in snapping me out of my homesickness.

Celina Fernandes was the tallest among us. I imagined that she must have taken after her father in height. She often appeared anxious, her brows knitted in bewilderment. She had a lilting accent, so typical of the Goan people and, unlike Sumitra, she always let her long hair fall free like a curtain, with just a bow at the back. Silva Derentz, one of the four Armenians in the class, made a mark on me too,

17

with her mischievous chuckles in class. I was amazed to find that she could speak fluent Amharic, the main Ethiopian language, but then she had been born here, like many of her compatriots. Sumitra was the most demure – it was a time of raging hormones for many of my classmates, but she always seemed serene and I used to look forward to seeing what colour sari she'd be wearing every day.

Lastly were Princess Mary and her sister, Princess Sihin, whom I sat beside in grade 5A, my first year at Nazareth. Sharing a class with two princesses whose grandfather was known as the Lion of Judah could be tricky. We were told to treat Mary and Sihin as normal girls, but that was at odds with their grandfather's status. He was considered divine by many Ethiopians and by the Jamaicans too. Rastafarianism comes from his name Ras (Prince) Tafari.

We had a bad case of head lice in the school one month, and as part of the treatment the teachers were asked to inspect everyone's hair and scalp. After everyone else in the class had had their inspection, Princess Mary quietly walked up to have her scalp checked. The look of horror and embarrassment on Miss Bouchard's face was a real picture.

"Oh no, no, I don't need to inspect your hair, I'm sure it's very clean," she squeaked. The rest of us chuckled at her discomfort.

*****

The need to be on your best behaviour with the royals extended to life outside school too. If one of the royal family's limousines appeared we soon learned that we had to stop our car, get out and bow. We children found it quite a lot of fun, but I imagine it was somewhat irritating and time-consuming for the adults: we had to bow deeply from the waist, as a slight nod of the head wasn't enough.

Visits by heads of states were major occasions, and every school child would have the day off. We would all line up beside the iron railings outside the Jubilee Palace in our class groups with the Ethiopian green, yellow and red paper flags to wave. You could tell when the Emperor was on his way back to the palace, as cheers would go up. Then the huge Rolls Royce with large windows would appear. The car's size made the Emperor appear even smaller as he sat perched on the seat with his prestigious guest beside him.

Next would come the black Mercedes of more junior members of the royal family and government officials. Finally, taking up the rear of the cavalcade was one of Haile Selassie's lions, gazing disdainfully at us from the back of an open-sided Land Rover. A thick chain encircled one of his paws, but as his yellow eyes looked down on the crowds there was no doubting who was king, and we all shrank from the barriers before he turned his magnificent head away.

Despite my initial homesickness, I soon settled into a routine. School began and finished earlier than in the UK, so we'd have plenty of time to play outside before the swift African sunset descended. It was a matter of no more than 30 minutes between light and inky darkness. Roy, Eric and I often wandered down to the river at the back of the hotel, to see what animals and lizards we could spot. Sometimes we were accompanied by the one of the stray dogs that hung around the hotel, waiting for scraps. They were full of fleas so we didn't encourage them to come near us. We'd jump across the river, which was quite narrow in places, and play hide and seek among the shrubs and eucalyptus trees.

At weekends we explored the city or ventured out of the capital. One Sunday we visited Addis Ababa's zoo, a small facility with mangy lions sitting yawning in tiny cages or walking to and fro out of sheer boredom. It seemed very cruel to me when Africa was their home, and they should be roaming free in the mountains and across the grasslands. We visited the zoo with a British colonel who'd moved into Villa Verde shortly after us, a man in his 60s with a handlebar moustache and a military bearing. I never found out what he was doing there – perhaps working for the army or advising the Emperor. That same afternoon we'd wandered up to Holy Trinity Cathedral, the main Orthodox Church just north of the city centre. We meandered among the gravestones and memorials, and mum called us over when she found a name she recognised.

"Come over here," she cried. "Look at this!" she said excitedly. "It's the grave of Sylvia Pankhurst. She was a famous suffragette who lived here for a little while."

"What's a suffragette, mum?" I asked.

"A woman who campaigned for women to get the vote," she explained. "They were very brave – they even went on hunger strikes and staged demonstrations outside the Houses of Parliament. The Pankhurst family were all involved, mother and three daughters."

After six months we moved to a bungalow in one of the suburbs of Addis, down a long cobbled road. Like all the European-style houses, it was surrounded by high walls with a tall security gate topped by spikes. Wide red tiled steps and a veranda welcomed visitors, leading to the mahogany front door and shuttered windows overlooked the road and the small community beside the house.

In the rainy season, when torrents poured down from the heavens onto the corrugated steel roof, the noise sounded like a barrage of gunshots. Outside, the road would be a swirling river of mud within ten minutes and we had to switch on the lights as dark clouds closed in overhead, punctuated only by shafts of lightning and the roar of thunder. Unlucky passers-by would be drenched in minutes - they ran past, often holding soggy pieces of newspaper over their heads, scant use against the deluge.

In the front garden was a large banana palm – unfortunately, the altitude was too high for it to bear fruit. Succulent plants grew all around, including canna lilies sprouting like weeds, their graceful wine glass-shaped heads tilted up to catch the sun's rays. On the left hand side was the garage, and behind the house the servants' quarters: two bare rooms and a very basic shower and toilet, where our sabanya - night watchman - lived. The other guard was our dog Sessan (Swedish for princess), a half-breed grey and black bitch who slept in a kennel beside the garage. A gift from friends, she'd hurl herself around the garden, barking like crazy at any stranger who dared come near.

Inside was a large lounge and combined dining room, three bedrooms and a small, square kitchen overlooking the back. We often had friends round to play, or we'd visit them. Within those walls I was introduced to the BBC *World Service,* and it became a habit to gather around it and listen to the early evening news, with the six pips which preceded the announcement, "This is the BBC *World Service,* and now the news at six o'clock Greenwich Mean Time."

The World Service was our door to pop music: I remember first hearing the Beatles' *Please, please me* and thinking what a great song it was. It sounded so different to the ballads of Frank Sinatra, Matt Monro and Perry Como, which my parents loved.

I really struggled to understand the great contrast between the rich and poor in Ethiopia - I had never encountered grinding poverty before. On the roads near the palaces and grand homes with their manicured lawns, donkeys and goats would jostle for space with women bent double from the firewood on their backs, which they would sell for a few cents in the market. Everywhere you looked there were beggars, unable to survive in the countryside. The worst were the deformed, some with hands missing from leprosy, others with the hugely swollen limbs of elephantiasis. I felt most sorry for those crippled by polio or cerebral palsy, who took their lives in their hands when crossing roads. They would somehow cross one leg over the other and swing across the tarmac using two wooden bricks with holes cut out for their hands, while impatient drivers hooted their horns. They were too poor for wheelchairs.

We'd been in the house for a few weeks when dad brought home a 'house boy', Matthew, whom he'd found wandering around the perimeter at Bole airport. After Matthew's mother died, his father had remarried. His stepmother turned out to be wicked, just like in the fairytales, and forced him to leave. She had her own children and didn't want another mouth to feed. He was thin, dressed in rags and not much taller than me, even though he was 14. We used to chat when we washed up after the evening meal.

My parents said I was wrong to talk to him, because I was encouraging him – but to do what? Perhaps it was this unspoken distrust that led him to steal some money and drink a little of our vodka and gin when we were away. So he was dismissed. Again he went out into the world on his own. I tried to imagine what it would be like to feel bereft and terrified – where would he sleep the next night? Perhaps, like others in his position, he turned to crime to survive, because no one had listened to him except an eleven-year-old girl. His disappearance was to haunt much of my life.

Beside our house was a small community of round mud huts - tukuls - that allowed us to have some contact with ordinary Ethiopians, rather than the wealthy or middle class whom my parents mixed with. I used to enjoy sitting outside on the back step and watching what was going on. Once a week the local butcher would slaughter a cow out in the open. Within an hour, he had skilfully cut the meat into portions and one by one families would queue to select and pay for their cut. Nothing was wasted, as the entrails were regarded as a delicacy. Having good fresh meat was always a cause for celebration. Later that afternoon, smoke from fires for the evening meal would drift over our fence. The tang of beef and spices used for the local watt hung in the air and always made me hungry.

Occasionally funeral processions would wend their way past our house. The mourners, all in black, would walk behind their relative's coffin, with the women wailing. The long, drawn out keening and 'la, la, la, la, la, la' used to make my hair stand on end, a fitting send-off for the departed.

Along with the hubbub of people walking by our gates, occasional cars and the ubiquitous gari, there was a constant sound of prayers. A Muslim Arab had a small hexagonal wood and corrugated iron shop beside our house, selling sweets, postcards, papers, cigarettes, lighters and soft drinks. Inside there was only enough room for one adult to stand or sit on a small stool. I would watch quietly as he took out his prayer mat, washed his hands and took off his shoes. He would face Mecca, stand and say his prayers and then kneel on the mat before bowing to Allah, all the while reciting loudly. It was good to see such devout faith first hand, as we no longer went to church and Sunday school was firmly behind us. In our family, religion was confined purely to school from 1962 onwards.

In July 1963, I wished my classmates a happy holiday and we travelled back to England for a month's break. I knew that most of my friends would be returning in the autumn, except for Princesses Mary and Sihin. They were off to board at Benenden School, Kent, the same one attended by HRH Princess Anne. I was sad to say goodbye, knowing that sitting beside a real princess had been a unique experience. Perhaps I would do so again one day.

Further information:

① Stuart Munro-Hay, *The Quest for the Ark of the Covenant,* p. 205,
      I.B.Tauris, 2005
BBC *World Service*   www.bbc.co.uk/worldservice

2 Mountains, lakes and lions

Returning to Addis Ababa felt a little more like coming home. It was good to see our house and Sessan, our dog, was overjoyed, swooping between our legs and jumping up and licking our faces. I buried my face in her fur and smelled the dust, rain and hot sun of the last month. It was comforting to return to school clutching my new red lunchbox, bought for five shillings in Woolworths, and be reassured that most of the faces would be familiar: perhaps someone else would be the new girl.

Life settled back into the normal round of lessons, homework, occasional trips to the cinema, meeting friends and getting out to the countryside at weekends in our VW Combi. International events didn't really touch us – there was only the radio, and dad didn't always buy the local paper. Mum would buy *Woman,* an English magazine, and the American publication *Life,* often three months out of date. I liked the latter, with its news photographs. We would regularly gather around the radio for the news at 6pm, but that was as far as our awareness of world events extended.

There were two occasions when the outside world had intruded. The opening of the Organisation of African Unity in 1963 was the first. With the growing desire for independence from the European colonialists and the right to control one's own destiny, the time was ripe for a pan-African union to make the continent's voice heard on the world stage. Ethiopia had already harboured guerrillas from Kenya's Mau-Mau rebellion, and Nelson Mandela had received military training there.

Addis Ababa was awash with visiting heads of states from all the African countries. We had more than one day off school, and Menelik II Avenue was decorated with the flags of the nations attending the opening.

The Emperor was careful to ensure continued harmonious relations with the US, as

Ethiopia was the largest recipient of military and civil aid in Africa, so the assassination of President John F Kennedy on 22nd November 1963 had a big impact. ① During the last break of the day, Celina and I were about to go back into class when one of the French Canadian Sisters came running along the first floor classrooms and down the steps, shouting, "President Kennedy's been shot!"

Tears poured down her face. I recalled the photos of the tall handsome man with his beautiful wife and young children from *Life* magazine and felt tears prick my eyes too. He seemed to stand for something good, and now it was gone – my American friends were very upset and some went home early that day.

*****

The Ethiopia that burned itself into my memory was the countryside. Weekends were welcome respites from struggles with homework. We had holidays in the Great Rift Valley camping beside Lake Langano, which stretched as far as the eye could see. It was two hundred miles or so from Addis, and after fifty miles the tarmac would disappear and we'd bump along on dirt roads. Sometimes I'd open the windows, but the dust from the roads permeated the air and they'd soon be closed. My parched mouth would long for a Miranda, an orange fizzy drink.

After four hours I'd spot the trees that hid the lake from passers by, and we'd turn left before bouncing up and down potholed tracks to reach the lake. It would take an hour to pitch the tent – my parents' sleeping quarters - while the Combi served as our bedroom and food storage area. Lions roamed the mountains surrounding the lake and hyenas would often search for remains of food around our tent, their laughing cries echoing in the night air. Once there was even a cheetah that bounded away when we shouted at it.

Although it was truly wild, it was close enough to Addis for an entrepreneurial couple to have built a small hotel, restaurant and some bungalows overlooking the lake. The local tribe the Oromo (then called the Gala) were friendly enough and encouraged my interest in their culture. The men still used spears to stalk wild animals, and their cattle were used for meat and milk and the skins for their leather garments.

I envied the brightly coloured beads of the women, made from conch shells and red, white, blue and green glass that they traded with other tribes. Beading was used for necklaces, hair decoration and amulets. As they walked down from their tukuls to fetch water every morning, I would lie in my sleeping bag hearing the rattle of their beads. Sometimes I crept out of the tent to watch as they appeared over the horizon, leather skirts slapping against their thighs as they carried the clay water pots on their heads. Their skin was an extraordinary colour – they used beef fat mixed with the red earth to create a rich, shimmering copper layer which both beautified and protected them from the East African sun's fierce heat.

As we didn't speak their language, nor they ours, I never managed to find out much about their customs, other than the fact that they regarded twins as bad luck. When twins were born, they would leave them out on the mountainside to die from over-exposure or to be eaten by wild animals. A Swedish and Ethiopian couple we knew adopted twin girls to save them from this fate. They would be over forty today – a lucky escape.

Lake Langano was where I practised my swimming. After almost drowning in a pool at Wolliso, a popular weekend destination, I vowed to become a strong swimmer. I would wade into the muddy brown lukewarm waters, my feet slipping over the smooth pebbles by the shore, and head far out to the centre of the lake. Bit by bit people on the shoreline got smaller, and I would only swim back when they were pinpricks.

I dreaded brushing up against a fish, or worse, an eel or snake, but although they were there, they never bothered me. It was peaceful out in the middle of the lake and I relished the chance to be away from my irritating brothers, surrounded by nothing but sky, the horseshoe-shaped mountains of the Rift Valley and the cool water surrounding me. This was where I felt at peace: Ethiopia marked the beginning of my lifelong love affair with nature.

Langano was also the place where I saw my first spirit. I'd woken up feeling stiff from the Combi's unforgiving plastic seat. It was very early morning, and the air was still as night turned into pale daybreak. Sitting opposite me was my English grandad, calmly smoking his pipe. I could only see his head and shoulders, but he looked content. I was shocked and kept opening and shutting my eyes, but there he remained for some minutes. I was anxious to hear whether he was ill and asked my father about it, without letting him know what I'd seen earlier. Dad reassured me that all was well with his father, and that he was enjoying going to Bristol Rovers' football matches with his new wife.

Swimming became part of our weekends. One Sunday we spent the whole day at Ambo, some hot mineral springs about 45 minutes' drive from Addis. I was wearing the pink gingham cotton swimsuit that mum had made for me, with elastic around the arms and legs. Eric, Roy and I jumped in and out of the pool and sat by the hot thermal springs, deeply breathing in the coppery wafts of minerals. It felt incongruous to be sitting by a hot spring while the sky overhead was a deep blue and the sun blazed down. I was pleased to see some of my teachers there - they were also on a day trip. They didn't swim though, their vows of chastity included not wearing swimming costumes. I felt sorry for them, for all the fun they were missing out on. Faith, it seemed, must be really important to make one give up such pleasures.

On another occasion we drove a long way south east, down to the Omo River, to a weekend retreat with a large swimming pool, a restaurant and a bar. The river was home to many weaver birds, their large, spherical nests hanging from willow trees over the river's banks. They darted in and out, feeding their young and making the most of the plentiful supply of insects that hummed and flitted over the muddy water. The male weavers found it difficult to enter the nest, as their tails were as long as their bodies, a luxuriant plumage with which to woo a mate. As we stood silently, dad pointed out a pair of eyes regarding us from the depths of the water. It was a hippo. Along came her baby: the protective mother gave a huge yawn, exposing large, stubby teeth and a chasm of a mouth. We took the hint and walked back to the swimming pool.

We sat and had our picnic a few yards away, tucking into lemonade, ham and polony sandwiches and jam sponge. Roy and I went for a walk up the dirt track we'd driven down earlier. We stopped when small boulders began rolling down the mountainside close by. Some trees shook, and then a wild-looking hermit stepped from behind them. He wore a lion skin thrown over one shoulder and another wrapped round his waist. His hair was long and unkempt and his skin was filthy from months or years of sleeping in the wild.

He stared at us in defiance and started muttering some words in a tribal language I couldn't understand. Frightened, we backed away. Then he walked towards the river and was gone, his brown form melting among the bone-dry trees. After he'd vanished, I peered up at the mountainside and saw the mouth of a cave above the line of trees. It was a very steep climb – how did he manage it without tumbling down?

The pool had been crowded most of the day, but towards the end of the afternoon it emptied and a party of Indian ladies took their chance to have a swim. All five of them waded into the shallow end in their saris, and, with the soft, translucent material of their skirts billowing behind them, began to swim gently to and fro. We watched transfixed as they got out of the pool, laughing and chattering, saris clinging to their bodies and wet hair streaming with water. Their children laughed, and after the women had changed into dry saris, they were gone in a trail of dust.

Along with lakes and its many rivers, Ethiopia also had a massive hydroelectric dam, Koka Dam, on top of a mountain just south of Addis. It was built by an Italian company, for which my classmate Azeb Fesseha's father worked. Overlooking the enormous expanse of water was a pleasant hotel, and we stopped there for lunch one Sunday. The manager explained that everything was cooked fresh to order and that we might have to wait for a while. We decided on chicken, and Roy, Eric and I went outside to have a look at the view.

Minutes later we witnessed the incongruous sight of the chef, cleaver in hand, running after a beheaded chicken. Its head hung on by just a small fibre of muscle but its nervous system was still sending out the signals to run away from the executioner! After another two minutes the chicken flopped onto its side, dead. Despite seeing it being killed, we had to admit that the flesh tasted good.

Ethiopia had become our home, and some of their customs became part of our lives, but it wasn't to last. Dad told us his salary simply wasn't enough: he resented the fact that the Americans who worked for TWA earned three times his salary, often with less experience.

We returned to Villa Verde once more. Now that we knew we didn't have much time left there, Roy, Eric and I took the chance to make more local friends. Outside the hotel was the railway line, the main line between Addis and Djibouti. We would often run outside as we heard the hoot of the steam engine's whistle, and it would hurtle past, smoke swathing some of the carriages. Smiling faces would wave and children would thrust their heads out of the windows while others, too poor to pay the fare, hung from ladders at the back.

Houses lined the road by the hotel, from little tukuls to more European-style homes. We made friends with a young couple who ran a little shop by the railway. They kept goats, and one afternoon they invited us to have a meal with them. This was a privilege, as normally we wouldn't be allowed.

The husband took one of the goats and slit its throat: within ten minutes he'd hung it up by its forelegs, with the intestines dangling like bloody strings of sausages between its legs. His wife prepared the large circular bowl for the injera, placing it over the fire to heat, and mixed the tef flour with water to form the batter for the unleavened bread. She left it to prove while she cut up the goat and divided it into two piles – one to be salted and stored and the other for our meal. She took each piece of fresh meat and rolled it in spices for the hot watt. We left them to cook the meal, returning in a few hours' time when the food would be ready.

It was a new experience for us to enter a tukul. We sat on little hand-carved three-legged stools there in the pale darkness, with the injera in a large circular serving dish between us and the watt placed in the middle of it. After washing our hands with some water from a can, we tore off pieces of the warm injera and dipped it into the watt. The flavours burst on my tongue – chilli, garlic, paprika and some Ethiopian spices I didn't know the names of. It was a truly delicious meal. Roy, Eric and I left an hour later, feeling really special to have been treated like adults and shown such hospitality by people who, by European standards, really didn't have much at all.

Further along from their hut was a small house with a sign outside: 'bar'. I was intrigued that so many men seemed to come and go there, particularly at weekends. One Saturday afternoon I saw the owner, a heavily pregnant Ethiopian with a half Ethiopian-half European toddler in her arms. Eric was with me: I took a deep breath, plucked up my courage and asked if we could go inside.

"Sure, why not?" she replied.

It was very bare. Plastic and metal chairs were arranged around small wooden tables with aluminium ashtrays in garish metallic reds, blues and silvers. In the right hand corner was the bar, with bottles of Coke, spirits and a large fridge. Grubby glasses sat on the counter. Through an open door, I could see rooms with beds inside.

"Why do you have beds in here?" I asked.

She laughed gently. "Sometimes our guests get tired and they want to have a sleep."

We'd come across the local brothel. And it had satisfied my curiosity about where some of the hotel guests went on a Friday night, after they'd had a few beers!

Two weeks before the end of term, Sumitra invited the rest of the class to her birthday party. Her family were wealthy: her father was the first manager of the Indo-Ethiopian Textile Company and the factory was in Akaki, about an hour's drive from Addis. It was a glorious day and we enjoyed good Ethiopian and Indian food and plenty of squash and games. After a game of rounders, I stood looking at my classmates and felt the familiar pang of sadness. Once more I'd have to say goodbye to my friends, and to the caring Catholic Sisters who'd given up comfortable lives and thoughts of marriage to commit to God and educating girls in a country far from home. The tears of those first months had turned to laughter: I started off standing alone in the playground, but now I was surrounded by friends, sharing lunches every day.

Our last evening was spent in a well-known, traditional Amharic restaurant, high up on the mountainside in Entoto, which overlooked the capital. We were there with Major Tebeba, who had become a good family friend. He was a sophisticated, friendly bachelor in his mid 30s who served in the Ethiopian Air Force. We enjoyed three different types of watt, and Roy and I got drunk on the local tej, or honey mead, which we kept pouring into our glasses and quickly downing when mum and dad weren't looking!

After the meal, I went outside with Roy to watch the view. Below us lights glowed orange in the night air, and the smell of wood smoke drifted up from fires as families cooked their evening meals. As I absorbed the sights and sounds of the city, trying to burn them into my memory, a huge moth flew by and settled underneath a bright light on a wall alongside the restaurant. Its wingspan must have been almost ten inches, an amazing sight, with a large skull shape on its body. It rested there quietly, enjoying the warmth from the light. I sighed in wonder and longing – Ethiopia was now in my soul forever.

*****

On my return to the UK, I began to lose my innocence and sense of wonder. English school mates couldn't really relate to me: Africa was a strange and dark continent to them, with no connection to their daily lives. Excitement for them was a trip to Paris, or a holiday in Benidorm.

We had a very short stay in Bushey, Watford before moving to Allesley Park in Coventry. That city, too, was just a staging post – in March 1966 we emigrated to South Africa, much against my wishes. The day dad informed us, I rushed at him, pounding my fists on his chest, raging with anger and despair: "I hate you, I hate you, I hate you!"

As I packed up my things and cleared my bedroom, I came across the old photo from Nazareth School. Gazing at the faces, I struggled to remember most of the girls' surnames, I could only just recall their Christian names. Taking a black pen, I carefully kept turning over the photo to write each name on the back, roughly in line with the classmate's head.

Putting away my pen, I noticed something glinting on the floorboards beneath the bed. Kneeling down to grope for it, I felt a piece of metal: pulling it towards me I discovered it was a small silver and marquisite cross. I put it in my pocket to keep it safe – a sign of faith and hope wherever I went in the world.

I made friends more easily in South Africa, as so many of us at Kempton Park High School in the Transvaal (now Gauteng Province) were immigrants. But I hated the apartheid regime with a passion and at 15, made it my mission to return home to the UK as soon as I had left school and had enough money.

In 1972, I was finally free of the family, and returned home. I met Rob five years later and did what was expected of me: climbing the corporate ladder and getting married. The most exciting thing that happened was giving birth to James in 1989, but despite that, I felt I'd lost something important: the connection to other people. All that mattered was money and appearances. Life was little more than power and comparison and I longed for relief from the relentless stress and boredom of it all.

Further information:

① Richard Pankhurst, *The Ethiopians: A History,* p. 264, Blackwell
   Publishers, 1998

II: PREPARING FOR THE ODYSSEY

3 The dreams push me onwards

The first threat of the storms ahead came in the summer of 1992, when mum was diagnosed with lung cancer. I gladly left my job to care for her. I had wanted time out from work anyway, and I felt this was the least I could do when she'd not only lavished her love on me when I was little, but also looked after James for a year when I went back to work.

In the caring of her, something inside had begun to creak into life, small and rigid after years of atrophy. I think it was my heart, cracking out of the glacier where it had been frozen for decades. It began to pump a little more each day, as I sat by mum's bedside in the hospice, stroking her transparent white hands, marked with spots from the South African sun. I talked quietly, as by this time, mum was unable to speak: the tumour at the top of her lungs had squeezed her vocal chords into submission.

My hands trembled as I carefully gave her a bed bath at home, using lemon balm soap and then mango butter body cream, which she loved. The room was festooned with spring flowers, some of which James had gathered for his precious 'nana' the day before. He was only three, and he couldn't understand why nana couldn't speak any more.

During the last family meal at mum's flat, he had sat in the gold velvet armchair in her bedroom, looking at her, concentration etched on his face. Mum had just two days left to live. Her breath rattled, as she drifted in and out of consciousness, stirring only to ring a bell for water, which she sucked slowly through a straw.

"Come, James, leave nanny, it's time to eat," Rob said, tugging at James's arm. "But I'm guarding nanny whilst she sleeps," he grumbled, easing himself off the chair. That was his last sight of his beloved grandmother.

My heart had broken into a thousand pieces at her funeral and all I could think as her coffin moved into the crematorium's furnace was:
"Why me? Why now?"

*****

It took me months to recover. What I missed most of all were the weekly phone calls, the shopping trips and going to her flat for Sunday lunch. James, too, wished he could still walk in the garden with his nana, and sit beside her as she read a story to him, pointing out the pictures and tracing the letters with her long fingers. Her Norwegian waffles were his favourite tea time treat, oozing with butter and strawberry jam – delicious with a glass of milk!

The pain welled up most when I thought about the little things I'd enjoyed with mum: the words of encouragement, the family jokes and the conversations about the past. She was always reading and often recommended books to me – biographies were her favourite. I can picture her now, sitting in the gold armchair by the lounge window, the light behind her: head bent over a book, black magnifying glass in hand. She was too mean to get herself stronger glasses!

After her death the dreams, which had once been so frequent in my late teens and early twenties, began to return. I had some counselling to begin to make sense of what had happened – both mum and dad were gone and I was now responsible for my own actions. Angela, the therapist, was very compassionate and listened as I poured out my woes – as much about my childhood and all the change in my life, as about my grief.

One morning, I rushed excitedly into the office where the sessions were held. Angela smiled as she looked up: I must have had a lot more spark than usual.

"I've got to tell you about this amazing dream I had last night, Angela!"

"What was in it?"

"I dreamt that there was a beautiful sun bird in a golden cage, with iridescent feathers. It just sat there, and had been silent for many years. But then the door magically flew open and it began to sing the most glorious song."

"What do you think that represented, Annette?" she commented, getting into counsellor mode.

"I think that little bird was me." I sighed wearily, "I'm beginning to realise that I always tried to bend to what mum and dad wanted – their approval was all important. Now that they're both gone, it's time I found out who I really am. I've finally got the freedom to do that."

 But first I had to pick myself up, get out there and return to work, to ease the grief and give structure to my daily life.

By January 1994, I'd found a challenging and exciting job, working for a start-up business. Soon, just like before, the temptation to work harder and harder and win the approval of those around me – apart from James and Rob – became too much. I gave in, and when I wasn't working, I was thinking about work: I was short-tempered at home, and irritated by James's normal demands to play. I didn't have time, apart from giving him a bath and reading him a bedtime story. Frequently, I'd lie on his bed with him and fall asleep afterwards. I was totally exhausted.

I began to listen to the arguments between my inner voices: the materialist – the hard, cynical, impatient adult and the spiritualist – the spontaneous child, full of wonder at the magic of life. At times, it was like world war III in my head, and I found it increasingly difficult to make decisions. I was losing my grip – my work status and the BMW in the drive began to seem pointless. The inner child was beginning to break free.

Plagued with insomnia, I tossed and turned between three and four most mornings – how to get out of the 'rat race' and do something I loved. That was now the big question in my life.

In May 1995, the answer finally came. I'd been thinking back to my teenage years, spurred on by my repetitive dreams of being back at school in South Africa, listening to the teacher drone on. The message seemed to be that I still had a lot to learn: perhaps I hadn't progressed since then.

But then an idea struck me – writing. I'd loved writing poetry when I was in my teens, as it helped ease the roller-coaster of emotions. I'd shown them to some friends, even hesitantly read them out loud a couple of times. Something in my words clearly touched them and my first small notebook of poetry had been buried with Louis, my first love, who'd died at 26 from a motorbike accident.

'Writer, I'll be a writer! That's it,' I whispered quietly to myself. But writing wasn't enough – it had to be purposeful. 'I know, I'll give half of the profits from my books to help the very poor.'

'Yes, now you're talking!', the little girl in me replied.

A flash of brown appeared, the drab brown of the houseboy's jacket, 14-year-old Matthew who'd worked for us in Addis Ababa. It was people like him I wanted to help – to let them know that there was someone who cared, someone who'd stand by them, no matter what.

I eased my aching body out of bed and stood up 'Yes, this is what I'll do with my life. The little girl was now jumping up and down on the spot ' Yay, yay, yay, she's finally got it!'

But this wasn't a whim, it was deeply serious – a call from the unknown. I reached down to a place I'd never been before and prayed from it: 'God, if I do this for you, will you help me and readers to create gardens of peace in the world? I would like the first one to be in Jerusalem, in honour of your son, Jesus Christ. Until we have peace there, I don't believe we can ever have world peace.'

My soul cried out in relief. I'd made a covenant with God and at last I'd found the purpose of my life.

*****

From that day on, the spiritual dreams increased in frequency. I also began to write, often at 3 or 4am, starting again with poetry. I had to learn to explore and open up, to find my voice once more, lost when I was 16. However, what I needed most was wisdom.

Stupidly, I ignored the covenant and tried to get on with my job, and accept life for what it appeared to be: exhausting and monotonous. After all, it gave me and the family the things we needed. But the little girl had other plans, and another dream popped up one night. This time, I was sitting in a cinema all alone. Only the image from the screen lit up the darkness – a black and white map of the world. As I stared at it, it began to fade into the centre until the black was just a small pinprick.

On waking, I decided that this meant I was to work internationally, rather than in the UK. In 1997, I left my stressful job to become a consultant, advising companies on internal communications and improving customer satisfaction. I knew a lot about the former, but not much about the latter, although it was a passion of mine.

Deciding this was my route map, I left the secure job and spent time researching the market for a suitable partner, which I found in Sweden. I poured acres of time and sweat into it, but very little worked – I was out of my depth, new business meetings didn't progress to the next stage and the partnership soon floundered when I asked for a contribution to the business costs. I'd been completely naïve and blinkered and by this time I had a huge business loan – over £30,000 - secured on the house.

The only way of paying it back was to sell our home, where we'd lived for eleven years. Rob was angry as hell and James was devastated.

"I was born here, I want to die here: it's the only home I've ever known," he shouted at me with tears in his eyes.

Devastated and ashamed, I couldn't face them, nor my stupid, stupid self. One Tuesday morning in July, after we'd sold the house, I decided to commit suicide – that way I wouldn't have to endure their criticism. Rob was young enough to find someone else and James would soon forget me. Whatever lay on the other side, I'd face when I passed on.

I mulled over the method – knife or pills? I planned it for the following week whilst James was at school. The kitchen was the best place – the tiles were easy to clean. I realised bleeding to death was too messy and could affect the house sale, whereas pills were cleaner, perhaps just some vomit to clean up afterwards. My soul, though, had other plans.

That night, another clear dream appeared. It was dark: I was alone in a room with no windows. To my left a small, triangular sliver of light shone on the floor. It seemed to come from a door, left slightly ajar. I walked towards it, curious as to what lay behind. As I opened the door, the most heavenly rays of light poured all over me: the feeling of deep love was overwhelming. Complete and unconditional love for who I was right then, in all my misery, shame and suicidal thoughts. Standing there, I felt my life change - I knew I was in God's presence.

I woke up, crying. The message had been so momentous, so clear, that I gave up all thoughts of suicide and decided to travel through the pain to a new life beyond.

*****

The stay in our next house in Granborough, Buckinghamshire was short – just over two years – hastened by another redundancy. But I managed to take my first, unsteady steps towards peace and returned to Norway in 1998, 23 years after my last visit. Mum had fallen out with my aunt in a dispute over my grandfather's will and relations had ceased. I was curious to see my relatives and the country again and wanted to introduce James to his Norwegian roots. We were to spend a few days in Oslo with Odd Inge Skjaevesland, a journalist and my second cousin, and then drive south to Kristiansand.

Plans had to be changed at the last minute when Berit, Odd Inge's wife was suddenly taken ill, so we had to stay elsewhere. Odd Inge booked a room for us at the Holmenkollen Hotel, which overlooks Oslo fjord – he told us that this was where the Oslo peace accord had been developed between Israel and Palestine in 1993. A small spark lit up in my heart when I heard that – it was a place of great peace and beauty, with a wonderful carved Norse roof, reminiscent of Chinese pagodas.

Greeting my aunt and uncle, Olga and Arvid, in Kristiansand made me cry. Although six inches shorter than my mother, Olga was her spitting image and I wept as I hugged her: for the pain of mum's passing and that I would never be able to embrace her again. The big family news was the imminent appointment of Olav, a second cousin, as Bishop of Agder and Telemark in southern Norway. The holiday was a real breakthrough, and since then, we've developed a strong bond.

In November, 1999, we moved to a smaller house in Buckingham, so that the mortgage was affordable, no matter what changes lay ahead. Better to plan for it, than be a victim, Rob and I decided.

I discovered it was exactly the right move when, going round to introduce myself to our new neighbours, the door was opened by a very familiar face. Roger was now our next door neighbour - a former colleague I'd once shared an office with seven years ago! I didn't appreciate it then, but that marked the beginning of increasingly synchronous events which would finally push me towards my true destiny.

*****

Fireworks exploded in the deep blue wintry sky on Millennium Eve. Rob and I were celebrating it at a party and, buoyed up by a few drinks, he danced around kissing complete strangers. I stood close by with renewed hope in my heart. I had a new job, James was settled in at school and my first book of poetry would be completed later that year.

Billions of people around the world were celebrating too. I had now learnt to acknowledge my covenant with God. Deep down, I prayed for peace in the new Millennium: peace for all mankind.

4 The voyage ahead

Less than two and a half years after that party, I sat slumped in the study, weeping. My high hopes and idealism lay in tatters around me. Redundant once more and plans to celebrate my 50th birthday in Australia with the family dashed. How good were the prospects of finding work again, when I was 49? My efforts there had seemed doomed to failure since mum's death.

A glint of blue disturbed those fatalistic thoughts. Shimmering in my study window was a blue glass dove, hanging from a delicate thread. I'd bought her two months before the redundancy in a little café and gift shop in Thame, Oxfordshire. I'd fallen in love with the way the light had shone and reflected through the handmade butterflies and doves.

I'd got chatting to the café's owner and discovered that she'd worked for the Norwegian Ballet in Oslo for five years. I responded: "I'm half Norwegian and my second cousin, Odd Inge Skjaevesland, is culture correspondent for *Aftenposten,* the daily newspaper. Did you ever meet him?"

She shook her head, "No, but it's a small world." With a wry smile, she continued wrapping the glass memento.

These small connections always lit up my day, and I remembered laughing as I walked towards my car for the trip back to work.

Seeing the dove now reminded me that I was on a journey, and that it was time to stop crying. I'd been brave and told Ken, my boss, of my plans to bring water to

Ethiopia. 'Stop fussing,' I told myself, 'and get on with it.'

Reaching for a blank sheet of paper I decided to map out the things that would be important to me in the time ahead, even if some were little more than hazy impressions. I placed an arrow at the top – N for north – along with the words 'water' and 'peace'. Peace brought to my soul by finally doing something that I found truly meaningful and magical: that was my destination.

I considered what mode of travel I should use for this mythical odyssey, and chose a tall ship. The sight of their sails billowing in the wind always made my heart sing, and reminded me of 'Treasure Island' and the pirate stories that I'd read in my childhood.

Ships need wind to sail: I wondered what would serve this purpose for me. I decided that my winds were the still clear dreams I'd had since 1970, starting when I was 18. They were very different to my normal dreams, always completely unconnected to the day's events, beginning with complete silence, out of a mist. Then came sounds, followed by the sharp images, smells and finally the feelings I experienced as I dreamed.

My first dream had been about Jesus, the second about the homeless, the third about spirits, and the fourth about God's love for me when I was suicidal. Finally in April 2000, there was the one about water. I drew the dreams at the sides of my map as faces, blowing my majestic ship towards its destination.

At which islands could I cast anchor? I would need time to draw breath, get new provisions for my journey and consult my map. After all, I was both captain and crew, and would need all my strength. Would the islands be lush and full of tropical vegetation and food, or barren, with sharks ploughing the waves a few yards from shore? I chose the questions that I'd harboured for many years - some since childhood - as my islands.

There were three unanswered questions that had plagued me for some time. Did my father's experiences in Palestine in 1946 have anything do with my journey? Dad was a very private man. He rarely let out emotion, apart from his anger, which was very quickly stirred, and occasional bursts of happiness, when he sang with a lovely tenor voice. He'd never spoken about his war time service in the RAF – the only souvenir was a pilot's helmet that I'd worn for fun when I was little.

Secondly, what of Coventry Cathedral's role in my story? We had lived in Coventry for eighteen months before emigrating to South Africa, and we'd often take family and friends to see the new cathedral. It seemed odd that we never worshipped there: we just wandered around the ruins from 1940 and into the cavernous new church. I would sometimes stop and sit on one of the pine wooden chairs looking at the altar, marvelling at the huge tapestry of Christ looming over me, a life size man at his feet.

The final niggling question was equality. Although our standard of living had been very good in South Africa, I'd hated the country with a vengeance for how the apartheid laws created such a struggle for existence among the black and coloured communities. The system was so arbitrary that Japanese were regarded as honorary whites, while Chinese were deemed 'coloured.' All in the name of trade, of course! After 9/11, the whole world was becoming more and more suspicious of the stranger in our midst and all our wealth and technology had made barely any dent in poverty levels in the developing world. We were increasingly just seeing the label: black, Jew, disabled, asylum seeker, Muslim, beggar, rather than the human being to whom we applied that term.

Drawing them on the map, I had three places to rest: Israel/Palestine, peace and equality.

What about the hardships I'd encountered? As I stared back into my past they felt like shards of glass, stabbing me in the heart each morning when I woke up, assuming that life was the same as it had been before. On the map, these shards became perilous rocks looming out of the fog against which my tall ship could suddenly be dashed, despite all my efforts to turn her around. Sometimes it had taken years to repair the hull before I could set sail again, as in the case of my mother's death.

Friends' faces appeared before me, the people who'd helped and supported me through the tough times – true guides. They didn't just show up in daylight hours either, but also at night, in my dreams. There was Queen Elizabeth II, whom I'd met for tea along with the Queen Mother. To me, she symbolised loving duty. Then there was George Harrison, the Beatles' guitarist. He represented true spirituality, and he'd always been enthusiastic about my plans. In the first dream, he'd encouraged me in my writing, and offered to write the foreword for me. In the second, in December 2001, he was very shocked that I'd not finished my book yet. He told me how important it was: 'after 9/11, the world needs a book like yours' he'd declared. These were my real and metaphysical guides, whose role it was to show me the stars and new navigation routes to the next island.

Flags were needed for the tall mast, to declare what I stood for. I decided to have three pennants rather than a single large flag. At the top was a pale blue one on which was a dove of peace with an olive twig in its beak – it would never be lowered, no matter how stormy the seas. The second was the Norwegian flag, representing fairness and water – the lakes, streams, waterfalls and fjords - that made it the most beautiful country on earth for me. And last was the Ethiopian flag – the glorious green, yellow and red bands echoing the proliferation of those colours in nature.

Preparations were almost complete.   But I'd not considered how to avoid sandbanks and jagged rocks in the dark. I needed lighthouses to show the way and chose inspirational people to guide me: Mahatma Gandhi, Martin Luther King Jr, and Nelson Mandela. I chose Gandhi and King for peace and non-violence and Mandela for resilience and forgiveness. Finally, there was Bobby Kennedy, the brother of JFK, who'd given several brave speeches in South Africa in 1966, the first year we'd lived there.   They had all dedicated their lives to equality amongst all humanity.

There was one final lighthouse: Sam Wanamaker, the Hollywood actor whom I'd come across in 1980, whilst working for a building products company. Sam had asked for help with achieving his dream: the reconstruction of Shakespeare's Globe Theatre in London. When he visited the office, I'd gone out to meet him. He stood up from the leather couch, hand outstretched in greeting. Determination and focus shone from his piercing blue eyes and he broke into wide smile: "Hi, good you could see me at such short notice."

Trying to appear nonchalant, I replied, "Good to meet you, too, Sam. Come and meet my boss Tom to tell us more about your project." Opening the double doors to our office, I ushered him through to some comfortable seats by Tom's desk.

After coffee and some pleasantries, Sam leaned forward, getting straight to the point: "I've been coming to the UK for many years to perform in theatre, and now it's my home. The most challenging and exciting parts have been in Shakespeare's plays. For me, he's the world's greatest playwright. I couldn't believe that London didn't have a theatre dedicated to his work!" he said incredulously. We nodded, unsure of where this was going, but carried away by his obvious enthusiasm.

"I was thinking of the Globe Playhouse by the Thames, where his work used to be staged. It's my life's dream to recreate it, so audiences can experience Shakespeare as people did in the 1600s."

Southwark County Council, he told us, had donated some land a couple of hundred yards from where the original Playhouse stood, and now he was looking for plasterboard so the project could move onto its next step.

Tom and I looked at each other, then he replied: "Sam, I'm sure we can help. We'll need to make some arrangements, but give me your card. I'll let you know when it's ready to deliver. You have a wonderful dream - we'd like to help you make it come true."

Sam grinned broadly: "That would be terrific: I look forward to hearing from you." I was already bowled over by this charismatic man. In that moment, I could see just what the camera saw. He must have felt it as he turned to me, "And Annette, how about coming down and taking a look when it's done?"

"I'd love to," I blushed. "Thanks so much!"

Two weeks later the plasterboard was delivered, and I took up Sam's offer. He showed me around and introduced me to some of his team. They were as energised about his vision as he was. Sam told me about his fundraising efforts, touring in plays to get finance and support for the theatre. The whole encounter left a lasting impression on me – I'd never realised how one person's dream could electrify and stimulate so many different people across the world.

Remarkably, eleven years later I shared an office with Mike Abbott, and was very envious to hear he'd been offered a secondment to work for Sam as PR manager for the Globe Theatre. I told Mike about the inspiring meeting with Sam and marvelled that these coincidences could happen so randomly in my life.

With Sam's lighthouse shining for me, the map was complete, and in May 2002, I was ready for the voyage ahead.

Further information:

Shakespeare's Globe Theatre: www.shakespeares-globe.org

5 New guides and tests

Scrabbling around in the pocket by the driver's seat, I jubilantly fished out the cutting I'd torn out of a magazine two years previously. Now dog-eared and crinkled, the astrology feature included an interview with an astrologer, Christeen Skinner. I wanted to have a reading with her, to make sure that this time, I was heading in the right direction.

A few weeks later, we sat opposite each other. On the table between us lay Christeen's charts, laptop and the detailed questionnaire I'd had to complete.

"This is very interesting, I see you've got a failed business behind you."
"Yes, but why would that be interesting?" I responded defensively.
"It shows you're prepared to take risks – that's good," Christeen looked up, smiling.

She continued: "There's no doubt this redundancy was meant to happen, you're being repotted. Your chart shows that you can work globally, not just in the UK. See here," she said, turning the chart towards me. "Here's a very strong writing seam for you – you'll get lots of inspiration from East Africa and Madagascar. The book will have a lot of interest from Eastern Europe, Australia and New Zealand. The Japanese will lap it up too, just like the Americans."

I leaned forwards – this was just the encouragement I needed.

"So, what do you think about using funds to provide water in Ethiopia?" I queried.

"It's a very good one. In my analysis of the planets, I've already predicted that there will be water wars by the end of this decade. It's going to become more important than oil."

Before the session ended, she gazed around me. I wasn't sure what she was looking for – her eyes seemed to be tracing an imaginary outline. "There's an aura of magic about your future. I think you're getting a helping hand in the spirit world. Do you know much about your relatives – perhaps there was someone who'd died early and always wanted to take a big risk like you?"

"I've got no idea, really. We had so little contact with mum's and dad's family."

Pursing her lips, she commented: "Well, there's definitely someone out there helping you in this venture, I can really sense it."

Christeen's analysis and pep talk gave me the encouragement I needed, and sometimes I played the tape of our meeting as I drove to and from home and Milton Keynes station. By July 2002, I'd managed to find contract work through a friend of mine. I'd been worried about how I'd be treated: maybe work that no one else wanted would be tossed over to me? Perhaps I wouldn't be invited out for drinks after a hard day at the office? But my fears proved groundless. On my first day at Axa Insurance, a big company in the city of London, I was delighted to find three colleagues who knew friends of mine. That was a real boost. In fact it was exactly what I'd hoped for - some connection with my past.

Almost inevitably, I slipped into my old habits and was soon working the familiar long hours. It wasn't what my heart wanted, it didn't represent my new life, but the long neglected part of my brain in which my intuition lived began to creak and old connections re-established themselves. I now had more courage and told a handful of people about my Ethiopian dream. For now though, the inspiration for the book was missing, but I was much more patient. I knew I had to wait for it to appear, I couldn't force it. This was completely at odds with how I used to behave, pushing things forward too forcefully at times. It had earned me a reputation as being bossy and a pain in the neck: I learnt to listen more carefully and only comment when asked for an opinion. In any case, work was no longer a career, just a contract, and a stepping stone to the person I wanted to become.

In October 2002, the family got to explore more of my roots when we visited South Africa for my 50th birthday. Uncannily, we came across another connection with the past when we had a one-night stopover at 'De Poort', a small, remote guesthouse a few miles outside Oudtshoorn. At dinner, the owners seated us opposite another British family, whose son was a year older than James. Initially despondent – I had wanted to get away from Brits on holiday – my mood thawed because John and his wife were very chatty. The talk turned to stories about our journeys to work, an obsession with the British, particularly in the south east of England.

"My journey's a long one, I take the M1 north, then the M25 west, before I join the M40 heading to Bourne End," explained John as he sipped a glass of wine.

"Bourne End – who do you work for?" I responded, intrigued. It had been the corporate head office location of my previous company.

"Lex, or should I say RAC plc," he responded.

"Well, that's amazing, I used to work for them too!"

As the conversation continued, I learnt that John was Head of Risk Management. His face was a picture when I told him that we'd spoken to each other via a conference call that February! He was clearly uncomfortable when he heard I'd been made redundant, but I brushed it off and told him how I enjoyed the freedom of contract work. That night, I slept soundly, feeling I'd passed another small test.

Another link with peace appeared out of the blue, a few days later in Montagu. The guesthouse where we'd wanted to stay was fully booked, but the manager recommended Kingna Lodge nearby. The owners were rightfully proud of the immaculate Victorian lodge and peeking into one room, I saw a plaque commemorating Nelson Mandela's stay there, the former South African President. Rob and I chose another room, in which Mandela's ally had stayed: Frederik Willem de Klerk. In 1993, they had been joint winners of the Nobel Peace Prize. My intuition had twigged that it was these seemingly random coincidences that were now important to my future – far more so than anything I planned.

*****

In February 2003, as the days began slowly lengthening into spring, conversation at work turned to events in Iraq. Most of the team were *Guardian* newspaper readers and felt very strongly that the invasion was wrong. We all agreed that the US and UK governments should wait until the UN weapons inspectors had reported back on their search for weapons of mass destruction. Putting our beliefs into action, five of us went on the 'Stop the War' march in London, joining hundreds of thousands of people from every corner of the earth marching towards Hyde Park.

On that sunny, bitterly cold day, it was hard to appreciate that war, real war, was probably just around the corner. There was a carnival atmosphere: drums were beaten, whistles blown, chants cried and placards danced in the wind as demonstrators climbed up lamp posts to take photos of the march. I learnt the next day that we had been part of the largest global anti-war demonstration since the Vietnam War.

Mulling over the impending war, I felt extremely distressed, gripped by the same hopelessness that had overcome me as I waited for mum's imminent death. My thoughts were with the innocent civilians, some of whom had suffered enough under Saddam Hussein's harsh regime. In today's wars, 90 per cent of victims are civilians rather than military – how could their massacre ever contribute to the development of a peaceful democracy? It seemed ludicrous to even think that. The British public had shown enormous resistance to the war, but Blair hadn't listened. I felt betrayed – both Bush and Blair claimed to be Christians, but where were their values? How would they react if their family were under threat from bombing raids? And what was the real motive behind the invasion, was it about enabling a secure pipeline of oil to a fuel-hungry world? In all the rhetoric, nothing was clear, nor transparent any more.

The weekend before the Iraq invasion, Rob and I visited Buckingham garden centre, looking for new plants for the tubs in the back yard. It was busy – Sunday was a prime gardening day, and shoppers wheeled their low flat trolleys around, picking up packets of seeds, plants and shrubs. At the back of the store was a colourful display of houseplants: small African violets, bushy white gardenias, busy lizzies, deep red and pink cyclamens, tall rubber and cheese plants.

Lilies have always been my favourite. Lifting up the ones I found most appealing, I spotted a tall plant with white leaf-shaped flowers, long knobbly stamens and more leaves than usual – wide, fine and long. Fumbling for the label, a small stick protruded from the pot, on which 'Peace lily' was written. Taking it home, I placed it in a decorative pot by the French doors. I hoped it would mirror my determination to always keep peace in my heart, no matter what.

The bombing of Baghdad began at 2.30 British time on Thursday 20th March. I hadn't slept particularly well, worrying about the families who'd made their final preparations for war. The wealthy and middle classes may have been able to escape to neighbouring countries or to the west. But what about the rest: what about those who had no cars, not even bicycles, and just enough to eat? Where could they hide?

I turned on the radio to get ready for work at 6.30, and the worst was confirmed. We'd invaded southern Iraq and the bombing of Baghdad had begun. Normally I avoided breakfast TV, but that morning I ran downstairs and switched it on. The sombre newscaster confirmed that the invasion was underway. As she intoned the headlines, footage of air attacks appeared on the left hand side of the screen. It was a nightmare scene from a Middle Eastern city: in the distance, date palms and flat roofs were illuminated to an almost daylight brightness by the magnitude of hundreds of bombs exploding on the ground, dropped by US and British fighter jets. Flames licked bombed out buildings and flashed over broad avenues.

Something in my memory clicked – I'd witnessed that scene before. Out of nowhere came a crystal recollection of my first prophetic dream in 1970, the one with Jesus and the angels descending on clouds to collect the faithful from those streets, while people howled and screamed in anguish. I found it hard to marshal my thoughts – it was 33 years since I'd had that blinding image in my sleep, and here it was being played out for real. Of course there were no angels to be seen, nor Jesus, but as I stood by the couch, looking at the sight unfold, I imagined millions of people all over the world praying for peace and an end to war. I was fortunate: I could just press the remote control to switch it off.

*****

A few weeks later I was hurrying up the steps at Milton Keynes station, in a rush to get to the dentist's. Walking towards the exit, I heard a voice calling my name: "Annette, Annette." It had an unusual timbre, neither male nor female, and was very insistent – almost imploring. I turned around to look for its source but there was no one around. Shrugging, I let the moment go.

I understood whose voice it was the following Saturday, a week before Easter. Rob and I were hard at work, landscaping the back garden. My job was painting the fence panels sage green, which would take several days. As Rob placed bricks around the edges of the circular lawn he'd created, I was in and out fetching glasses of water. It was a warm April day. Stopping to choose the next panel along, I glanced past the shrubs we'd just planted. On the panel, within the whorls of the wood, was unmistakably the face of a man. He had long, wavy hair and a short beard, and on his head was a crown of thorns. As he looked at me, tears began to stream from his eyes – it was the face of Christ. He gazed at me so pitifully, in intense pain because of the horrors we were inflicting upon our beautiful world.

I jumped back, alarmed. I must be going mad. I shook my head and averted my eyes – I was really seeing things. This was crazy! But his face stayed there all day, looking at me mournfully, crying from time to time. He knew that this image would be burnt into my soul forever. Jesus was the second of my guides to step forward.

Further information:

Stop the War coalition: www.stopwar.org.uk

You may find these books useful to explore what happens to your life when you enter the flow. I found "Synchronicity" particularly helpful.

Joseph Jaworski, *Synchronicity*, Berrett-Koehler Publishers, San Francisco, 1996
James Redfield, *The Celestine Prophecy*, Bantam House, 1993
Dr. Wayne W. Dyer, *The Power of Intention,* Hay House Publishers, 2004

6 The awakening

Shortly after the Stop the War march in London, I'd gone to a homeopath for a remedy for ongoing skin problems, probably caused by the stress I'd suffered since 1997. Sitting in the bright, modern consulting room, I'd answered the usual questions about health and then emotional problems.

I explained to Helen, the homeopath: "You know, what I really need, what I ache for, is the inspiration for my first book, to help raise funds for water in Ethiopia. It's so frustrating, it's been almost a year now since I decided to leave permanent employment, but nothing, nothing's showed up." As usual, tears had welled up, and I felt very despondent.

"I think we'd better concentrate on that first then, rather than your skin," she answered, looking for a remedy which would help unblock things.

Within three weeks I was firing on all cylinders, in top form, and felt full of energy, more than I'd had for many years. On the day I'd seen Jesus's face on our garden fence, I'd written my manifesto, the things I stood for, earlier that morning, which I called the 'Concept of Enough' (see chapter 29). This was the first time I'd ever done this – usually I was helping senior managers and directors do this in their companies – but now what really mattered to me was my purpose, my manifesto. I emailed it to a few friends at work to see what they thought about it: did it make sense, did it touch them?

It did: some had cried at what they read, which wasn't what I'd been expecting. Others agreed, but said big business and governments were too apathetic to change, so what was the point? By all accounts, liberal, questioning people in ten different countries had received the material – far more than I'd dared hope.

Fired up by this success, on the Tuesday before Easter 2003, I went to see the vicar at the church close to work: St. Botolph's, beside Aldgate tube station in London. Even at 9am, I had to negotiate my way past two drunks, who sat sprawled on benches outside the church doors, cans of cider by their side, swearing and cursing me for disturbing them. As my eyes adjusted to the dim light inside, I saw two men and a woman deep in conversation, service sheets on the table in front of them.

"I'd like to see the vicar please," I remarked, my legs feeling rubbery with nerves, but trying to conceal it. "I have a message from God." They looked taken aback and looked me up and down – an affluent nutter, that was a new one on them!

"Wait here a moment, he's in his office." My knees were knocking together and my throat dry as I waited for what seemed like half an hour. The vicar appeared, approaching me anxiously – 'better humour her' seemed to be written on his face.

"Hello, I'm Brian Lee," he said firmly. "Come this way, please, we'll talk in my office."

I followed him up some stairs to a large, shabby office, where he motioned me to sit down. I told Brian about my broken life since mum had died, and he listened patiently. Moving on to the dream and the previous weekend's event, I handed him the Concept of Enough.

"Do you think you could include some of that in your Easter sermon?"

"I've already prepared it, some weeks ago." My heart sank, was there no room for spontaneity in the church any more?

Reading my expression, he said with a resigned tone: "Leave it with me, I'll take a look at it later and get back to you." I'd included my mobile number, but I never heard back from him. I dropped a short letter in the letterbox two days later, asking him to reconsider, telling him that a publisher would be in the congregation that Easter: someone who didn't normally worship at St. Botolph's.

*****

Things came to a head over that Easter weekend. I was sleeping poorly, had lost my appetite and all I wanted to do was drink water. At night, I could feel an electrical storm in my brain, as old, worn out connections were replaced with new, particularly near my left ear. I could almost hear the fizzing noise the small neurons were making in my sleep.

Travelling down to Sidford, south Devon, where Roy and Jill, my brother and sister in law lived, everything seemed connected. It was just extraordinary, as though I was on another plane on earth. We stopped at a pleasant pub just off the main road in Wiltshire and I found it was run by Israelis! I tried hard to conceal my excitement, as Rob wasn't feeling very well. We sat outside, enjoying the spring sunshine and words leapt towards me: 'Hope' on the bike leaning against a wall, unusual car number plates and my whole being seemed to expand, radiating in the sunlight.

I decided that the best thing was to establish a company: 'Universal Power' or UP for short. The next thing that sprang into my mind was the need for a worldwide Peace Concert. I texted some friends, and suggested the 15th June. One, Claire, a devout Christian, replied telling me that it was the day of the Pentecost, when the Holy Spirit descended down from heaven to the disciples, filling them with faith and joy. Marie, another friend, had lots of contacts in the music business, as did Simon, my boss. They were intrigued and amused and initially humoured me. They thought it was a good idea too!

I barely slept that Saturday night and on Sunday morning was up at 7.45, creeping downstairs to go out to the local church, St. Peter's, only a few yards down the road. Finding the church warden positioning chairs for the service later that morning, I asked him where I could find the vicar. He pointed up the road, to the rectory.

Knocking at the door, full of energy and hope, I was relieved when it was hurriedly opened. As I introduced myself, I could see that David – the vicar - was rather startled to see someone at his door so early on Easter Sunday. Again, I had the 'concept of enough' with me, and asked him to read it.

"This is one of the busiest days of the year, I really don't have the time. But," he paused, glancing at my disappointed face, "I can see you're a good soul."

Ushering me into his study, he scanned the contents: "Well, this looks interesting. Communism didn't work, and neither has capitalism, but it's impossible to include anything now. If I'd had it a few days earlier..........." His voice trailed off. In the letter at the back of the document was a plea, and a statement that a film or TV producer would be in the congregation that Easter Sunday.

I went back to Roy's feeling a bit deflated, but also realising I needed to become more grounded, the feelings I had been experiencing for almost two weeks were just too intense, too other-worldly. John Sentamu, Bishop of Birmingham, was on the TV that morning, leading the Easter service – he seemed a jolly, devout man.

We left to return home later that morning, and as we travelled down narrow lanes, my ego disintegrated and I felt that I was in the middle of a giant eye, looking at the earth, in awe at everything that had been created. Trees, shrubs, hedges and flowers glowed intensely - almost luminous in the spring light. Sparking from each one were clear energy fields and I saw their roots and the skies, it was 360° vision – nothing was hidden, nothing was separate and everything was connected. The true beauty of the earth floated towards me and enveloped me. I was part of it, and it was part of me.

On reaching home, I threw away the homeopathic pills, I was burning up so much, after which things thankfully returned to normal. I apologised to the people whom I'd texted and emailed that weekend, explaining that I'd been given too strong a remedy for a skin complaint. A few had been very concerned, but more than half asked: "What were you on, because I'd like some!" But those two weeks had been my wake up call, or being 'born again' as we say in our faith. From that time onwards, everything changed forever.

*****

Five hundred people got to their feet. Applause rippled and then filled the room as an elderly South African was helped to the stage. Nelson Mandela, one of my lighthouses, made his way slowly to the steps, nodding his head in appreciation at our welcome and waving to familiar faces. Hilary Benn was in the audience, along with Michael Buerk, and David Blunkett, then Labour Home Secretary, and his dog.

Lindsay, a tall, slender, quietly-spoken South African, and I had seized the opportunity to hear from 'Madiba' the architect of the new South Africa, who was such an icon of resilience and forgiveness for millions. Nelson Mandela was guest speaker at the British Red Cross "Humanity Lecture", a week before his 85th birthday, in July 2003. He stood before us, in his trademark leopard print shirt, no tie, and white hair, like small cotton wool balls, framing his beaming face.

In his speech, he criticised President Bush and Prime Minister Blair for invading Iraq and as he did so, more rapturous applause broke out. I had to fight the urge to punch the air and shout: "Yes, yes!"

As he spoke of the care and compassion shown to him during prison visits on Robben Island by the International Committee of the Red Cross, an image emerged from our South African holiday in 2002: the bull-necked taxi driver who'd taken us from De Waterkant Lodge to Cape Town's waterfront one evening. All the drivers from Seapoint Taxis had been unfailingly pleasant. This man was different: I could sense his resentment of 'bloody rooineks' (red necks) as Afrikaners used to call the British, enjoying a few days holiday in his country. He was a dinosaur Afrikaner, adrift in a sea of change. Everything he'd held dear - his white supremacy, the ability to walk into any job because of his colour and language, the Afrikaners' beating of blacks and coloured with impunity – had disintegrated forever.

The next day, I'd mentioned his surliness to the Asian owner, who had explained his behaviour. "Ag, well, Gert was the last prison warder to leave Robben Island: you can imagine how it is for him now."

*****

In August 2003, we holidayed in Norway. During the first week, I met the third guide - in a dream. He was Terry Waite, who had been special envoy to the Archbishop of Canterbury and one who'd spent many months negotiating for the release of hostages particularly in Lebanon, before he, too, became one. As the dream unfolded, I was standing by a layby, waving at traffic and Terry pulled in hurriedly. He wound down the window and leaned out: 'What do you want?' I told him about my journey and the book. 'Sounds like a good idea, but it's important that the stories are told with integrity, not embellished for the west. Sorry, Annette, I've got to make a move,' he shouted above the car's accelerator and then he was gone.

My dreams alerted me that they were as important as the events which took place during the day. In this voyage of destiny, everything mattered, no matter how incongruous at the time. My senses were becoming more finely tuned to what was important – a message – and what wasn't. I had to ready myself for these messages though, and respond immediately: that meant living completely in the moment. Illusions and past experiences counted for very little, as they could block the clear stream of particles coming towards me, to which I must remain sensitive.

So it proved during a conversation with Odd Inge, my second cousin, a week after the dream with Terry Waite. He is pragmatic and realistic, and was very dismissive of my plans for a best-seller, to bring water to Ethiopia. "Who do you think you are, my dear?" he sniffed in an upper-class English accent, as he rinsed some salad for our lunch at his house in Oslo. "Not even Clinton, with all his fame, could sell the millions you wish to."

Hanging my head, I had to admit he was right. The old me would have noticed the critical tone and been cowed by it, giving up. New me - the brave sailor – needed to only hear the words and mull them over, ignoring the emotion and energy around them, choosing to use them as a gust of wind to move the ship further forward. The book of poetry and reflections I'd finished in 2001 was irrelevant to this odyssey. I desperately needed a new story, one that had to be simple and linked to Ethiopia, to make it captivating and magical to as many people as possible.

As we drove down to Kristiansand to see my aunt and uncle, I thought about the place where I'd last encountered many different nationalities. Suddenly, the connections sprang up like sunflowers lifting their heads to the sun: 'Ah ha, Ethiopia.' I paused: 'Addis Ababa.' And then in a burst of inspiration: 'Nazareth School for Girls.' There and then I decided to go back to my old school in 2004, to track down some of my former classmates and write about what had happened during the intervening 40 years. It seemed a magical idea, and a hundred per cent right.

With that thought, three symbols appeared within three minutes. Three white butterflies flew towards the car; three signs for churches appeared on the road, and over it all, hung three circular clouds – the only ones in a deep blue sky. Three times three – my soul confirmed that I'd made the correct decision. This time, I knew I was finally on the right road.

Three days later, I opened the Kristiansand newspaper, *Fedrelandsvennen,* and read about a family called the Toppstads, who were travelling to Ethiopia the following day. Thom was a plastic surgeon and Helene a nurse; and their eldest daughter was the same age as me when we'd travelled out to Ethiopia. This was a very good omen indeed, and I decided to track them down when I was back in Addis Ababa.

Thom and Helene Toppstad, middle and right, with their children and nanny. Photo courtesy of Trygve Skramstad, Fedrelandsvennen, Kristiansand.

Further information:

St. Botolph's, Aldgate High Street, London EC3   www.stbotolphs.org.uk
International Committee of the Red Cross: www.icrc.org
Fedrelandsvennen: www.fedrelandsvennen.no

7 Choices

As the late August sun splashed across the sitting room's wooden floor, images and noises from class and the playground filled my head. In my hands was the old school photo, bent and yellowed after 39 years. There were over thirty young women standing on the classroom steps with our teacher, Miss Bouchard. Early memories had already begun flooding back: Celina and I in the playground when the teacher came running down the steps, weeping and shouting, "President Kennedy's been shot," the tinkling of Sumitra's gold bracelets, Kathy's freckles, Silva and Fanaye's unusual laughs.

With just the Christian names on the back, I realised this would be a tough challenge, requiring all my ingenuity. Most of the women would have married, and probably had children. Were some dead? I felt that some were bound to be, it was the nature of life. I really wanted a story that would combine many different nationalities and faiths and prayed that some may have converted to Islam, or perhaps married Ethiopian Jews. But that was just a quick thought – the important thing was to start to tracking them down.

Using my wise intuition to guide me, it seemed right to begin with someone who was easy to find, then hopefully the remainder would appear from there. It had to be someone high profile, a woman whom others still spoke of, so people might know where she lived. The most sensible thing would be to look for Mary, Mary Asfaw Wossen, Emperor Haile Selassie's granddaughter. The only trouble was that she wasn't in the photo – in November 1963 she would have been shivering at Benenden School, southern England, along with her sister Sihin. They were in the same year as another monarch's daughter: Princess Anne.

That decision made, I compiled a list of the others, based on my hazy recollections. Silva was important. Out of all the Armenians I remembered her best, with her bell-like laugh. Next was Phoebe, the ample Egyptian with the thick plait, who was so good at maths. Then Celina, the graceful Indo-Portuguese with the lilting voice; next Sumitra with the colourful saris. Kathy was an obvious choice, the friendly American with whom I'd corresponded for a year afterwards, until that too had fizzled out. Finally, I needed an Ethiopian. I decided on Fanaye, the small slim girl who always wore plaits pinned on top of her head: her scratchy laugh had cheered me up when I'd been feeling homesick. Seven in total – lucky number seven. That would do for now.

In the back of my mind, I realised with a sinking heart that the biggest trial would be asking others to help. There was no way I could do this on my own. One of my old beliefs was that it was weak to ask for help. This had been drummed into me by mum and dad, perhaps because they were so far away from their families and thus, had to be self-reliant. By my early 20's, I'd completely absorbed the lesson, which had resulted in stress and working unduly long hours, because being independent and doing it myself was the best way. What a load of rubbish that had been!

Now was the time to chip away at these old fears and beliefs, which were part of the voyage's hazards. I needed to find the right partner too: a charity already providing water in Ethiopia, which had the contacts and infrastructure and – most important of all – worked in a way which involved the very poor, respecting their knowledge and needs.

*****

First things first, I had to find an Ethiopian willing to help, someone who may know Mary. I couldn't go running up to passers-by asking: "Excuse me, are you Ethiopian by any chance?" I rang my half sister Gill, to whom I'd become very close after mum's death. She was taking a diploma in International Studies at Birkbeck College, London University. She had friends from all over the world: if anyone could help, it would be Gill.

By happy coincidence, it turned out that one of her lecturers was an Ethiopian - Theodros Abraham. I contacted him and we had dinner together – he was really eager to help. He understood the dream's importance straight away and grasped the adventure of finding former classmates. Theodros then involved Kidist Dagnew, a lively Ethiopian in her early 30s, who worshipped at the Ethiopian Orthodox Church in Battersea - along with one of Mary Asfaw Wossen's relatives! The trail began to appear.

Kidist and I met up in the reception of Red-R, a charity for whom she worked. Walking towards me, she beamed: "Annette, how good to meet you at last! Come, let's go for a coffee."

Over a sandwich, we chatted about Ethiopia, her family and whom she knew at the church, where she worshipped every week.

"I think Mulugeta Asrate Kassa may be able to help," she paused, putting down her cup. "I know he's a member of the royal family – he may be related to Mary. How about I call him and see if I can get you two together?"

"That would be just fantastic, Kidist!"

Theodros Abraham and Kidist Dagnew, my first Ethiopian friends

As I smiled at her, my heart could feel the connections strengthening as I got used to asking for help, something I was very proud of. We hugged each other outside the café. She promised to get in touch as soon as she had some news.

Wolde Absa, Ethiopian Airlines general manager, UK

I hurried home - I wanted to see if there was a letter from Ethiopian Airlines: I'd written to them asking for a discount ticket for my return to Addis Ababa. I'd mentioned my dream and dad's connection with them, hoping it would result in a positive response. Lying amongst the post by the front door, was a white envelope with a familiar green, yellow and red logo – EAL had replied.

Trembling, I picked it up, then pressed it to my heart, yearning for a yes. Ripping it open, I scanned the brief reply from Wolde Absa, the airline's general manager in the UK. It was a qualified 'yes.' He was happy to help, but I needed to contact their head office in Addis, who would make all the arrangements. I jumped up and down: another step forward. Tears ran down my face – these days, I cried more in joy than sorrow. 'Thank you, thank you, thank you, Lord,' I acknowledged – it was now my deep faith giving me the necessary courage and energy for each step.

I rang Wolde the next day to thank him. "No problem, Annette, it's the least we can do. But I hope your book sells well – it's very important to us."

Discount ticket almost finalised, I now needed to find a reputable, long established charity with whom I could work to channel funds for permanent clean water in Ethiopia. I searched on the internet and googled 'water' and came up with over a billion entries, and water charities, twelve million. But the answer dropped out of the Sunday paper the following week: a fund-raising leaflet for WaterAid. Checking their website, I found they managed projects in Ethiopia too. Full of anticipation, I emailed the London office, and was in put in touch with Helen Pankhurst, Ethiopia's project manager.

Pankhurst, Pankhurst – where had I heard that name before? An image flashed in my mind: mum standing by a gravestone at Holy Trinity Cathedral in Addis Ababa reading out the name and dates of Sylvia Pankhurst's life. Helen turned out to be Sylvia's grand daughter, sending shivers of delight through me. I asked her if it would be possible for me to spend a few days with them, visiting their rural projects. Helen readily agreed.

*****

Returning to work for a few short weeks, I found corporate life had lost much of its appeal. I did the work in a hum-drum way, focusing on the money I'd be earning, although the stupidities of people's egos and power struggles irked me. I managed to conceal my impatience and worked through projects which could have taken hours, but instead turned into days, because of politics. The four days a week we'd agreed, stretched into five and a half and I wasn't having it any more. I quit after eight weeks.

It wasn't all plain sailing. Rob was concerned, fearing a return to the scarcity of money we'd experienced in 1997 after my business collapsed. I reminded him: "I promised you when I decided to do contract work that I'd pay half the bills and fund all my travel without taking any loans. I've kept my promise so far, and – well, you can see there haven't been too many problems finding work," I added quietly. There was no point sounding too confident with Rob, he was very cautious and would often try to deflate me if he thought I was being too optimistic. He called this being realistic. In many ways, we were complete opposites.

"I suppose so," he muttered unenthusiastically. "But I don't want this book and journey going on and on. Remember, I'm the one that has to look after James and the home when you're away."

"Yes, I appreciate that," I conceded. "But I'm around more often these days, and I think it's much better now I've got time to cook decent meals in the evenings. It gives you a break too, doesn't it? All those meals you cooked the past few years."

"OK, just be careful with your money though, don't go on one of your wild shopping sprees," he warned.

With time on my hands, I could confirm my plans for the return. In my head it was written in capitals: RETURN. As I radiated out 'Ethiopia' so my mind became attuned to anything mentioning the country. Visiting the Christmas fair at Stowe School, the BandAid song: 'Do they know it's Christmas?' began blaring out the moment I entered. This was my life now, lots of inklings and waves of intuition, every nerve in my body alert to slight movements and energy fields which pointed to the way ahead.

*****

The most scary decision was returning to church. I'd not worshipped properly for 41 years: they were places to celebrate weddings, funerals and occasional christenings, nothing else. I felt compelled to rejoin, because the amazing synchronicity which dominated my life made me feel very humble and thankful, and for that, I wanted to thank God. This was all too powerful and quick to be random. Anyway, I owed it to him after eight years of a neglected covenant.

Walking into the entrance of St. Peter and Paul's Church whose steeple dominated Buckingham's vista for miles around, was very, very daunting. I needn't have worried. The man beside me in the back pew singing so confidently turned out to be one of the church wardens.

"Hello, I'm Mark Whitehead," he remarked, proffering his hand. "Have you just moved to Buckingham?"

"No, we've lived here for four years, but I've not been to church for 41 years," I said, shamefaced, a flush warming my neck.

"Really, that long?" he replied, as his eyebrows shot up. "Welcome back!" he remarked with a twinkle in his eye. "What's brought about your return then?" Mark was clearly intrigued, even as he acknowledged others with a wave of his hand and a smile as worshippers left the church.

I explained about the dream and the need to worship and acknowledge who was guiding it all. Mark responded: "If it's God's will, which it sounds as if it is, it will all come into place for you. You just need to put all your faith in him."

The following week I met Kevin Ashby, the rector, a tall man with thick greying hair, a wonderful sense of humour and contagious laugh. I was relieved that vicars had lightened up since I was last a church-goer. Mark had introduced us and Kevin was very curious. He had sensed there was more behind the journey than just one dream and invited me to the rectory, a modern house a few minutes walk from the church.

After making a cup of tea, we sat in the church meeting room, making polite talk until he asked: "Tell me about your faith, Annette."

"Well, I was brought up in an agnostic family, although the three of us went to Sunday school when we were little. I've always had deep faith, particularly in Jesus Christ – I suppose I see him like an older brother. So much has happened to me which is more than coincidental since my mum died in 1993. And then there are my dreams."

He listened intently as I related them: his slight nods told me what I had hoped to hear. "Well, God has clearly given you a big challenge, Annette, but he chose you because he has given you the faith and gifts you need to meet it." Dreams and spirituality seemed to be accepted unconditionally by Kevin – a wonderful endorsement.

November 2003 finished with a treat: Bob Geldof's concert at Aylesbury's Civic Theatre. It was very good – better than I expected. The eloquence of the man was extraordinary, each song evoked a story – Ethiopia had touched him very deeply and he spoke of visiting Africa for a TV series he was producing for the BBC.

*****

Kidist called: "Annette, Mulugeta would be very pleased to meet you. I suggest we meet at Victoria station and then I'll leave you, as I'm going out to dinner with a friend."

Rounding the corner, I saw Kidist first sitting outside the Reef café bar, deep in conversation with another Ethiopian. The man nodded politely as she spoke. As I got nearer, I could see he wore a cravat, which dad had often worn: especially when socialising in Africa!

Kidist turned at my approach, and stood up to hug me: "Hi, Annette, good to see you. This is my friend, Mulugeta Kassa Asrate."

Mulugeta too stood up: I could see the royal family's patrician bone structure in his face. "Before we start, what would you like to drink, some wine or a coffee?"

"White wine please, Mulugeta."

Kidist and I exchanged a few pleasantries and then she put her hand on my arm. "I need to go now, you're in safe hands here, Mulugeta's very interested in helping you."

"OK, Kidist, I'll see you soon. Remember I'd like you and Theodros to come round before I go back to Addis, I want to show you some old slides."

"That would be good, give us a call. And if I don't see you before, have a lovely Christmas!"

Dad had left virtually no money when he died, but mum had done me a great favour by giving us his enormous collection of slides, along with the projector and screen. Rob had got on well with dad, and mum had given him his lion of Judah ring and lovely cufflinks: the gold lion offset by black onyx.

"Kidist is a nice lady, isn't she?" I asked Mulugeta, wanting a bit of breathing space before the real questions began.

"Yes, she's very devout, I'm not in church every week, but every time I go, Kidist is there."

"Kidist seemed to think that Mary's your mother, but if so, she must have had you when she was ten!"

"Oh no, no," Mulugeta laughed. "My mother lives here in London, she's quite elderly. Mary's my second cousin. You know, I'm second cousin to Emperor Haile Selassie." I sensed Mulugeta still traded on his royal connections, which seemed very complicated, but most Ethiopians came from big families.

"Where does Mary live now?" I was impatient to get to the heart of the matter.

"Mary lived here for a while, but she's been back in Addis for quite some time," Mulugeta was more relaxed, leaning back in the plastic seat. "Tell you what, what I can do is get you her address and phone number, so you can get in touch. That way, you will at least have one interview in the bag before you return."

"Tell me", he peered, as he shifted in his seat, "you look foreign. Are you Scandinavian by any chance?"

"Yes, half, my mother was Norwegian, from Kristiansand in the south."

"Thank God for that!" he said, sounding relieved. "You know, a Norwegian family was so kind to me when I was languishing in prison, along with other members of the royal family. We were all imprisoned after the Emperor was deposed in 1974."

"That must have been terrible, Mulugeta," I scrabbled to recall the details after the Emperor's deposition, but couldn't. All I could remember was the killings and the rivers of blood during the Derg's cruel rule, people had even been shot in churches in the late 1970's.

"It was, but I was lucky," Mulugeta interrupted my thoughts. "Amnesty International campaigned for the royal family's release and a Norwegian family sort of adopted me. They sent cards and letters and some funds: I even met up with one of the family right here, at Victoria station. Sadly, we lost contact. I can't remember his name any more."

"That is sad." I murmured sympathetically. I wasn't surprised that a Norwegian family had helped out: along with the Swedes they were the most generous Europeans when it came to charity.

"Yes, I'd like to find him again one day," responded Mulugeta, curiosity flickering on his face. "In any event, I was released after nine years in jail, in 1983. I joined my sisters and brothers here in the UK. Along with Mary, we campaigned for the imperial family's freedom."

As Mulugeta spoke, I had the strangest feeling on my face, like an angel blowing on my cheek. This was something I'd never experienced before – a touch of the divine. I tried to stay focused on Mulugeta's story: "How did you go about it?"

"We lobbied a lot of people and spoke to the media, to try and keep attention on our family back home. I even met Terry Waite in January 1987, to see if he could help negotiate for their release. At that time, he was the Church of England envoy to Robert Runcie, the Archbishop of Canterbury – do you remember that?"

"Yes, he was doing lots of work to release hostages in Lebanon, wasn't he?" I tried hard to suppress an inappropriate smile. The company where I'd been so stressed out in the mid-1990's had run an advertising campaign in 1996, featuring one of the Beirut hostages whose release Terry Waite had tried to negotiate: the journalist, John McCarthy.

Mulugeta continued eagerly : "Terry Waite was a very kind man, and promised to see what he could do. But then two weeks later, he himself was taken hostage in Beirut." His tone became more business like: "Now, do you have the school photo to show me?" I carefully pulled it out from the hard-backed envelope I now kept it in, for safety. Handing it to Mulugeta, he began laughing. "Oh my, look at those hairstyles – thank goodness they're long gone!" He pointed to Phoebe and muttered: "Now she looks so much like Boutros-Boutros Ghalli, the former UN secretary-general: I wonder if she's his niece?"

Who knew where the connections led, and who was related to whom? The main thing was that soon I would be in touch with Mary. Potentially, I now had two appointments confirmed: a week with WaterAid and a meeting with Mary. It was only on the train home that I realised another connection: Terry Waite. His face shone before me, from my dream four months earlier. How accurate the metaphor had been – people wanted to help, but most were very pressed for time.

*****

With the twentieth anniversary of Michael Buerk's chilling and moving coverage of northern Ethiopia's famine in 1984, news about the country began appearing once more in newspapers, TV programmes and internet sites. Just before Christmas, there was a special edition of the BBC TV gardening programme: *"Ground Force"*. It always featured a trio of presenters designing and transforming neglected eyesores into beautiful spaces, within two days. In this instance, Alan Titchmarsh, Charlie Dimmock (a lady) and Tommy Walsh had travelled to Addis Ababa to create a garden and play area for the Concern charity. Rob and I had laughed to see the British ambassador, Myles Wickstead arriving in his white Land Rover, Union Jack pennant fluttering, to inspect their work. He never got his hands dirty, I noticed, although he'd lent the team some of his gardeners for the project! Myles had taken the team out for a celebration in a restaurant where they were entertained by tribal dancers. Tommy's eyes were standing on stalks as he ogled the lithe Ethiopian women.

*****

Mulugeta was as good as his word and rang me with Mary's details. He also invited me to an international awards event, the Worldaware Business Awards, which were taking place at the end of January. Mulugeta felt it important that I met Abebech Gobena, head of a large orphanage in Addis Ababa, who was to receive the top accolade: 'Humanitarian of the Year'.

The guest list was impressive, lots of journalists, corporate sponsors and attendees from over twenty countries. I didn't know anyone there, but Mulugeta introduced me to Fisseha Adugna, the Ethiopian ambassador, who was very intrigued about my dream. He shook my hand firmly, stating: "If there's anything I can do to help, don't hesitate to contact me". He also invited me to a reception to honour Abebech at the Ethiopian embassy later that evening

I also met Abba (Father) Bogale Tiruneh, the representative of the Ethiopian Catholic Church in the UK. A tall, beaming man, he wore his faith quietly: there was nothing showy about him, he stood quietly in a plain grey suit over the black shirt and dog collar. He asked about my connection with Ethiopia and appeared captivated by the dream and my vision of a Garden of Peace in Jerusalem. Immediately, he offered to write a letter to Sister Weynemariam (Wine of Mary) Tesfaye, the head teacher of Nazareth School whom he knew well, as it was an important school in the Addis diocese.

Jon Snow, the Channel 4 News presenter, was hosting the event. Hilary Benn, the International Development Secretary had been due to present the awards, but had been called away. Instead, Baroness Valerie Amos, leader of the House of Lords, was presenting them: she was the sister of Colleen, my first boss at Axa Insurance! I shivered in happiness at all these fleeting connections.

Each of the award winners gave a presentation about their project, usually with photos. When it came to the final awards, Mulugeta translated very eloquently for Abebech Gobena, a quiet, motherly figure in her mid 60's, who wore an elegant shama with green and yellow borders. She spoke about the work that her charity, AGOHELD, did with orphans, and the schools she'd set up with the resulting funds. Since 1980, they'd cared for half a million orphans, an incredible number. They also ran four projects in small towns outside the capital, helping provide further education to students who'd not done as well in their final exams as expected (and would therefore find it difficult to get jobs), and gave assistance to families suffering from Aids. She richly deserved the top award.

At the Ethiopian embassy later that evening, I bumped into Myles Wickstead, the British ambassador I'd seen on BBC TV's *"Ground Force."* We had a brief discussion: he told me that his tour of duty had finished as he'd been called back to become Head of the Secretariat for the Commission for Africa, an organisation set up by Tony Blair to investigate the causes of the continent's endemic poverty and to make recommendations. Bob Geldof was one of the commissioners.

Abebech proved to be a real inspiration. She was very humble and thanked God for all the success she had had with her charity. Offering my congratulations, I asked if I could stay with her when I visited Addis in March. She was eager to agree.

The three weeks were now filled with plenty to experience: the first week in Addis, including my meeting with Mary Asfaw Wossen, my former classmate; the second week out in the provinces with WaterAid seeing their project work and the final week at Abebech Gobena's orphanage.

*****

Marshalling high-profile support for my dream was important. Ethiopian Airlines had been the first step, and then I contacted Michael Buerk, the well known BBC TV reporter who'd reported from the famine in northern Ethiopia in October 1984, which had inspired Bob Geldof to write the BandAid song *Do they know it's Christmas time?* and organise LiveAid in 1985. I wanted to see if Michael had any ideas how to promote the old school photo on TV. He was kind enough to reply, but told me that TV was too difficult: he suggested that BBC Radio 4's programme: *"Woman's Hour"* might be able to help. On reflection, I decided it was far too early to contact them.

I had better luck with a man of peace, Archbishop Desmond Tutu. After lunch at Waterstone's book store in Piccadilly with Ken and Linda, with whom I'd worked at RAC, I'd ambled down to the third floor to their religious and spiritual section. Tutu's beaming face caught my eye on the cover of his latest book "God has a dream". ①

I read it from cover to cover within a day and decided to write to him about my dream. His editor at Random House was kind enough to forward on my letter to the great man, and two days before my departure for Addis Ababa, his reply arrived. 'I read of your dream with great interest and wish you well with the writing of you book An Ethiopian Odyssey.' My last task before I packed my bags for my travels in Ethiopia was to photocopy the letter: I felt sure it would come in handy.

Further information:
Ethiopian Airlines: www.ethiopianairlines.com
① Desmond Tutu, *God has a Dream,* Rider, an imprint of Ebury Press, 2004.

III: RETURN TO ETHIOPIA

8 The return

Orange light suffused the cabin. A few travellers had given up on sleep and had opened the blinds to look at the view. Below, the sand was the same colour as the sky – we were flying over Egypt and the Sahara Desert, heading south towards Addis Ababa. Harsh rocks jutted out of flatness, breaking up the unrelenting desert. Occasional circles of green relieved the dry monotony: peering intently, I could just make out roads leading to oases and date farms. The magic of irrigation in the desert!

I'd made as many plans as possible for the three weeks ahead: visiting Nazareth School on Tuesday: meeting with Mary Asfaw Wossen on Wednesday: a few days out on the road visiting projects with WaterAid, and spending the final week at Abebech's orphanage. In the midst of these pragmatic thoughts, I could hardly believe I was actually going to be landing in Addis after forty years. And I had done this all by myself, on the strength of my dreams alone. Each day had been a step on the journey, a few yards in my tall ship, steering towards the final destination: water and peace.

I also acknowledged hesitant and nervous gnawings in my belly: the language barriers, the need for support for what I was doing, being insecure as a woman in a strange country. But I pushed these fears aside and chose to focus my thoughts on finding kind guides who'd show me the way, in return for a meal or a coffee. I'd brought fifty friends with me via the blog site I'd set up, and in my handbag were sixty addresses for people I'd be sending postcards to - probably the only postcards they'd ever receive from Ethiopia.

A few hours later, the plane descended towards Addis Ababa. There were the majestic mountains I remembered from my childhood, and the occasional patchwork fields. As the soil's fertility increased, so did the dwellings – the little round tukuls with their thatched roofs and the fences made from rough, chopped wood, bound together with metal wire if there was enough money. Otherwise, tall cacti did the job of deterring strangers, wandering hyenas and the occasional lion. The landing was perfect: and I could see the new airport buildings close by. There were only 50 or so of us on the flight. A few were intrepid travellers, but the majority were Ethiopians home for a holiday.

Outside, bright sunshine bade us welcome and porters looked anxiously for faranj (foreigners) who would give them a few birr for a tip. I changed some money, using my last £10 note, and walked outside to haggle for a taxi. The Lonely Planet guide ① recommended not paying more than 30 birr to get into town, but I knew my hotel was on the outskirts seven miles away, so when one persistent driver agreed to 40 birr, I let him take my case after some muttering, and sat in front of the beaten up old green Mercedes. My backside acclimatised to the re-covered seats and I had to ignore the lack of seatbelts – a feature of most of the old cars around Addis. It was a wise decision sitting up front, as the back door flew open when we hurtled around a corner.

The smells and sights came flooding back, igniting my memory – bodies unused to clean water, much less deodorant, the throng of humanity walking on the roads alongside donkeys, cars and trucks. The young women bent double under huge piles of wood that they'd gathered at dawn to sell at the market to richer city dwellers; the lack of shoes; the unplanned way in which pavements seem to appear and then disappear, like missing teeth. As we drove along, I wound down the windows and the pungent smell of open sewers filled with rubbish wafted into the car.

Stopping for a short time at a traffic light, two boys in rags stood beside us, laughing and playing on a small island in the middle of the road. When they saw me, their faces changed to instant despair, and then came the tears and: "money, please, I'm so hungry." I had no change, and besides, I knew this would be the first of many such requests. I had to harden myself, and keep my eye on the bigger picture of what I was trying to achieve.

Addis's population seemed to have grown five-fold since I was last there. Tin shanties were squeezed in everywhere, and the open spaces down by the Jubilee Palace were no more. The garis (horse drawn carts), too, had disappeared. In their place were blue and white Toyota people carriers, which served as the local buses. Conductors leaned out of windows, bawling their destinations. Queues formed in a random fashion, but when the bus stopped people hurried up to pay their money before being allowed on – he who pays first gets the seat. Once the maximum possible number had been squashed into the back, they set off.

Rusty, corrugated iron roofs shimmered in the sunshine, and local entrepreneurs sold their wares outside many small huts – whether it was iron beds, furniture, tyres, or welding, most seemed to have some kind of business going on. We drove up a series of hills, passing the old Menelik Palace, where Mulugeta and Emperor Haile Selassie had been imprisoned all those years ago. Finally, after driving along a winding crescent, the taxi driver turned left up the steep, potholed road leading to the front entrance of the Ras Amba Hotel.

An old sabanya (night watchman) saluted me and offered to help take my suitcase. The hotel was a plain, three-storey structure set into the hillside north of the centre. I'd chosen it because of its views over Addis from the roof terrace and its large satellite TV, so I could keep up with the news. It was popular with others too – lots of sports fans would descend for an afternoon's or evening's hard drinking whilst cheering for their favourite soccer team. Manchester United seemed to be number one, and David Beckham was a local god.

My room was clean and airy. I opened the door on to a small balcony to get my bearings. Below, houses of all sizes tumbled down the hills towards central Addis. The more expensive ones had concrete walls with iron railings above, built cheek by jowl with little tin shacks and occasional tukuls. Car ownership was reserved for the very wealthy, so small dirt paths wound between the houses. Traffic noise was constant: lorries grumbled their way up the hill towards the north, and every other car was a people taxi discharging its human cargo on the way to or from work and school. I lay down to try and catch up on some sleep.

*****

The phone's shrill, insistent ringing interrupted my dreams. I groped sleepily for the receiver. "Tanasterlign Annette, and welcome to Addis!" It was Helen Pankhurst.

"Hi Helen, great to speak to you again," I sat up to make myself comfortable.

"Notice many changes since you were last here?"

"Many? They're innumerable, Helen, I hardly recognise anything!"

"Well yes, Addis has changed quite a lot since 1964!" chuckled Helen.

We chatted for several minutes, and Helen confirmed the various arrangements she'd made for the week. She'd already organised a reliable guide to help me, a former civil servant who spoke good English: Tirlaye Gebre Medhin. Tirlaye was to accompany me over the next few days. In return, it was the custom to pay for his travel and any food. We also agreed to meet up on the Thursday in WaterAid's office near the Globe Hotel.

Wide awake now, my stomach rumbled and I changed into a clean T-shirt, to find the hotel's restaurant for lunch. I chose a table on the terrace from where I could see for miles to the mountains on the south side of the city, which planes skirted before arriving and departing at Bole airport. Ethiopian eagles swooped in the sky and tiny hummingbirds beat their wings a thousand times a minute while their long, thin beaks sucked nectar from the flowers on the terrace. I sighed happily in recollection – this was the Addis I remembered and loved.

A waiter in a dapper black and white checked jacket approached with the menu. I giggled at the thought that he looked just like Geoffrey, the butler from the American TV series Fresh Prince of Bel Air. After giving him my order, I asked his name.

"Girma," he smiled.

His teeth were dazzling against his blue-black skin. He told me he was a trainee manager there. As I looked at the menu, I could see that it was strictly European food. That was disappointing: I'd been looking forward to tasting injera and watt again and drinking the rich, sweet Ethiopian coffee. Never mind, I mused: this trip was one of discovery, and I'd have plenty of time to do things and go to places that felt right. My intuition had become my trusty inner compass.

Later on, Tiringo Lemma, the restaurant manager, came to introduce herself. Small dimples played around her mouth as she asked directly:

"Tell me, are you here for a holiday, or on business?" When I told her she sucked in her breath, and asked how she and Girma could help me.

"I'd like to go out for a walk this afternoon and get some exercise after the long flight. Could you take me to that church I can see over there?" I pointed to a white dome on the right, jutting out amidst the tall eucalyptus.

"Yes of course," she replied, dimples lifting her cheeks. "If you wish, we can show you some other churches. Depends on how much time you have – we're both free this afternoon. Then I'll take you to my home for a coffee ceremony. Would you like to taste some real Ethiopian coffee again?"

"Yes, yes please, that's so kind of you, Tiringo." I was taken aback by her instant hospitality, but I shouldn't have been. The kisses and hugs from daily greetings in the playground crept into my memory once more.

"You're welcome, very welcome," she smiled.

Girma and Tiringo were waiting in reception when I came down. Tiringo wore a casual netallah (shawl) around her shoulders, a long skirt and flip-flops: Girma sported a bright red polo shirt with 'Village Ethiopia' sewn on the chest. It was the logo of a tour company run by a friend of Helen Pankhurst's, and Girma explained that he had visited one of their villages the year before. I realised then that I'd found the right guides: two friendly, spontaneous Ethiopians willing to spend an afternoon helping a lone tourist.

We meandered along the roads heading up towards the church. There were no pavements here and little children ran along crying "faranj, faranj!" I replied "tanasterlign," - 'may health go with you' - the only word of Amharic I could manage that day.

Hundreds of mourners poured through the church gates of Holy Trinity Cathedral, Addis Ababa's main church, where Haile Selassie was buried. How fortunate that I'd found the right one straight away – this was something I could ask Mary about in a couple of days. It was an Ethiopian custom for anyone who knew the deceased to pay their respects. Their devotion was very dramatic: worshippers prostrated themselves on the church steps and again at the entrance. Many stood kissing the frames of its huge wooden doors, and shoes were removed before they went in to pray. But just as I was focusing the camera to take some photos, a man marched up to us, looking annoyed and gesturing to Girma.

"What did he say?" I asked.

"That you can't take photos, or if you do, you have to pay a hundred birr."

"That's just too much, I'll leave it."

We walked to two other churches: St Gabriel's and Be'hta le Mariam, (St. Mary's) close to the old Menelik Palace. The latter was a circular building with a three-tiered roof painted in the colours of the Ethiopian flag: green, yellow and red, including the decorative metal work around the roofs' edges, like an ornate wedding cake.

From there, it was a short distance to Tiringo's bedsit. In those brief minutes I felt at home once more: donkeys still chewed grass at the roads' edges, goats bleated, mangy dogs slept curled up in the sun, their coats the same colour as the dust. Street hawkers squatted by their wares and children looked inquisitively at the strange woman with white skin. The beggars were everywhere, more populous than in '64. They assailed you with hands outstretched: "Money, money," "I need food to eat." If you gave to one, the rest would flock like birds around you. I found it better to wish them each a Christian greeting: "Ekserstelign" – God give you.

Tiringo's bedsit was in the same courtyard as a local nursery. Splashed along the corrugated iron fence were English letters in bright colours, with the Amharic ones below. She shared a toilet and outside tap with two other families in the small compound. The room was dark as we stepped inside and she hurried over to the window and opened the shutters, letting in the light. On uneven wattle and daub walls hung Ethiopian religious posters along with photos of her and her boyfriend, who was away working in Harer. They'd been together for almost three years.

Tiringo lit a small fire in a pan on the floor. She reached into a cupboard to retrieve the coffee pot, with its narrow spout and rounded base for heating on charcoal. The coffee ceremony commenced: Tiringo advanced with a flat tray on which the green coffee beans nestled, prior to roasting. Girma nodded approval, and soon acrid smoke filled the room before the delicious tang of coffee wafted in the air. Taking the pan off the stove, Tiringo fanned the aroma towards us – an important moment. Taking my cue from Girma, I murmured appreciation. Tiringo then ground the beans using a pestle and mortar. Fetching some water from the tap outside, she spooned the coffee into the coffee pot before adding water. The pot bubbled away on the coals .

"Here, have some popcorn," Tiringo urged, pushing a big bowl towards us. "Go on" she prodded as I shook my head. I was still full from lunch. "It's the tradition with coffee." I took a couple of handfuls and the three of us sat companionably around the small fire, Tiringo on the bed with its crocheted doily-style bedspread and Girma and I on a hard sofa. The room was very simple, but she had everything she needed in there.

After the coffee was poured, with mine being poured first as is the custom with guests, we discussed the main changes that had happened in the country since 1964, especially its poverty. I described some of the sights I remembered, but they were coloured by nostalgia and were, perhaps, too positive. Neither of the pair had been alive back then – Tiringo was 32 and Girma just 28.

Girma was convinced that the main problem was the population explosion. It had grown by 250 per cent since 1964. Children are regarded as gifts from God, and when you don't have much money, having free labour is very important. Both Girma and Tiringo wanted small families – two children at most. We talked about work and life at the hotel, and I asked, "What are your dreams?"

"To have my own restaurant one day," replied Tiringo. "Serving good food – Ethiopian of course. And for my boyfriend and I to live together." Her expression was poignant: "He's been away over three months now and I really miss him. He has his own place, but I'd like us to be together."

"And you, Girma?"

"To work in a holiday or tour company. I enjoy meeting people and using my English."

"Your English is very good – far better than my Amharic!" I laughed.

He chuckled: "Yes, but we learn it at school from the age of twelve. I would also like to travel overseas. I've never been on a plane before. Sometimes it's difficult to find the money to even go home to my family – waiters aren't paid much here."

By now it was almost evening, and they took me to a local taxi rank where Girma introduced me to Yalikel, a friend of his, a tall, handsome young man. "If you like, you can hire me for half a day," he grinned. "I will give you a good price." On the dashboard was a photo of his girlfriend, a beautiful woman with long dark hair. "She's Muslim, but she will convert when we marry: I'm confident of that," he added.

*****

The next day I met Tirlaye, the guide organised by Helen Pankhurst. He wore a homburg hat, square, gilt-framed glasses and a dark brown suit that had seen better days. He leapt up from the chair as I approached, a man of the old school. He was very knowledgeable and told me about the various foreigners, including some ambassadors, whom he'd tutored in Amharic. He had worked with Helen before and knew her father, Professor Richard Pankhurst. Richard had moved to Ethiopia in the late 1950's, accompanying his mother, Sylvia, where they'd made Addis their permanent home.

Yalikel sat outside in his blue and white taxi – this was the best arrangement, as Tirlaye didn't have a car. We drove up and down hills for several minutes. I didn't recognise much until we came to a wider road and headed down a sloping avenue, along which were several large schools. Yalikel dropped us off: he wouldn't be joining us. I knew the railings of Nazareth School for Girls the moment I saw them: I sighed with relief when I saw that it was still standing. In my bag was the introductory letter from Abba Bogale to Sister Weynemariam Tesfaye, the head teacher. Nostalgia threatened to turn into tears, but I brushed them away.

Now, there was wooden boarding behind the iron railings, presumably for privacy and to protect the pupils during the time of the Derg, the oppressive military junta that ruled Ethiopia after the Emperor was overthrown. Tirlaye had a few words with the sabanya and he opened the metal gate to let us in. As he pulled open the squeaky gate, I was overwhelmed – virtually nothing had changed. The steps where we'd stood for our class photo still remained, as did the double metal doors to reception, but the rubber tree in front had grown another twenty feet in forty years. Walking inside, I could see the library at the back, where I'd once sat with other pupils having lunch that first month. Even the anteroom to the head's office was exactly the same.

"Excuse me, I wonder if it might be possible to see Sister Weynemariam this morning?" I asked the receptionist who sat behind a sliding glass window.

"Do you have an appointment?"
"No, but I've come a long way, from England. I was a pupil here, back in 1964."

The receptionist shrugged and informed us that the head teacher was in a meeting. I gave her my most polite smile, gulping back sudden nerves that I might stumble at the first hurdle. "Please tell her that a former pupil has come all the way from England to meet her."

Sister Weynemariam Tesfaye and Marta Asrat (right),
my former classmate

Tirlaye and I returned outside to wait in the rubber tree's shade. Although it was normally autumn in March, a fierce sun beat down and its thick glossy leaves gave us respite from the heat. As we talked, an Abyssinian eagle swooped from above and landed a few feet away. With its large wings folded in, it looked far less dangerous, almost friendly.

"It's alright, I can see you now," announced a short, bespectacled woman who hurried out to greet us. Sister Weynemariam didn't look much older than some of her pupils. "I had a meeting with some parents but they'd forgotten their papers, so we had to cancel it," she explained. "Now, exactly why are you here?"

She ushered us into her office. Behind the desk, a stinkwood cabinet was crammed full of trophies won over the years. Ethiopian art was displayed on either side. As she motioned us to sit down, I gave her Abba Bogale's letter, which she read carefully before turning to me.

"I see you know Abba Bogale," her smile was definitely warmer now. "How can I help you?"

"Sister Weynemariam, I need your help in finding the surnames of seven former classmates, whom I last saw in 1964. I'm hoping to write about their lives for a book to bring water to Ethiopia." I paused to hand over a copy of the old school photo.

Sister Weynemariam stared intently at it. A flicker of recognition ran across her face. "Hmmm... I think I might have one of your classmates in the room behind us!" She rose quickly to her feet and began knocking at a door by the display cabinet. "Marta, come and meet one of your classmates from the 1960s!"

Out of the door walked Marta Asrat, wearing a quizzical expression. I was shocked and amazed, nerves tingling throughout my body. Staring at me, she smiled hesitantly. Then her grin got larger. "I think I can just about remember you. I work here as school secretary!"

What good fortune - I was hoping she could help me find the missing names. We hugged each other and she drew up another chair. Sister Weynemariam handed her the old school photo and Marta's face lit up.

"Oh yes, I can still recall most of them." She began rattling off names, far too quickly for me to jot down.

I interrupted, "That's why I'm here, Marta, to find the classmates' full names. Do you think you might have them still in your archives? It's such a long time ago."

"I'm sure we have, I will ask one of my team to help. The old files are down in the basement."

As she stared at the photo, she pointed at one of the faces. "That woman there, she's Hiruth: Hiruth Girma, the daughter of our President, Girma Wolde-Giorgis."

With that remark, the list of women I needed to trace had grown longer. I decided to add Marta after my good fortune in finding her, and I couldn't leave out Hiruth, the daughter of such an important man. Sister Weynemariam told me that the school was celebrating its 50th anniversary that year, but they had no formal plans to commemorate it: funds were limited. She also described how they'd educated the daughters of Colonel Mengistu Haile Mariam, the former Derg leader, who'd fled into exile in Zimbabwe just before the Ethiopian People's Revolutionary Democratic Front marched into Addis Ababa on 28 May 1991.②

"Frances Bring had been head at the time. We had had long discussions about it, but she pointed out that it was our role to stand by what we believed: to bring education to girls of all nationalities and religions, regardless of background. His two daughters were very smart, very respectful girls, and I'm sure their values would have rubbed off on him."

As I shook her and Marta's hands before I left, I was completely shocked and awe-inspired. The meeting had been successful beyond my wildest dreams.

*****

Later that evening Tirlaye, Yalikel and I drove west from the city centre, looking for Villa Verde, the hotel my family lived in. Yalikel told me it had changed – it was now an Ethiopian restaurant called 'Agelgil' (bread basket) with tribal music and dances. In the darkness the streets teemed with people, as we bounced through deep potholes past brightly lit shacks and little shops where locals bought their groceries. Most of these dwellings had been built after I'd left Ethiopia. As we crossed the railway line, my anticipation increased – we weren't far from the building where I'd spent a year of my childhood.

Driving in, I could just about recognise the exterior: the same marble steps were there. Now thatched umbrellas and tables were placed outside for lunchtime snacks and weekend meals. The corridor we'd walked through to reach the restaurant had been transformed into one long bar. As we followed the manager to our table through those familiar double doors, I saw that everything had changed: the restaurant with its cappuccino bar in the corner was transformed into a dance floor with small tables around it. A thatched, decked area had been built beside the double doors where the band now played, and water trickled over rocks and lichen-covered stone down one wall, with a corner seat for a musician.

Something inside me clicked – I'd seen this recently. Then Tommy Walsh's raucous laughter echoed in my ears – this is where Myles Wickstead, the British ambassador, had taken the *Ground Force* team in the episode that had been shown on TV over Christmas on BBC 1!

The service and food were exemplary, and the two tribal dancing couples mesmerising. How they managed to change their costume ten times in an hour, I'll never know. There were influences of Egyptian, Russian and Indian movements, but unique to Ethiopia were the shudders which ran from head to toe, like a Jewish harp.

Yalikel, Tirlaye and I celebrated two productive days with some St. George's beer and red Ethiopian wine – what a night! I silently toasted my brothers and parents and the many happy meals we'd enjoyed at Villa Verde.

Further information:

① Lonely Planet *Guide to Ethiopia and Eritrea,* Lonely Planet Publications, 2003
② Harold G. Marcus, *A History of Ethiopia,* p 217, University of California Press, 2002 edition

---

9 Bringing back smiles

The small six-year-old boy turned away as I walked into the paediatrics ward at Yekatit 12 hospital, north east of Addis city centre. Helene Toppstad was accompanying me – the Norwegian woman whose family photo I'd seen in *Fedrelandsvennen* in Kristiansand last August. The boy's parents had gone for the day, and he was all alone and ashamed of the gaping hole in his top lip – the cleft lip and palate that would be operated on the following day. An older boy waved and smiled. He'd been operated on two days ago, and was getting used to trying out his new, joined-up smile.

These boys were just two of the reasons why Helene and her husband Thom had decided to leave their comfortable home overlooking a fjord in Kristiansand to practise plastic surgery and anaesthesia at the hospital. Thom had qualified as an ear, nose and throat (ENT) surgeon in 1992 and became a qualified plastic surgeon in 1995. He and Helene had met in 1991 while working at Vest Agder hospital in Kristiansand and married two years later.

Thom's love affair with Africa had begun in the Gambia when he volunteered to work for St. John's School for the Deaf in Serrekunda for several weeks each year. He went on to establish an ENT outpatients' department at the Royal Victoria Hospital in Banjul, where he was responsible for training surgeons in ENT operations. After the Gambian project which lasted six years, it seemed a natural step in 2003 for Thom to accept the contract in Ethiopia.

In Addis, he'd joined another Norwegian, Paul Gravem, who headed up the project. Since 1986, Paul's dream had been to establish multidisciplinary treatment for patients with cleft lips and palates (CLP), including surgery, speech therapy and orthodentistry. The condition frequently isolates sufferers, when villagers and sometimes even family members ignore, ostracise or tease them because of their facial appearance.

The hospital chosen for this venture was Yekatit 12 and the improvements were funded by NORAD, a Norwegian non-governmental organisation which provides long-term aid overseas. Originally named the Haile Selassie I hospital, it had been built in 1923. All the royal children and grandchildren had been born there, including my classmates, Mary and Sihin. The Emperor had his own private building and church in the hospital grounds.

Thom and Helene's decision had to include their three children: Eline, ten, Lars-Mathias, five and little Mathilda, two. They had settled in the Norwegian compound with its own Lutheran church and lovely gardens. Just across the road was the Norwegian and Swedish school, opened on 11 January 1965 by King Olav of Norway. This meant that the children could continue studying the Norwegian curriculum: Addis was now their home from home.

As I knocked on the wooden kitchen door, a smiling, blonde Norwegian appeared: Helene, tanned from the seven months in Ethiopia. The house was comfortably furnished, everything bought from local shops, and we sat and chatted companionably for half an hour. Eline was at school, while little Mathilda was out with the nanny, and Lars-Mathias was enjoying the snow back home in Kristiansand with his father.

As Yalikel lounged in one of the chairs, reading the local paper, Helene showed me the before and after images of some of Thom's patients on their PC. It was remarkable the transformation that his surgery wrought and all this cost the patients nothing. In fact, the hospital gave the patients the greatest gift – a normal life once more.

Over lunch with Eline and Mathilda, Helene described her role as anaesthetics nurse, a difficult one with the old equipment they had in the hospital. Finding the safest way to anaesthetise patients required real resourcefulness, and raising funds for new equipment was high on Helene's priority list. Her role now included working with the architect for the new 18-bed CLP unit, making sure that the interiors and equipment were the same standard as in developed countries.

Yekatit 12 had large grounds and lovely gardens, improvements introduced by another Norwegian plastic surgeon, Dr Einar Eriksen, who had been born in Ethiopia. The hospital had general surgery, gynaecology, paediatrics, medical, burns and cleft lip and palate wards. Both the burns and CLP projects were funded by NORAD. As with many highly indebted poor countries, the Ethiopian government didn't have the budget to fund all the improvements needed.

Before we left, Helene showed me the women's burns ward, where six beds were occupied. One patient, with burns to over half of her body, had only been admitted the day before. Her life hung in the balance: following a heated argument, a neighbour had thrown kerosene over her and then lit a match.

After the visit Helene dropped me back at my hotel, where I was meeting Tirlaye. We had an important appointment that afternoon with Abune Berhaneyesus Souraphiel, the Archbishop of the Ethiopian Catholic Church.

*****

'May peace prevail on earth' was inscribed on the tall, white metal pole in the church gardens outside the simple offices. Abba Bogale had given me the Archbishop's phone number and I'd rung his office that morning, asking to meet him and explaining the English connection.

I had assumed that arranging an audience would take several days, but Abune Berhaneyesus was curious: "This sounds most interesting, Annette. Abba Bogale wouldn't have recommended you speak to me lightly. When are you free? I have some time this afternoon – is four o'clock OK with you?"

I was delighted: three days in, and already so many things were beginning to slot into place. I wanted to explain my journey and dreams to the Abune, to get his blessing. Sometimes what was going on felt so extraordinary that I had to stop on the way and ask for prayers from religious leaders. In fact, I'd found that one of the most momentous occasions was when someone prayed for me, that my dream might be fulfilled. It was very humbling, and tears would often trickle down my face – heartbreaking in the best possible way.

As we sat on small wooden chairs in the passageway outside the Archbishop's office, Tirlaye explained church protocol and the need to bow and kiss the cross that the Abune would be holding. A small sign hung from the doorknob of his office: 'Bless all who enter here.'

We were ushered in, where Abune Berhaneyesus sat behind a large mahogany desk. Resplendent in navy blue robes, with a fuchsia pink belt and hat, he had a gentle face and a silver grey goatee. Around his neck and in his hands were the famous Lalibela crosses of Ethiopia in solid silver. Tirlaye bowed and kissed the cross, and I followed suit. I wasn't used to kissing crosses and wanted to make sure I got it right.

"Annette," he murmured in a rich voice. "How good to meet you. How did you meet Abba Bogale?"

Tirlaye Gebre Medhin, my trusty guide with Abune
Berhaneyesus Souraphiel

"It was at the Worldaware Business Awards in London, in January," I replied. "He was there with the Ethiopian ambassador and several of the embassy people. Abba

Bogale was so trusting and helpful to me: he recognised straight away that this was a holy journey." The words had gushed out and I felt myself blushing, but the Abune neither laughed nor looked away.

"Tell me this story of yours, and about your dreams," he said gently.

He motioned us to sit on the red velvet and gilt chairs. I sat opposite, feeling anxious: would he believe me? As I related the dreams I'd had since I was a teenager, the events of Easter 2003 and the abundant coincidences that had populated my life since then, the Abune listened thoughtfully, occasionally nodding. Peace seemed to glow around him: I couldn't imagine him ever raising his voice in anger.

When I had finished, he cleared his throat. "I'm delighted to hear that Nazareth School has such a devout former student. They are a very good school and an important part of our diocese." He smiled gently. "I do believe that this is indeed God's will, Annette. This is an amazing blessing that he is showing you and it's clear how his will is working through you."

This was praise indeed, and warmed my heart when I thought of how sceptical other people had been: but now was no time for arrogance. Silence descended and he bowed his head to pray both for his people and that the journey might have a successful conclusion – water for the poor in Ethiopia and peace in the Holy Land. The Abune returned to his desk and sat there smiling. We had to leave as he was due to give a service shortly. My mind raced back to the conversation I'd had with Marta and her comment about Hiruth Girma, the President's daughter. Summoning my courage, I asked one more favour. "Abune, do you by any chance have the phone number for the President? I would very much like to contact him to see if it's possible to find out Hiruth's whereabouts before I leave Addis."

"Somewhere I think I have his details. Let me check my box - ah, here they are."

He read out the number as I scribbled it in my notebook. Escorting Tirlaye and me outside, he shook my hand firmly and with his blessing "May God go with you," the audience was over.

Further information:
NORAD   www.norad.no
Ethiopian Catholic Church: www.ecs.org.et

10   A Princess's tale

The old, gold Mercedes estate car had come to collect me at four. Inside, it was immaculate, although the springs had long ago lost their firmness. In the late afternoon sun we drove quietly through central Addis to the Bole area, which is more affluent, with many grand houses hidden behind eight-foot high concrete walls and impenetrable iron gates. When we turned into a broad road full of embassy residences, I gazed in awe at the Malawian compound, replete with two giant satellite dishes and an imposing three-storey house. I wondered how that compared in size to the average Malawian home: diplomats should be accorded respect, but they also need to be in touch with the rhythm of daily life, both at home, and in their host countries.

The driver hooted and the sabanya opened the metal gates. In front of me was a bungalow with a pleasant veranda facing onto an L-shaped garden. I walked up the steps, very aware that this would be my first interview with a former classmate. But this wasn't a time for nerves.

Princess Mary, or Mary as she now prefers to be called, stood watching on the veranda. She wasn't much taller than when I remembered her, perhaps two inches or so. She wore a shimmering lilac cotton shama and netallah and dainty gold sandals, with toenails painted the same colour as her clothing. With her slim legs, she reminded me of a bird of paradise perched on a branch, resting.

"Tanasterlign, welcome to Addis! At last we meet, Annette." She extended her hand, and I shook it, unsure of protocol.

Mary showed me into a comfortable lounge and introduced me to her mother, Crown Princess Medfrish Worq, now in her mid-70s. Photos of her father, Crown Prince Asfaw Wossen, and her sister Sihin stood on the mantelpiece by the fireplace. There were some Ethiopian artefacts dotted around, but the impression that I got looking around the plain, painted walls of the room was that it was a place where people stayed for a while, rather than a permanent home. There was a loneliness present, like a hotel suite waiting for the next guests.

The Crown Princess, a tall, statuesque woman with white silver hair and a bright, inquiring mind, asked me lots of questions about my journey, and how I found Addis after forty years. She was fascinated by the idea of someone acting on what they'd seen in a dream to help the poor. A maid came in to serve tea for us, on little tables in front of us, along with biscuits from Saudi Arabia. Then Mary helped her mother to her room, so that we could sit and talk at length about her memories from the past fifty years.

Settling herself beside me, Mary asked brightly: "Would you like me to begin with our childhood and life at the palace?"

"Yes please," I said, "you never told me any of this when we were schoolmates. I think I spoke more to Sihin than to you."

She laughed. "That's true! Hmmm, well, my first early memories are of our birthday parties. I used to share them with Sihin, who's a year younger than me. All our relatives would come around to our house, about five minutes drive from my grandfather's palace."

"We had an English nanny for four years and she introduced us to British birthday party rituals: we would play musical chairs and have treasure hunts. All the music was European and the guests would always sing Happy Birthday to us both. We'd have a big cake, biscuits and popcorn. Those were a big treat, as Ethiopians at that time generally didn't eat much cake or sweet things. There'd also be balloons and those curly whistles you used to get: lots of noise, in other words!"

Mary had quickly got into her stride: there was little point stopping her whilst she recalled the early memories. Her bright, clear voice filled the large room where we sat. "I remember we'd always get new clothes just before our birthdays. It was the one day of the year when we could go into town and pick out exactly the clothes and shoes that we wanted to wear."

She turned to look at the black and white photo of Sihin and her on the lawn with their father: two young girls dressed in frothy organza dresses with puff sleeves and big ribbons from the belt which fastened at the back. They looked like little princesses enjoying a wonderful day with their father. What saddened me was that it was one of only two photos in the room.

She continued, "My grandmother, the Empress Menen, would always give us a nice piece of jewellery. One year I got a lovely amethyst necklace: it was mostly always gold and made by local jewellers. My grandfather the Emperor would give us gold ingots, which my parents would put somewhere safe for us.

"Until we were nine and ten years old, we were educated at the palace by an English couple, Mr and Mrs Jerry. They taught all 14 grandchildren, and lessons would start at 8.30am: Mrs. Jerry taught each child according to his ability. It was taxing but fun. We'd play rounders and tennis. The girls also studied ballet and learned to play the piano." Listening to her was like listening to the BBC *World Service* in the 1960s. Mary's English was polite and formal, a throwback to the Jerrys' education, perhaps.

"Every Christmas, we would stage a play or musical: some sort of entertainment to mark the start of the festive season. All the parents would come along and watch the production. I was always excited when the end came, because then I knew it wouldn't be long until Christmas Day and presents.

"Do you want me to continue?" remarked Mary, turning towards me.

"Yes, Mary, these stories are interesting," I urged.

"Let's have a little break for a moment. Your cup is empty - I think you need another another pot of tea, don't you?" She called out to the maid, who hurried into the kitchen for more hot beverages.

Stirring her coffee slowly, she stared through the lounge windows. "Although the Ethiopian Christmas is celebrated on 7th January, the Western Epiphany, the Emperor always made the 25th December a special day for us and all the diplomats' children in Addis at the time. We had a Christmas tree at home, but my parents were under strict instructions from His Majesty not to give us any presents until we went to the Jubilee Palace on Menelik II Avenue – the newest of the Emperor's Palaces.

I noticed that Mary still referred to her grandfather as the Emperor or His Majesty. I wanted to ask whether she'd ever called him 'grandad' but decided it was inappropriate.

"At midnight at Christmas Eve, we would go to Estafanos Church and then return home to feast. This was a tradition in most Ethiopian homes. But we weren't allowed to open our presents until we went to the palace at four on Christmas Day. All the diplomats would be there with their families, and we'd be ushered into a big room with a large Christmas tree. There seemed to be hundreds of presents!" Mary's eyes lit up, as if the cascade of different wrapped shapes were still in front of her.

"On display would be lots of cakes and biscuits and a big Christmas cake: one year camels brought in the presents, something that every child attending must remember! My grandfather would give us wonderful toys, and for the occasion we'd have special new dresses, made from silk in lovely pastel colours by Madame Hal. The boys would each get a new suit."

Mary's early memories appeared idyllic: being a member of Ethiopia's imperial family was a privilege that she was aware of and appreciated. But her tone changed as she recalled the events of 12 December 1960, when the first cracks in support for the Emperor began to appear. People were beginning to become impatient at the slow rate of economic reform and the Emperor's autocratic rule.

"Life changed for me on my twelfth birthday. We were at home with my mother and waiting for my father to return. That night, he didn't."

Emperor Haile Selassie was out of the country on a State visit to Brazil, when a coup d'etat was staged. The ringleaders were Germame Neway, a senior civil servant, his brother Brigadier General Mengistu Neway, the head of the Imperial Bodyguard, and Colonel Workineh Gebeyehu, His Majesty's Chief of Security. They stormed the Guenet Leul Palace and imprisoned most of the ministers they found there: the coup was also supported by university students, who were becoming increasingly militant. (Today the Guenet Leul Palace houses the Institute for Ethiopian Studies on Addis Ababa University's campus.)

Anxiety filled her voice as she recalled the fateful event. "It was very frightening. Our house was surrounded: all the schools were closed. I heard gunfire blazing all night long as the Imperial Bodyguard and the General's forces battled it out between them.

We were kept safe in the cellars with our cousins, including Mulugeta Asrate. The insistent gunfire would sometimes be punctuated by the sound of fighter jets bombing close to our house. We had to have all our meals in the cellars: sometimes we were let out for two or three hours to play between lulls in the fighting. We were all very worried about my father and didn't know what had happened to him."

The Guenet Leul Palace where the 1960 coup d'etat ended

Emperor Haile Selassie learnt of the coup and was advised to fly first to Asmara, the Eritrean capital. From there, he returned to Addis Ababa, where he met the Crown Prince. The abortive coup ended: but not before most of the ministerial prisoners were killed in the Guenet Leul Palace, besides which stood the imperial children's former school. One result of the fighting was the decision to educate Mary and Sihin at a private school, and then later in Europe. The Emperor also decided on another change: he moved to the Jubilee Palace in Menelik II Avenue, built in 195, to celebrate his silver jubilee.

"In 1961, my mother told us that she'd decided that we should mix more with other girls of our age and go to Nazareth School. The school offered the best education that girls could get at the time, but I was still a little nervous about having to meet so many girls. But that was the beginning of a happy period for me.

"We were plunged into the deep end, joining at fifth grade in September 1962. We would always go home for lunch.   However, through classwork and games, we gradually got to know more girls and shared things with them. I especially liked the samosa pastries that some girls brought to school! From those early days, we both made lifelong friendships."

"Do you think you were treated specially?" I interrupted, wanting to see if her memories differed from mine.

"No, I don't think so." Mary stopped and took a sip of coffee – the porcelain cup had bands of gold and an Ethiopian pattern around the rim, stories from ancient history. "There were times when I'd have to kneel, hands stretched out in front of Mrs. Blake, our maths teacher, for a rapping, because I'd got too many sums wrong. We took part in games sessions and I also enjoyed being part of the choir – two things we'd not had at the palace."

While Mary and Sihin settled in at Nazareth School, friends of her parents were searching for a suitable boarding school in Britain for them. The Scott-Browns, both doctors, visited a number of suitable public schools, and sent a telegram telling Crown Princess Medrish Worq that they'd found two places at Benenden School in Kent, the same boarding school attended by Princess Anne, Queen Elizabeth's daughter. Mary and Sihin were the only Africans to attend the school at that time, but not the only royals: Princess Basma Hussein, the youngest sister of the late King Hussein of Jordan, was in the same year. It meant that they'd be away from their family for the first time ever.

"How did you acclimatise when it was your first time away from home?"

"We'd been allowed to take some Ethiopian snacks with us: dabo, small baked balls of bread; kollo, a cracked, roasted barley, and kwanta, dried meat. After the first two weeks, I wrote to my mother, 'Please tell Miss Clarke not to force us to eat porridge.' Along with the school uniform, which I hated, I found the weather a complete nightmare!" Mary shuddered as she remembered the cold.

"It helped that we always returned home for the school holidays. Part of our education as members of the imperial family involved attending some of the Emperor's meetings. Twice a week he held a public court called Chilot, or Supreme Court. We would stand behind the Emperor and listen to the arguments between the defence and prosecution. This taught us patience and discipline.

"Sihin and I would also be invited to official dinners at the Palace, where we would often be seated beside foreign officials and other dignitaries. This taught us protocol and how to converse with people from other parts of the world. My grandfather taught me responsibility and to take leadership seriously. Above all, he passed on the lesson of being involved in our country and community, and to love and serve Ethiopia."

Mary completed her A-levels at Millfield School, then trained as a Montessori teacher in London and taught at the Montessori School in St John's Wood, London. In 1972 she returned to Addis Ababa.

"How did you meet your husband?" I was curious to know whether it had been an arranged marriage and how lavish the wedding celebrations had been.

"Just before I left England for good, Professor Edward Ullendorf of the School of Oriental and African Studies, (SOAS), who was also Honorary Chairman of the Anglo-Ethiopian Society, introduced me to Seifu Zewde. We had dinner together at the Hilton Hotel in Park Lane, after which we lost contact.

"A year later we were reintroduced by Rahel Mesfin, a cousin of mine. One evening, we decided to go to the new disco at the Ghion Hotel after dinner. That second meeting was more fruitful and romance blossomed," she smiled wistfully at the memory.

"How did you celebrate your wedding?"

"We had a huge celebration which lasted for three days," recalled Mary. "It was at St. Mary's Church, Sidist Kilo, close to where I'd been born. I didn't wear a traditional Ethiopian wedding dress, instead I had a European bridal dress with hat and veil. After the wedding, we went to my grandfather's palace to say goodbye to our close relatives. The following day, my husband's family gave a huge dinner and the day after that, my parents reciprocated. We had traditional Ethiopian food with dishes from all the provinces, and wine and tej (honey and barley mead). The final celebration was with the diplomatic corps, after which we left for our honeymoon in China."

The winds of change were blowing across the world during the time of Mary's wedding. Students went on marches and demonstrations throughout the 1960s, particularly against the Vietnam war. As more of the world became industrialised, the oil-rich states discovered the true value of their black gold and an oil crisis was declared early in 1973. This meant long delays at petrol pumps: in London, where I worked at the time, offices were only open for three days and when the power cuts came, we worked by candlelight. News of this spilled across to Africa, where prices also rose, and Ethiopian students became more impatient for change.

In December 1973, teachers went on strike for more money, and in February 1974 the prime minister and the cabinet resigned. They were replaced by an interim government that lasted five short months. Because of the oil crisis, Ethiopian grain prices rose dramatically and ordinary families could no longer afford to buy grain at the market. The drought of 1973/74 had resulted in a failed crop for many, and the first tales of famine began to be reported outside Ethiopia. In the corridors of power, Colonel Mengistu Haile Mariam had been marshalling his forces and building alliances: they were to declare themselves leaders of the Marxist state of Ethiopia in September 1974.

Mary got caught up in events, which resulted in an urgent return to England.
"Ethiopia had become a nervous place in which to live, but life carries on, and in August 1972 I had the first of our three children, Maria. Here in Ethiopia, birth is a natural process, and we didn't have a big party to celebrate her arrival. Things changed dramatically in January 1973, when my father had a massive stroke, which affected the left side of his brain. We realised that he needed care overseas as quickly as possible, and Queen Elizabeth II arranged for us all to be airlifted to London. My father was treated at the National Hospital for Nervous Diseases in London. After the surgery, he had to have significant rehabilitation to help him recover his speech.

"Together with my mother, we found a flat in Grosvenor Square, close to my father. It was a very difficult time: we were concerned about him and the escalating events in Ethiopia. To remind us of home, we combed local shops for suitable flour with which to make injera and spices for the watt. The only places we could find that stocked suitable substitutes were Indian shops."

In April 1974, Sorra, the first of Mary's sons, was born in Geneva, where she had moved while her husband worked for AFRA, the African Airlines Association. However, her happiness was short-lived. In September 1974, Mengistu declared, "We are the ones in control."

Her shoulders visibly drooped at the impact on the imperial family. "I heard it on the BBC News on TV and read about it the following day in *The Times* and *The Guardian.* On 12 September 1974, my grandfather the Emperor and fourteen members of our family were arrested." One of these was Mulugeta Asrate.

Mid-flow, there was an insistent knock at the door: the driver was waiting. Two hours had passed and the story was not complete. Slipping on my jacket, I hugged Mary, and we agreed to meet in a fortnight's time.

Further information:

The best website I've found for information about the Imperial Family is:
http://www.angelfire.com
You will find many images of the Emperor and his family there

---

11 The new Jerusalem

Even here, in the hot, parched north east of the country where many famines had begun, there were patches of green. As we came in to land at Lalibela airport, one field looked like the horn of Africa with a hungry child crying: beside it was a tukul surrounded by greenery, in the shape of a heart. They brought back the haunting images of Michael Buerk surrounded by thousands of starving people in 1984.

Taking my overnight bag, I disembarked from the small Fokker Friendship plane and walked through the airport, looking for the Jerusalem Guesthouse guide. Lalibela was my rest and recreation, reputedly one of the holiest cities in Ethiopia and a UNESCO world heritage site, famous for its rock-hewn churches. I had booked the guesthouse on the recommendation of Richard Pankhurst, Helen's father. The trip also included a tour of the churches.

A young, smartly dressed man stood by the exit with a small sign bearing the guesthouse's name. Alan, my guide, introduced himself and we walked quickly to the car. Time was pressing: I was only there for 24 hours. Business was obviously good: the people carrier was fairly new and the weekend shouldn't be too taxing for him, as I was the only guest to disembark that Saturday lunchtime.

Speeding up the tarmaced roads to Lalibela, we passed small kebellehs – neighbourhood communities - nestling in the foothills of the mountains that ringed the town. Alan gave me a brief run-down of the history of the city, which had been created by King Lalibela in the thirteenth century. He had been very devout and travelled to many countries, visiting holy churches and shrines and bringing back symbols and drawings of their architecture – inspiration for the churches which he then had carved from solid rock. His fame had spread far and wide and the town had been named after him.

Investment had poured into the city in recent years – the airport, roads, electricity and fresh water for the residents. Tourism was brisk, and I learnt that both Bob Geldof and Princess Anne had visited Lalibela before Christmas.

"Look up there!" Alan pointed. "That's our mount of olives." It was completely unlike any photos I'd ever seen of the world's holiest city, Jerusalem. There was no wailing wall, no gleaming dome of the Al Aqsa mosque, no Jewish gravestones dotting the hillside. Just a green mountain, looking like an upturned basin on top of a flat plateau some two thousand feet above us. But Ethiopians consider their country as divine as the Holy Land: many of their legends go back to the time of the Old Testament. At that moment my heart yearned to see the real Jerusalem – peace was always on my mind, along with water, and it was my plan to visit the city of peace at some point, divided as it was. I wasn't sure when it would be, but here was the first spark of a connection.

When I'd told people about my odyssey and its purpose, some had been critical, telling me to just focus on Ethiopia and water, not 'mess it up' with peace in Jerusalem. In fact, when I spoke about peace, this wall of resistance appeared from quite a few – others just laughed or walked away. But it didn't matter: I had to honour my covenant and this passionate voyage of my heart, for which I'd given up everything. Nursing constant thoughts about peace since 2000, I prayed about how I could achieve it. The answer came softly over the ensuing months: "Like Gandhi, you have to be the peace you want to see in the world."

"Do you know Michael Buerk?" Alan's voice brought me back down to earth.

"Not personally. Although I did have an email from him in January. I'd written to him to see if he could help with some publicity for the old school photo."

"He was here in October. Solomon the guesthouse owner and I were his guides. We took him to the special feeding stations: there are still problems with famine around here, though not in Lalibela itself. He's a good man, I think: this publicity can only help the people who need it here."

I nodded, remarking, "Yes, I watched the documentary he did. It was broadcast the day after I got that email from him. Isn't that a coincidence? I'm very pleased you're my guide too, Alan." We chuckled together, joined by the driver whose name I didn't catch. I performed imaginary cartwheels of happiness – the right place at the right time.

Potholes and dirt appeared out of the blue. The tarmac only went as far as the town's outskirts. We bumped along, avoiding the biggest holes, and people showed little interest – they were obviously used to tourists. The guesthouse was the other side of Lalibela. The bedroom was sparse but clean, with breathtaking views over the countryside to the south: trees, mountains, small tukuls and a path running by to a neighbouring kebelleh. Constant movement and motion, plenty to look out on and meditate over.

After lunch was served in the large tukul used as a bar and dining room, Alan took me on a tour of the nearest and most famous Lalibela churches. Hewn out of solid rock, they were like ancient treasure chests, doors and windows carved over months and years. Inside they were surprisingly clean, most with carpets and pews, full of colourful iconic paintings of Jesus and carvings of ancient Orthodox saints on the walls.

One of the churches had crosses from all four corners of the world, including the Scottish cross of St Andrew and the Indian version. The latter was very familiar – the Nazis had taken it and transposed it to create their symbol of hatred and might.

Reserving the best for last, Alan took me to the Church of St George over ground. I had refused to negotiate the pitch-black underground tunnel to its chapel, so I'd only seen the outside. St George was constructed in the shape of an equal sided cross, the only trapezium church in the world, where the bottom was wider than the top. It was awe-inspiring, its roof level with the ground we stood on, the bottom some sixty feet below. The cross's symmetry echoed that of the International Red Cross logo – always there in times of crises.

In the distance, little dots of people finished their Saturday afternoon trading at the local mercato (market). Above them wheeled a flock of doves in a giant circle. I pointed it out to Alan, who told me it was an unusual sight. To our right, a man in a green jacket and trousers appeared to be listening.

"It's such a pity that most of the world only knows Ethiopia for its famines," I commented. Alan nodded slightly. "There was another documentary shortly after

Michael Buerk's," I continued. "It was done by an African journalist who'd lived with a family for a month, eating what little food they had, helping in the fields. He'd lost a lot of weight, but was a brave man for doing it. I think it was called "Living with Hunger", or something like that. I know the PR woman at the Ethiopian embassy in London, and she told me many people cancelled their holidays after seeing it."

"I know who you're talking about," the man in green exclaimed. I hadn't realised my voice had carried so clearly. He came over, right arm extended in greeting and left hand holding the elbow – a sign of respect. "I am Josef, and I was the Sierra Leone journalist's guide. His name is Sorious Samura."

We spent the rest of the afternoon together: Alan, Josef, an American woman and me, in a small tej house. Lalibela tej is famous, brewed from pure honey, water and barley. Three small bottles went down very well, and the driver took us back to the guesthouse for a small supper and an early night. As I collected my thoughts, light shone in the distance through the windows of a few tukuls. The connections were beginning to form a clear pattern: water, peace and plentiful guides.

Further information:

Sorious Samura, "Living with Hunger": www.insightnews.tv.com

---

12 Water for life

We'd been on the road for over 24 hours and there was no respite from the dry heat still burning up the countryside. We were over 200 miles south of Addis in the depth of the Southern Nations and Nationalities Province – SNNP. WaterAid's driver, Berhanu, negotiated the large potholes and rocks which gashed the road: by now my back had submitted to the constant bumping and ricocheting from side to side. Earlier, I'd jokingly suggested that the first funds should go towards a helicopter. Berhanu had laughed and told me about one faranj lady who was so traumatised by the roads, she'd insisted in returning to Addis by plane!

In the distance were swirls of dust: was someone repairing the road, or a tukul? We were on our way to Wolle Dagna, a small community in the heart of the Alaba woreda (district), not one of WaterAid's current projects. As we approached the dust storm, I saw men, women and children standing by a big hole. Slowing down to take a closer look, I asked Berhanu what on earth they were up to.

"Digging a reservoir," he replied. Several men hacked at the ground with spades and any other implement they could find in their efforts to carve out the giant space. They'd dug down about ten yards, in preparation for the rainy season.

"How deep would they have to dig to find water?"

"Well, around here, about 200 or 250 metres." A mile further we came upon another group, doing exactly the same. I thought about how they'd go home exhausted without the means to have a shower, or wash their dusty clothes, as water for drinking and cooking was the highest priority.

Soon, we turned right on to smoother mud tracks leading to the community. We parked by the cactus fence and waited for someone to appear. A teenage boy put his head outside the gate. He ushered us in after Endris Adulmegid, the project manager of WaterAid's community scheme, explained why we were there. By this time, several people had ventured outside their tukuls, and the sound of bleating goats greeted us. Young kids stood crying for their mothers in a small enclosure by a tukul. All around us, everything was bare except for some scrub. On top of the tukuls' roofs stood small crescents, the sign of a Muslim community.

The villagers brought out seats and a small table, so we could sit in the shade of the largest tukul and talk. A tall, ebony-skinned man stepped forward and shook my hand. He was Mamali and told me that he had a wife and two teenage children. He described their daily routine without water to me.

Mamali and his family (2nd - 5th left)

"Our whole life is concentrated on finding water: the women and children collecting water have to leave the kebele at 7am with the donkeys. They take two 25 litre cans with them: usually they arrive about 10am and each family takes it in turns to fill up the cans, load the donkeys and perhaps wash some clothes or wash themselves.

They return about 2pm, which leaves very little time to prepare the fresh food for injera and watt. It also means that, even if we could afford to send all the children to school, we have to keep at least one at home to help with fetching water.

"The water isn't good: animals drink from it and sometimes there are dead dogs or goats upstream which we can't see. There are little worms in the water and even after boiling, they can get into our stomachs and make us ill, particularly the young children. Also, we have to give the donkeys a rest every other day: the jerry cans cut into their flesh and we must allow it time to heal between trips."

As he spoke, the 15 or so villagers nodded in agreement. As Muslims, cleanliness is an extremely important preparation for worship. Often it wasn't possible to worship because of the lack of water. Among such devout people, that could only increase their feelings of helplessness and resignation.

An older man interrupted, "If it wasn't for God's will, we would all be dead from the inconvenience and sickness brought by the river water."

Another mused, "Well, we don't know what causes our illnesses, it may or may not be water. But it is God's will whether we live or die from these sicknesses."

I wanted to talk to one young mother, who was suckling a two-year-old, to find out how the women coped with childbirth when there was no clean water. She stood apart from the crowd listening quietly, with her netallah covering the half-sleeping toddler who lay against her breast. She smiled shyly, willing to answer the faranj's questions

"It becomes more difficult to collect the water as you get heavier, so sometimes you have to rely on neighbours, and they can only give you what they have left over. Of course, husbands will help too, but often they are out looking after our goats.

"When the baby is born, the first priority is to use water to clean it, to give him the best start. Depending on the birth, it may be five days or so before the mother can get to the river to clean herself and her clothing: it's something we just have to put up with. What else can we do?" she added, with a shrug of her shoulder and a sad smile.

Mamali's water supply - limited and polluted

I tried to end the discussion on a positive note and asked them how they thought their lives would change if they had water. Everyone was eager to give their views and the conversation got much livelier.

"The family will always be clean."

"We'll have more time and be stress free because we won't be spending it looking for water."

"Our animals will be in better health, because they'll have all they need to drink when they want. At present, they drink too much, which causes them pain."

"We can make more money as it will be easier to sell our animals at market because they'll be in better condition."

"At long last, we'll be able to grow plants and vegetables and have our own irrigation system. So we'll have better meals and perhaps, some food to sell at market too."

I asked why WaterAid weren't helping, and Berhanu informed me that they simply didn't have the funds. 1,200 people are affected by lack of water in this outlying community. They were completely reliant on the government, WaterAid or another charity's help to provide them with water. Unfortunately the finances for the water sector from government and non-governmental organisations is far from sufficient to meet the massive need of these people. We shook hands with everyone before we left and I put away my notebook and camera.

When we got back in the car, Endris read my thoughts.

"Of course, now we have raised their expectations. They have seen this nice faranj come to talk to them and ask lots of questions about water: they are praying for you and for the book to sell well to help them." I nodded and sent my prayers heavenward as we set off for our basic but clean hotel, with running water, in Sheshemane.

*****

By way of contrast, Berhanu took me to one of WaterAid's completed projects in Robe, the capital of Bale within the Oromia Region. It is a bustling town with 35,000 inhabitants, and shops and small tradesmen along every street. There were also a wide variety of bars, cafes and restaurants to visit, along with some small hotels. The town and surrounding area had suffered from acute water shortages, both from erratic rainfall and the growing population.

The main local water supply was from the Shiya River, which carried many diseases, including three different types of water-borne worms. In Robe, the water wells piped from the river were also polluted. In the rainy season silt from the river would block the pipes, while in the summer months the water levels were just too low for a regular supply. In addition, enterprising local water salesmen were spreading the diseases by taking water out of big barrels, transferring them to small containers to sell and passing them off as clean water.

A local water board had been established in 1991 and began lobbying the government for clean, accessible water. They also raised money towards a water fund. In 1993, things began to progress when WaterAid got involved. After consulting with the local people, by the end of 1994, the project design was complete and construction began on a way to provide water to 14 kebellehs or peasant associations. This was a complex project, involving 147 kms of pipes being laid underground: thus extensive excavation was involved. By 2001 the project was complete, and a year later, the Robe community project office was opened.

Coincidentally, on the day of our visit, the local water board were holding a meeting that day. Zeyitu Aliye, a woman, is the leader, and she was quick to explain just how clean water had transformed her life.

"I live in a small village called Amalema, where the wells were just too far for us to walk to, so we had to use the local Webb River, which was polluted. Not only that, but we had to compete with animals for water – including lions. As a result the whole family had to go, so our income was very, very small, because there was no time to work. After talking to other families about our problems, we agreed that we needed to do something to get proper, clean water. Along with some others from my community, we met local and regional officials and we were always asking when we'd get water. WaterAid has been so good in providing the funds through their overseas donors and in helping us educate local people about hygiene: washing, the preparation of food and use and cleaning of latrines.

"Water is miraculous: what cleans a person's body is very important, for hygiene, for worshipping in mosques, and especially for women. Now cleansing during and after periods and childbirth is no longer a problem and we have water in barrels outside the latrines, so we can wash away the waste afterwards. Life is very good, and I am pleased I could help my community in this way."

I wanted to see the effect on rural communities, so we set off for the Sinja kebele, one hour from Robe. As the Jeep veered sharply from left to right along the deeply furrowed road, the horizon was empty, apart from mountains unfolding, peak by peak in front of us. I was transported back to my early memories of Ethiopia. Occasionally, small children stood by tukuls, alerted by the sound of a car, a rare occurrence. Some would run out and wave and shout jubilantly "faranj, faranj!" I waved in reply. Other small children just smiled and raised a hand in greeting. To rich westerners they appear to have so very little, but they smile readily and have a zest for life that is hard to find in our so-called 'developed' world.

The queue of women outside the community standpipes told us we had arrived at the right spot. Endris had decided to introduce me to a local family, and so we knocked at the gate of Aberash Feleke's large compound opposite the standpipes. In this kebele, 48 kilometres of pipe have been laid from the water table 80 metres underground. Water had been diverted to the community water points.

How it should be. Clean water on tap!

Aberash was initially reluctant to let us sit down in her large tukul. She thought that a faranj would find it too basic. But inside it was dry and clean, with curved wooden seats along the walls, a small wood burning fire/stove for the injera and watt in the centre, and plates and cups neatly lined up in a roughly hewn cupboard. Two bedrooms led off the main room, and there was also a day bed close to the fire for cold days. It looked very neat. Aberash's daughter and daughter-in-law, whose tukuls were in the same compound, sat listening - their three young children beside them.

"It's a wonderful world we now have. We can now wash ourselves, our clothes and our cooking things regularly. The family is clean and neat, that is very good. I remember, before the water arrived, that we would walk for one to two hours to the river, and sometimes the queues were so long we returned home with empty jerry cans after seven hours. That was truly heartbreaking.

"In ten years time, I hope we can further increase our quality of life and be the same as all families throughout the world, with clean water, good health and the means to educate all our children, including daughters, so that they in turn can have a better life."

We walked outside to take a look at the latrine at the far side of the compound. It was immaculate, and what I had mistaken for the latrine near the gate was in fact a tap: Aberash was middle class by local standards, and able to pay for privately piped water. I took some photos of her with two younger generations of her family, as a thank you. In Ethiopia photos are very precious, and I promised to laminate them so they will last a long time. When I return, I will probably find that photo hanging in pride of place somewhere in the front room of her tukul – family comes first!

WaterAid Ethiopia team with Helen Pankhurst in the centre

WaterAid

The group began life as a charitable trust on 21 July 1981. Today, WaterAid has programmes in 17 of the world's poorest countries and over 8.5 million people are helped through their projects. Their target is to help one million more people have access to clean water and sanitation each year.

WaterAid began funding small projects indirectly in Ethiopia in 1983, through the Ethiopian Red Cross Society. A country office was established in 1991 and began to develop its relationship with EOC/DICAD (Ethiopian Orthodox Church Development Inter Church Aid Department). Gradually the charity took on larger and larger projects and it facilitated the formation of a special non-governmental organisation, (NGO), Water Action, in May 1995. Initially dependent on WaterAid, Water Action is now attracting funding from other sources and is one of the most respected NGOs in Ethiopia's water sector.

By 2002, WaterAid had financed 23 rural water supply and sanitation projects and five urban projects in six out of the ten regions. To date, almost a million people have benefited from these projects. Today the charity has a team of 21 staff, with a modern and efficient head office in the Debre Zeit area of Addis Ababa.

Throughout my discussions with employees, they emphasised the need for collaboration with many different partners in order for expensive water projects to work and to be sustainable in the long-term. That means working with the Ministry for Water Resources, the people in the regions and in particular with the local people at the woreda (district)   level. WaterAid works with partners and establishes links to their offices both in Addis and at project level. Consultation is vital all the way through, about where boreholes and standpipes should be sited, how the local community will run the water scheme, who will be trained to carry out small running repairs and how funds can be raised to pay for maintenance once it's up and running. Income from the water also goes to the local community: ten cents for each jerry can soon adds up. A major water scheme can take up to six years to come to fruition and over £1 million investment (for the very large schemes like Robe), so getting it right through constant discussion is essential.
www.wateraid.org
WaterAid, 47-49 Durham Street, London SE11 5JD

Further information:

www.unorg/waterforlifedecade/
United Nations Environment Programme: www.unep.org

A very good, current book about global water problems is:
Constance Elizabeth Hunt, *Thirsty Planet*, 2004, Zed Books, London and USA

13 Love and self-reliance

I awoke to a chill in the air: a welcome relief from the summer heat. In three months, rain would be pouring from the sky in torrents, with people dashing for cover. I was looking forward to my last week, spending five days in Abebech Gobena's orphanage near the Mercato in Addis. I'd met her two months previously at the WorldAware Business Awards in London – she'd received the top award for her humanitarian work, caring for almost half a million children in 24 years! No wonder she's known as the Mother Theresa of Africa.

After packing all my bags and having my last breakfast at the Ras Amba Hotel, I went back to my room to call the orphanage to confirm the arrangements to stay. I had butterflies in my stomach as I lifted the receiver.

A polite voice answered, and when I asked for Abebech, I discovered that she wasn't there and I was put through to a man called Tesfaye Tekle-Haimanot, deputy manager of projects. He was uncertain about the idea of me staying for a week. I told him about the email confirmation I'd received from them in the middle of February, agreeing to my visit.

Even as I said the words, I realised that perhaps he hadn't sent the reply to me, or perhaps the other person had forgotten to tell the team. My heart plummeted – learning about how Abebech worked with the homeless and orphaned was an integral part of my journey. But I decided to make my way there anyway, leaving my suitcase behind at the hotel. If the worst happened I'd just have to stay where I was, although after two weeks I'd grown tired of the never-changing menu, and I wondered what I'd do to pass the next five days before my flight back to London.

My first task, though, was to find an internet café with a fax so I could request an audience with President Girma Wolde-Giorgis, to find out the whereabouts of his daughter Hiruth. I'd been so fortunate in meeting up with Princess Mary again and hearing her fascinating story about the past 40 years, and also in my extraordinary luck in finding that Marta was still at the school as school secretary. These successes gave me extra impetus to try and track down the next missing classmate. Neither Sister Weynemariam nor Marta had been able to enlighten me as to where Hiruth was now. I hoped that if I included the purpose of the book and the letter of support from Archbishop Desmond Tutu, the fax would do the trick.

I walked down the rutted track from the hotel to the road leading to Arat Kilo, one of the main commercial centres in Addis. As it was a Monday just after 9am, it was too early for beggars, and most children were at school. Passers-by stared at me, but I got none of the 'faranji' calls and shouts I normally attracted. This was virtually always done in a spirit of curiosity and friendship: others shouted 'hello sister', or 'good afternoon'. I used to correct them according to the time of day, or shout back 'hello brother', which made them laugh good-naturedly.

I crossed over the bridge by the rotting refuse: plastic bags of rubbish, old food and scraps of material had been flung over the banks of the river. I saw a dead dog, gradually decomposing in the sunlight, but there weren't any flies around and the overwhelming smell was still of stale urine. Just the other day, I'd seen an old man stop and relieve himself there.

I ambled past the small shops with their Coke signs and the mechanics sitting squatting by the roadside, waiting for motorists to drop off punctured tyres for repair. Tyres were stacked haphazardly on top of each other, some as bald as an old man's head, to advertise their business. Alongside was a video hire shop: posters from Hollywood films flapped in the breeze and popular Ethiopian music wailed from the interior. Singers usually sang in a high nasal tone, recalling Arabic music: flutes were the main accompaniment, along with organs and drums. The sound and rhythm were still uniquely African, not something you could easily dance to unless you knew the local steps and cadence.

At the Lemon Café, which advertised 'fax and internet' on its windows, I hurried up the steps to send the fax to the President's office. As it was still early, there was only one European there, sitting composing an email. The fax machine whirred into action, and the three pages went through without any hitches: I paid a few birr and left.

I was determined to find a taxi driver who would give me a good deal both to visit the orphanage and return to the hotel for my bags, should all go well. As I walked down the long rank, it appeared that all the drivers had gone for a coffee somewhere. One car gleamed in the sunshine: good, a well-maintained taxi, which was a relief after the ones without any springs in the seat, or windscreens shattered by stones, but never repaired. 'God is Love', proclaimed a sign in the rear window. Many had such religious statements: people weren't afraid to show their faith here.

I negotiated a rate with the young driver and we set off for the Gojeberende area, where Abebech's orphanage was. All I knew was that it was somewhere near the Mercato, Africa's largest open-air market. We had to stop several times and ask passers-by for information, and the journey took us to a much poorer area of Addis. We turned right, by the Ministry for Health Education, up a very rocky track and the cab lurched past the usual small shacks with curious toddlers outside.

We could see we were heading in the right direction when a sign saying 'AGOHELD Photos' appeared before us. At the end of the short cul-de-sac was a very large metal gate. Knocking on it, I asked to see Abebech, and the sabanya opened the gate.

The compound wasn't what I'd been expecting: a few buildings a bit the worse for wear, with children running around, shouting and playing. The sight that greeted me was in complete contrast – a wide range of buildings around a cobbled road, edged by lovely trees and shrubs. At the end stood a modern office block and a large hall, and everything was immaculate. The sound of picks on concrete echoed around the compound: builders were slowly chipping away at the concrete floor by hand to make way for more new offices.

I wandered up to the offices and asked to see Abebech, but was told that she was out at a meeting: instead, I was ushered into the office of her deputy manager, Eshetu Aredo. I could tell by the number of people coming into and out of his office that he was an important man: he had the weary look of someone who always had something to do and somewhere to be, but he alternated between looking at me and signing invoices and letters. He didn't know anything about my arrival, but when I explained that I would like to include something about Abebech's orphanage and good work in the local community in my book, in return for free board and lodging, he began to listen properly.

He ummed and ahhed: he'd been distracted while I talked to him and I wondered how much he'd heard. He explained carefully that they relied totally on donations to keep the orphanage and other ancillary businesses going. There was no money forthcoming from the government. His hands went through his thick grey hair in discomfort, but then he stood up and put on his woollen waistcoat and ushered me outside. There, standing in the bright sunshine, was Abebech. Without hesitation she embraced me, and gave me the three hugs, two on my right and one on my left, deemed essential Ethiopian etiquette when greeting friends. I turned around and Eshetu was smiling.

She ushered us into her office. Against one wall there was a four metre wide wood and glass cabinet, full of the prizes she'd won for her humanitarian work in the past decade - a wonderful testament to an amazing woman. In the corner was the finely carved wooden bowl, her most recent trophy, from the Worldaware Business Awards in London In January.

I explained once more why I was there, and showed her the letter from Archbishop Desmond Tutu. Eshetu translated: Abebech's English was as halting as my Amharic, but that didn't matter: we understood each other, and she had far more important things to do than learn English.

"God bless you, the orphanage is delighted to welcome you. Please treat my home as your home," she smiled before agreeing that I could stay for a week. We left her office and walked down the hill to the accommodation block, where she showed me to the room I would occupy: as big as a hotel suite, with two beds, a coffee table and chairs and a shower and toilet. It was right beside the kitchen where I'd have my meals with her each day – so the loneliness of the weekend would be over.

*****

Abebech had been born in the small village of Shebel about 150 kms north of Addis Ababa in 1937, she believes (it's only recently that Ethiopians have been required to register births, so many are unsure of their exact birth dates). Sadly, a month after her birth, her farmer father was killed by the invading Italians and she was brought up by her grandparents. Like many young girls from her community, she was married at a very early age – eleven. This custom enabled many families to get rid of another mouth to feed. Abebech was desperately unhappy. One night she managed to escape from the tukul she shared with her husband and made her way to Addis Ababa, where she got together the money for vocational training until the age of 16. She remarried, this time for love, and became a quality controller at a coffee and grain company.

A devout woman, Abebech went on a pilgrimage in 1980 to the church of Gishen Mariam In Wollo province, north east of Addis Ababa. This was a time of severe drought in Ethiopia, and famine had already come to the province. She distributed the loaf of bread and five litres of holy water she had taken with her on her pilgrimage to the victims. While walking along the road from the church, she saw a woman lying in the dirt with a child suckling at her breast. Thinking the woman was asleep, Abebech tried to shake her awake. She discovered, with a shock, that she was dead. She'd starved to death. Although Abebech had succeeded in turning her life around after her inauspicious start, she instantly felt that nothing she had fought for mattered more than taking care of this little orphaned baby. She returned from her pilgrimage not only with him, but also another orphan: by the end of 1980 she was caring for 21 children.

Initially her husband indulged her, as they were relatively well off and couldn't have children. But as the numbers of orphans increased, so did his annoyance. He and his family thought she was mad. Abebech was forced to move out with the children into a little poultry house, in the same compound where her orphanage stands today. There she built a bed out of mud, and to keep the children fed, she sold all her jewellery and made and sold injera bread and other food to whomever she could. From a relatively carefree existence, albeit without the children she longed to have with her husband, she was now getting up at 5.30 each morning to start cooking injera to sell, to raise funds to feed her growing brood.

This was not a role anyone could study for: it was a calling from deep down. As the children grew older, so her idea for them and the orphanage began to crystallise. Her vision is that everything at AGOHELD is centred around the child while encouraging each one to become self-reliant. Gradually, through her persistence and the love and care she bestowed on each child, she got help, and in 1986 her orphanage was registered by the government.

AGOHELD has grown throughout the years. From its start just caring for orphans, it now provides practical solutions for social and economic problems experienced by the poor and destitute in the four communities it serves. Today it owns land and buildings within a half kilometre radius of that original poultry shed. The charity has built three schools, a clinic, 346 houses, 27 latrines and 14 water points within the local community. Since 1990, it has also served local communities in Fitche, Guder, and Bourayu. They have even refurbished local houses. Most impressive of all is the constant focus on self-reliance and education: beneficiaries can always work their way out of grinding poverty.

Abebech and Eshetu were keen to show off the facilities. There were special counselling and play rooms, where the orphans can talk to professionally trained counsellors. Alongside was a modern office block, where the communications and marketing people worked and further down, through a narrow gate, the garden, girls' and boys' dormitories and Abebech's accommodation. Abebech loves all the children she cares for: she is especially fond of the little babies and toddlers and her bedroom is right beside theirs, where you'll find the under-fours in double-stacked cots lining three of the walls. She still gets up at night if a little one is restless or teething. The children are undoubtedly her life.

When I peered into the nursery, two baby boys lay in their cots, silently drinking their bottles. Outside, young toddlers played in the garden courtyard and there were nursery nurses in attendance to wipe runny noses, feed them and give them a cuddle. I walked to the girls' dormitory which, despite having 12-14 beds to a room, was spotless. The girls had to make their own beds, and by the pillows lay soft toys and pyjamas. Once over eight, each child was responsible for a younger one before and after school. When they reached 15, they were expected to cook for the boys or girls in their dormitory. This ensured good domestic skills and enabled the boys to be as independent as the girls. (This is unusual in a country where most men do no housework at all: it is women's work and looked down on.)

Lower down the hill were the boys' dormitories, arranged in exactly the same way as the girls', alongside were the showers and a large laundry. Every day was a washday with almost 170 children to care for! Washing flapped in the breeze and small shirts decorated the fence by a deep gully through which a small river flowed. As with many in Addis, it appeared rather polluted, but at least here, there were no dead dogs lying in the water.

By now it was 6.30pm and time for our evening meal. The children played in and around the courtyard. Homework had been done and they'd had their meal. The kitchen staff had prepared fresh vegetable soup, a nice salad and bread for Abebech and I. As it was Lent, most Orthodox Christians were fasting: that meant no dairy produce, eggs, or meat, just fish and fresh vegetables. They were really strict about it, so it was bread without butter. The salad was the first I'd tasted in Ethiopia: it was made from vegetables grown in the compound, watered and rinsed with clean, unpolluted water.

Abebech had changed from her work clothes into a nightdress, her hair tucked underneath a small turban and a warm netallah (cheesecloth shawl) over her shoulders. I tried not to stare as one of the staff came with a bowl of hot water and towel, knelt down and started to wash Abebech's feet. I felt embarrassed and looked away. However this custom was common in Ethiopian homes where they treat visitors in the way Christ cared for the disciples. It was very humbling to see a Biblical lesson in practice in 2004. After a few minutes, the young woman turned to me and asked if I wanted my feet washed.

"No thank you," I replied, blushing furiously. "But you must," Abebech insisted.
This was the first time I'd ever had my feet and lower legs washed by someone else, apart from mum, and I didn't know whether to laugh or shrink with shyness.
I decided to follow Abebech's example and act as if it happened to me every day. I took off my socks and lowered my right foot gingerly into the water. The woman washed my feet and legs willingly and with care, an experience I will remember forever.

We chatted companionably with the help of Hanna Alemu, our translator, a 15-year-old who had been in the orphanage since birth. A slender young woman, Hanna was wise for her age, and had an easy way of translating adult conversation. Abebech paused frequently to allow Hanna to turn the phrases into passable English. It was Hanna's ambition to be a translator when she leaves school, but her real passion was football. Girls can play the sport while at school, but nursing a dream to become a footballer was definitely not encouraged.

We finished supper and at 7.15pm, slowly children poured into the courtyard in front of us. They lined up in four neat rows. When the children were all assembled, the chants began. One child chanted a line, and the others answered: even the little ones of three were word perfect. Some stood and bellowed, others recited the words quietly, and the chanting sounded magical: like a multi-layered organ recital. One solemn girl of about six held an icon with a picture of Mary in her hands: another boy had one of Jesus. After five minutes or so the children knelt down and bowed before God. There was no sound except breathing and chanting: even the sacred ibex birds appeared to be listening as they flew silently overhead, their curved beaks silhouetted against the purple dusk.

A tattered Bible was handed around, and each child kissed the cover: this was followed by the icon of Mary, the serious girl ensuring that everyone touched it twice, first with their foreheads, then with their lips. After the Lord's Prayer and more chanting, the ceremony was over. The rows broke up and laughter punctuated the air once more.

Abebech took one of the plates full of kollo snack food and called the children: they queued up on the steps to see her and she gave each one a handful and wished them a good night. They have a specific word for her: 'edaye', which means special mother in Amharic. At eight we all retired to bed.

Abebech Gobena with some of her charges. Hanna Alemu is on her right

At 3am I was awakened by barking dogs once more – the dog chorus as I called it. Invisible by day, the dogs came out to chatter loudly in the small hours and as each dog called to another, the howls and barks reached a crescendo. After a while there was no point being irritated: they were too far away to throw a shoe at. I drifted off to sleep once more.

*****

The following morning, as grey light filtered through the net curtains in my bedroom window, the children's chanting began again. It was just 6am, and this was the way each child began the day: in praise of God and the good life they were now able to live. I lay listening in the half-light, transfixed.

At breakfast, everything was already laid out in the kitchen and I helped myself to tea with lemon and a bowl of porridge. The maid was clearing up the breakfast things from the communal dining room where the children ate. She came in and greeted me, pointing at the food with a quizzical expression. "Isshi, amersegenalhu," – "OK, thank you," I responded in my pidgin Amharic.

After breakfast I heard a sweeping noise: I looked out the kitchen door expecting to see one of the maids, but instead a young schoolboy was stooped over a small brush made from twigs, cleaning the yard before he went to school. This was another habit Abebech taught the children - to keep their environment clean - and it was spotless.

I walked up to the offices to meet the children's affairs head Tedessa Beyene, who was to show me the rest of AGOHELD's facility. Our first stop was the clinic, which provided free, basic healthcare for the children and local community. I learnt that one of the orphans was very ill from AIDS and not expected to live much longer: she would be the third to die in the past 12 months. It was very likely that she was born with the disease, and she was the last of her family to die. The clinic also treated young babies and toddlers who were malnourished because their parents couldn't afford to give them enough to eat.

We then walked past the new clinic which was due to open in May 2004: a very impressive facility where they'd be able to provide additional medical services for the destitute. Further up the road was the Abebech Gobena School for grades 1 – 8, where both the orphans and children of local families living on the breadline were educated. AGOHELD paid the latter's school fees and provided their uniforms: parents were expected to fund school exercise books and equipment. Without this investment, families became dependent on AGOHELD, something Abebech and her team wanted to avoid at all costs.

Tedessa introduced me to Getahum Wolde-Semayat, school director for the past five years. The school had 339 pupils, of which 50 per cent were orphans. We entered one of the grade 1 classrooms and the little ones sat up and said welcome. The teacher encouraged them to sing a little song for me. It went something like this: "You're welcome, you're welcome, welcome to our class," and finished with the words, "We love you so much." The children really knew how to pull on heartstrings. I thought back to my dream about the homeless in 1974, people standing in rows applauding me – why they were doing so, hadn't been clear. These little children - the homeless – and Abebech were now showing me why I'd had that dream.

One of AGOHELD's catering classes

One of the classrooms was crammed full of women ranging from late teens to early 40s, dressed in green overalls and caps. Most of them were from poor villages outside Addis, lured by the prospect of a job and more money in the capital. Unfortunately they had found that the only jobs on offer were as prostitutes, or sex workers as they were known. AGOHELD recognised the size of the growing problem and the potential for further increases in HIV infections. Two years before, they had run a free six-month domestic science and catering course for vulnerable young women. This had proved such a success with hotels, middle-class families and the women themselves, that this year they were running two classes in adjoining classrooms. AGOHELD also provided 88 birr a month – about £6 - to each student, so they could buy food staples while they were studying.

Outside the school, we headed towards a sign reading 'Beauty Salon.' This was one of the mini-enterprises set up to provide jobs and an income for the 18-year-old orphans. The salon had everything needed for a beauty treatment, with all the latest African beauty products and hairdriers. We then toured the hub of Abebech's local enterprises, run by former students and people in the community.

In one hot and dark room, there were six wood ovens where women spent the late afternoon and evening cooking the flat injera bread that was the staple accompaniment to every meal. The best quality injera is pale grey, but it can vary to a rather unappetising brown – usually a sign of poor quality tef, or it being past its best. It was also here where the 15–year-olds learned the art of stoking the wood-burning ovens to the right temperature, mixing the ground tef with water and pouring it slowly in a circle onto the hot plate, so it cooked evenly.

Outside, the rhythmic thud of wood against wood greeted us. Two women pounded dried red chillies in a large wood vessel, while mounds of them were spread out on sacking to dry. Close by sat one woman, painstakingly de-seeding each chilli before it could be dried. In an adjacent building, more seeds and pulses were being quality checked before either being ground or packed for sale to hotels and restaurants, as ingredients for watt. The packing bay was next door and one of Abebech's former orphans sat packing and checking the amounts to be delivered the next day.

Further along were weaving and sewing workshops, where they made items for sale. Last of all was a woodwork area where young men built cabinets, beds, tables and small cupboards from wood and bamboo. I discovered that I was sleeping in a bed made by them: their work was of very high quality. Almost all of the people were either orphans who've now finished school, or local women who needed to earn some birr to feed their children. This was truly self-reliance in action.

*****

After the tour, I hurried back to my room to change – I was to meet Mary Asfaw Wossen to hear how she and the family had responded to the imprisonment of her family and grandfather, the Emperor. A small red Mazda collected me from

AGOHELD's gates, and Mary greeted me before giving instructions to the driver. We were off to the 'Blue Tops' an Italian restaurant and café very close to where Mary had gone to school in the Guenet Leul Palace grounds, in Sidist Kilo. In 1961, after the abortive coup d'etat, the Emperor donated the grounds to create Addis Ababa University and his former palace is home to the Institute of Ethiopian Studies.

"So, how's it all gone since we last met? How did you find the WaterAid tour?"

"Really, really good, and essential too, Mary," I declared. "There is nothing better than seeing the situation for myself and I now realise now how much it affects people's health and children's education, girls especially. It was also helpful to see the areas where WaterAid projects are complete, and the benefits they've brought to the communities. Water is the most essential resource for health, economies and self-respect. I agree wholeheartedly with their slogan now: Water for Life."

"Ah, sounds like it was a very worthwhile trip. Well, let's order and please remind me where our conversation finished last time."

"You were telling me about the imprisonment of the imperial family after the Emperor was deposed." A waitress approached and I chose a chicken risotto from the extensive menu. There were a few other diners in the restaurant, but no-one sitting close by.

Sipping her Coke, Mary reflected for a few moments. "It was a very difficult time for us. Although we were powerless to intercede in events 4,000 miles away, the Crown Prince and the rest of the family campaigned to bring the plight of our relatives in Ethiopia to world attention. The executions of 60 leading members of the aristocracy and middle classes in November 1974 had really shocked us. We saw this as just the start of a campaign of terror by Mengistu, not only against the educated classes, but against Ethiopians generally. So, our campaign began by lobbying MPs from both sides of the House of Commons.

"Who helped you?"

"I remember Sir Bernard Braine from Essex and Sir Chapman Andrews were particularly helpful and supportive. I think the big breakthrough was when James Callaghan, who was then Labour Prime Minister, saved my aunt, Princess Tenangne Worq, and cousins from certain execution when he made a speech at the European Community meeting in Rome. Mengistu's government knew then that the world was watching, and the likelihood of more aid to end the worsening famine would be in jeopardy."

Mary went on to explain how her family met and addressed meetings organised by Oxford and Cambridge universities, Christian groups, Martin Hill of Amnesty International, and Richard Luce, Minister for Arts in Heath's government.

"Although Ethiopians visiting relatives in the UK were forbidden to talk to us, we were part of a tight-knit Ethiopian community of 300 or so people, and had the support of most of them. We were shocked when we read that families whose relatives were shot by the Derg regime had to pay 150 birr (more than a month's wages at the time) to bury the bodies. This was to repay the government for the 'wasted bullet' used to kill their loved one." During this time of death and destruction in Ethiopia, Mary's third child, another son – Eyoha - was born in December 1976 at University College Hospital, London.

"Despite the desperate situation at home, I have very happy memories of their childhood: their first days at school, and birthday parties. We sometimes managed to get abroad for holidays, to Spain and also camping in Brittany. By this time, we lived in Cedar Road, Croydon. Croydon is home to the Immigration Service and I was able to help other Ethiopian asylum seekers escaping Mengistu's regime by translating documents into Amharic, or vice versa. The Immigration Service really helped many Ethiopians during this time."

In 1991, Mary, her husband and son, Eyoha, moved to the USA, where they had a second home amongst the large Ethiopian community in the suburbs of Washington. The two eldest, like Mary in her youth, stayed on at boarding school in the UK. She returned home to Ethiopia in the late 1990s, after the Derg had been routed by Meles Zenawi's Ethiopian People's Republican Party and the new federal government had become well established.

Considering all the powerful people Mary would have met, I was eager to know who had left a lasting impression: "Out of all the people you've met in your life, who influenced you the most, Mary?"

She thought for a while. "It was Benenden School's head teacher, Miss Clarke, who trained me to be disciplined. It was a spartan education, but it built strength of character. I wouldn't have gained the Duke of Edinburgh Award, enjoyed the variety of hobbies I've had, nor survived the turmoil of the revolution without the school. And then there was Dr Scott-Brown, our guardian. She encouraged my interest in

Mary Asfaw Wossen in front of her old school,
now the IT department of Addis Ababa University

opera, concerts, poetry and theatre. I considered her a second mother: I was broken-hearted when she died."

"And Ethiopia's future? What of the country now?"

"It lies in education," she said firmly, without a trace of hesitation. "We must find ways and means to increase the literacy rate, working with different organisations, including the Orthodox Church - so many people are devout Christians here and attend church regularly. Our priests are great educators. I think the way they teach children to repeat things orally trains their memories.

"And what about peace – and your hopes for the world?"

"I think women should become more involved in breaking down the barriers that exist between tribes and communities," she replied emphatically. "Violence is counter-productive: children have to learn to get along with each other. Through educating different groups together, we can begin to build world peace. We need to be far more proactive and discourage all the violence we see on TV and in Hollywood films.

"Terror is seeping into everyday life: children are recruited as soldiers from seven years old: there's violence in schools. If mothers got more involved and we increased respect and understanding of different cultures in primary and high schools, we could create a more cohesive, peaceful society."

Further information:

Abebech Gobena and AGOHELD: http://www.telecom.net.et/~agos/
Benenden School, Kent: www.benenden.kent.sch.uk

14   On the road again

On Wednesday morning, after the children's early morning prayers, I got ready for the day's trip to Fitche, about 115km north of Addis, to see the work AGOHELD does outside the city. Berhane Selase, the driver, was ready and extended a warm hand in greeting. We sped off towards the east of Addis to collect Eshetu, our guide for the day. At 6.45am the streets were already full of lorries dropping off loads for that day's market: porters balanced wide straw baskets on their heads while scurrying across roads, their strong neck muscles holding ten kilo loads in place, although they found it difficult to move their heads to see oncoming cars.

As we eased out of the capital, the traffic thinned and we approached Entoto, the roof of the city. A huge monument was erected by Emperor Haile Selassie on the northern approach, inscribed with the name of the city and the lion of Judah. This time the road was wide and smooth, a great relief after the potholes of Robe. We stopped for a light breakfast, parking by a bus stop: one of the local community guards walked to and fro, nursing an AK47 rifle in his arms. This was the rule of law, and people avoided him. As Eshetu got out of the van, he spotted two former pupils from the building course at Fitche: the men grinned in recognition, and after a brief conversation, Eshetu explained that they graduated two years ago and now have government contracts to build and refurbish buildings in the region – a great result.

We sat drinking our tea, looking out onto the main highway. After a few moments, a bus pulled up and people got on and off. Unlike in Addis, it wasn't a free-for-all, and the driver got out to unload packages and then packed away the bundles new passengers had brought with them. Within five minutes, the task was complete and the bus disappeared into the distance.

The countryside was lush, with cows grazing in the clear, sweet mountain air. In the distance, pale purple mountains stood majestic in the early morning light. There were fewer tukuls for each acre of land, a sign of wealth. Along with the noticeable drop in temperature, people's moods seemed better for not having to fight the constant heat, dust and flies all the time. Eshetu informed me that this area is the home to Fisseha Adugna's family - the Ethiopian ambassador to Britain - and also to Mulugeta Asrate's. All these connections: Eshetu added proudly that he had been to school with the ambassador's older brother.

The mountains seemed somehow gentler here and we passed a church by the road, built by a driver who **had** survived a dreadful crash when his lorry left the road. He raised money from other drivers, and today it's a sign that God looks after the men in his profession.

The AGOHELD Fitche project is housed on a very large compound, with half a dozen buildings around the perimeter. It has two main aims: to provide care for AIDS sufferers and their families, including paying for the children's education and preventing further spread of the disease, and to provide vocational skills training for students in their late teens and early twenties. After meeting some of the staff, we walked around to the classrooms where the skills training took place.

The training is aimed at students whose final exam grades aren't high enough for a good job, or those who have had to drop out of school, often because their parents could no longer afford the small fees. I learnt that training women is a priority: otherwise they'll often be exploited by employers or end up as sex workers in Addis. The very poorest students get free tuition, the others pay a small fee. The lessons include other general studies like civic responsibility, maths and languages, to ensure the students graduate as properly rounded, professional workers.

The year-long courses normally consisted of ten months practical experience and two months theory. In the knitting class, girls sat crocheting small table decorations. Pairs of students stood by knitting machines making jumpers of different colours and designs. Next door was the weaving class where they made fine blankets, netallahs and fota, the cloaks worn by men in winter. The craftsmanship was very good, the wool and cotton were organic and visitors could buy a blanket for as little as 50 birr, just over £3 - a real bargain.

The building course was a hive of activity, and obviously very popular. In one area, students were learning different bricklaying techniques: a quarter of them were women, I was pleased to see. Outside in the sunshine, students were using technical drawings, string, nails and wood to create floor plans for the kind of houses or small offices they would be building in real life in perhaps a year's time. AGOHELD also goes one step further and provides 300 birr seed funding for graduates to set up their own small businesses: another demonstration of its commitment to self-reliance for all.

Later on, Eshetu and I walked into a hall where around forty people sat waiting patiently for us – the AIDS sufferers and carers. One by one, a member of each family stood up and related their story. They were keen to tell me how the money from AGOHELD was helping to make their lives more comfortable, as they could now buy food staples rather than having to beg, and children could be educated, giving them a better future even if both of their parents died. Abebech and her team also provided training for the carers, so they knew how best to care for their relatives during the different stages of the illness. However, although their stories showed resilience in the face of great adversity, everyone there had lost someone close. One little boy, accompanied by his grandmother, was dressed in the same very smart suit that he'd worn to his father's funeral two days earlier. His mother lay in bed at home, also very ill with the disease. Nowadays, it's AGOHELD's experience that 90 per cent of those benefited by the project are women: either the grandmothers or aunts left to care for the orphans, or a mother who manages to hang on a little longer than her partner before also passing away.

The organisation also encouraged people to educate the community about AIDS, but it required great courage for people first to admit they had the disease. The first counsellor in the area was a woman, who had volunteered two years ago. A mother of three whose husband had died from the disease, she regularly spoke to school students, local women's groups and at coffee ceremonies.

The meeting lasted for almost an hour, as parents, aunts, uncles, and grandparents stood up one after the other to praise Abebech. When I thought we'd just about finished, one young teenager put his hand up. He introduced himself as Sentayehu Getye Cherenete and began by explaining that he was all alone in the world, as his parents had died when he was nine. His voice began to crack as he told us that he'd been forced to sleep rough as he had no one else to care for him. As he continued to speak, sobs began to escape from his thin body. Within seconds everyone in the room was sobbing, and when I looked at Eshetu sitting beside me out of the corner of my eye, I saw that he was crying too.

The boy stood there swaying and crying, and the sound of 40 people sobbing echoed around the thin grey walls. Not knowing what to do or say, I just got up and went to him and gave him a big hug. His face nestled into my shoulder and I thought how easily this could have been James, our son. I held him for what seemed like minutes until he understood that I wanted him to sit beside me while his sobs abated.

With the money AGOHELD had given him, he was able to buy shoe shine equipment and earn a living that way: he still lived on his own, and wanted to go to school, but he needed more money to do that. He also said that he was ill at times, and used his money to pay for medicine. My instinct was that he, too, had AIDS. He is one of millions left with nothing after this deadly disease, but each of the millions is a member of a family like you and I.

Sentayehu, whose parents died from AIDS when he was just nine

15 A call from the Palace

As I got into the car for the return journey to Addis, Eshetu turned round from the front seat and said with a sly grin, as though he was keeping a big secret, "There was a phone call for you today."

"Oh, who called?" I tried to think who it might be – perhaps Mary, or Marta Asrat from Nazareth School.

"It was the President's office. He can see you at 10 am tomorrow."

"Wow, that's just fantastic! Have others in the office heard about the call?" Smiles wreathed my face, and I wanted to punch the air with excitement.

"Yes," he grinned broadly, "everyone knows about it. We're very excited for you," Eshetu replied, squeezing my hand.

I called Tirlaye as soon as I got back to the orphanage. "Tanasterlign Tirlaye, I've got good news. The President can see us tomorrow."

"Oooh, Annette that's betam, betam turu – very, very good. What time would you like me to collect you?"

"Can you be here for 9.30 please and no later, as we must be on time." "Of course, your request is my command." "Tirlaye, one more thing," I added, thinking about the day before, when three men had had to push Tirlaye's borrowed car up the road when it had run out of petrol.

"Yes?"

"Please make sure you haven't been robbed by the petrol station and you have enough petrol this time."

"I will do," he laughed, "don't worry!"

Awoken the next morning by the dogs' barking and the children's chanting, I lay in bed, thinking just how amazing it was that I would be visiting the Jubilee Palace later that day. It was the same one that I'd stood outside as a young girl, with my classmates, waving the Ethiopian flag whenever the Emperor hosted a state visit. These weren't only from African countries, but European too – including Queen Elizabeth II. For the first time I would actually see inside the grounds and, perhaps, go inside the imposing Palace. It felt like a dream, but it was really happening.

After washing, I walked across to the cupboard and pulled out my black suit – the first time I'd be wearing it this trip. I completed the outfit with the silver Lalibela cross and my mother's Norwegian enamel brooch with the silhouette of fairies and a deer on it, for good luck. I left half my breakfast: I was feeling quite anxious and didn't want my stomach rumbling while we spoke. I tried curtsying a couple of times, but my back was sore from the rock hard mattress, which felt like sleeping on solid wood, so I decided that I would just bow. At 9.30, Tirlaye pulled up in the rather battered old gold Toyota. He got out and waved, standing there looking his very best, in a dark brown suit, white striped shirt and blue and silver striped tie. Like a gentleman of the old school, he opened the door for me.

"How are you feeling today, Annette?"

"Nervous and excited all at once, Tirlaye. I'm looking forward to seeing inside the palace!"

"Yes, this is a great honour for both of us. I, too, have never been inside those grounds."

Driving down the hills towards the Palace, I had time to gather my thoughts. I had three questions to ask the President, but I would have to see how the conversation went. I realised that, this being Africa, I had to wait before I asked them. My status, even as a white woman, would not be particularly high.

We parked in front of the Palace's metal gates, complete with shields and spears as I remembered them. The gardens were looking slightly the worse for wear because of the hot summer the plants and shrubs had endured. I could see a modern single storey office in the distance, which must have been a new addition in the past 40 years. Two soldiers stood sentry, a man and woman – the latter was comforting for me. Good to see the Army was an equal opportunity employer!

The security was thorough: everything in the car was checked, including beneath the bonnet, in the boot and underneath the seats. We were frisked too. I was worried when they took my camera, as I really needed to take a photo of me with the President, to show more sceptical people that I had actually met him. Fortunately it was returned, but I had to promise not to take any photos in the grounds.

President Girma's office was in the small modern block by the Palace. I felt a twinge of disappointment that I wouldn't get to see inside where Mary and her siblings had enjoyed their Christmas parties, but it was only used for ceremonial occasions now. Reminders of the Emperor's influence remained in the statues of lions, two guarding the massive front door of the Palace and two looking down from the top of the building.

We were ushered in through the double doors to the office. I said hello to his secretary and thanked her for arranging the audience. Tirlaye and I sat in a very formal reception room, with embossed wallpaper and Italianate couches. I casually flicked through a magazine, pretending that I met Presidents on a regular basis. Inside my stomach churned and I wondered about Hiruth.

Suddenly a smartly dressed man came out of the inner sanctum. "The President will see you now," he told us very formally.

Tirlaye stepped forward and said a few words in Orominya before introducing me: the President and he were members of Ethiopia's most populous tribe. I shook the President's hand and bowed my head as a mark of respect. We were in more modern surroundings, seated around mahogany table with all the accoutrements of a head of state around us: medals, a map of the world, photographs of the family and foreign dignitaries. On the large bookshelf behind the desk was a replica of the sign that stood in the Catholic church's garden: 'May peace prevail on earth.'

The President was a short man: with his kindly face and ample waistline, white hair

Meeting President Girma of Ethiopia, Hiruth's father

and moustache, he resembled a clean-shaven, black Father Christmas. He motioned us to sit down and asked how my travels had gone. I was very enthusiastic about the welcome and help I'd received from so many people. After a few pleasantries, he began to talk about Hiruth.

"You know, she was a very intelligent girl: she was the top student in all Ethiopia in grade 8 with a 98 per cent pass rate. She went on to win a scholarship to study art in Sofia, Bulgaria and from there she went to Bonn to train as a nurse. While she was there in 1973, we had such a big famine. Hiruth read about it and it upset her greatly. Together with a friend, she decided to raise what funds they could on the streets of Bonn. While she was doing that, she met a man called Bernd Dreesmann who ran a German charity: together they raised over two million deutschmarks in just over two months to help the poor. She was an amazing woman, we were so proud of her."

Was? His voice began to break as he spoke of her.

I interrupted gently: "President Girma, where is Hiruth today?"

"I'm sorry to tell you this, but she committed suicide in 1978."

The room fell silent: my heart sank, what could I do or say? Could this be it – the story ending here? He sat in front of us dabbing at his eyes, grief still etched on his face after all that time. I looked down at my feet, wondering how to break the silence.

My reply came without thinking, "I'm so very sorry to hear that, it must have been a terrible shock for all of you. But given all her good work for your country, I would like to include her in the book as a tribute to her life, if you would allow me to."

"I would like that very much," he said. "Please work with her sister Ghennet, who now lives in Paris."

I stood up, walked round to the President and put one of my arms around him. I couldn't take away the pain of losing his eldest daughter, but I wanted to show that I respected his feelings. He sat down heavily and rifled through one of his draws, giving me a business card.

"Here are Bernd's details. Do contact him. Tell him I asked him to help you with Hiruth's story."

At the end of that momentous meeting, I showed President Girma the letter from Archbishop Desmond Tutu. He was very impressed and said he would write a similar one for me. "Please come to the office tomorrow, I will find some photographs of Hiruth for you to include."

He was true to his word, and on Friday morning I was ushered in once more to collect some photos of Hiruth and a letter of support wishing me luck with the book. No, more than that – "I'm sure your book will do well" was his final sentence. I was very touched and humbled by that. Once outside, I left the Jubilee Palace grounds grinning like a Cheshire cat.

After lunch, Tirlaye and I visited Nazareth School to collect the list of classmates'

Hiruth's parents at her funeral

names. There was no need to wait this time: we were shown straight to Marta's office, where she sat peering at her PC screen as she typed out the exam syllabuses for the school. As we sat there, the sound of laughter lapped around us – it was break time.

"Well, we managed to get all the girls' names for you," Marta said, swivelling in her chair.

"That's wonderful news, Marta. Thank you so much – it'll help more than you can imagine."

As she smiled, I noticed the tiredness around her eyes and the grey tinge of her skin: all the preparations for exams and typing test papers must be exhausting. I told her the sad news about Hiruth, and she was silent.

"Of course, three or four of the class are dead, Annette. It's so sad when parents have to bury their children." She paused. "Let's see now, where did I put the list? Ah, here. Do you want to go over them and see who you remember?"

I drew up a chair and we sat together, checking off the names. I hadn't realised there were as many as 38 in the class. As I scanned the names some more faces floated towards me, but half were a complete blank. I wasn't concerned – there were only nine people on my list. Even as I thought that, disappointment crept in. I should, perhaps, be more ambitious and aim to recreate the old school photograph. Now wouldn't that be great – what a party we could have afterwards!

"Marta, you've been a real star. You know, I think that one day we should try and get everyone together and recreate the old photo. What do you think about that?"

"It would be amazing: what memories we could share – I think that's a great idea."

We hugged and tears pricked my eyes.

"I hope to see you when we launch the book here, Marta. I couldn't have done it without you."

"No problem, and God bless you on your journey, Annette. You have been given a very special mission."

*****

The last morning in Ethiopia began early. Stretching under the heavy blankets, I wondered what time the children would start their prayers on a Saturday. At 6am the intonations began: the same time as every day! I could hear the little voices breathing deep before the next verse: the quieter voice of the child who led the chant/song and the others answering: a few bellowing out in the chilly morning air. I had packed my suitcase the night before and collected the dried spices for Mulugeta, and Fisseha, the Ethiopian ambassador in London. Abebech had wanted me to take a very heavy suitcase full of spices – it was impossible to lift! We agreed on a more reasonable ten kilos.

I made my goodbyes, walking around the dormitories: I was hoping to see Hanna, the translator, and she arrived wearing a little cloth cap for her cleaning duties in the dormitory. She gave me eight letters from other 15-year-old girls all seeking pen pals, and a lovely drawing of a rose for me. I was very touched by her shy friendship and thought how tough it must be when you have no family of your own. I hugged her closely and promised to stay in touch. I was also yearning to embrace James too – it had been three weeks since the last one.

Tirlaye arrived to escort me to the airport: like Abebech he had adopted me and was keen for my return, with the completed book. He chatted away in Orominya, the language of the Oromo people to Abebech's adopted son, Isak, who drove us to Bole airport. Abebech had adopted Isak and a little girl and she now has two grandchildren. In every cloud there is a silver lining, and she was an honorary mother to many Ethiopians, who now lived all over the world, connected through the orphanage to her deep, abiding love.

I had a lump in my throat as we approached the airport: the invisible deep cords of Africa tore at me every time I arrived or departed. Inside, perhaps, I was still that small 11-year-old leaving Addis for the last time, or the 19-year-old flying back to the UK after six and a half years in South Africa.

As the plane soared heavenward, the fields of Ethiopia turned from green patchwork to brown, scorched earth. In the middle of nowhere, with no clean water, no prospects, no time, no money for education, just scraping the bare bones of a life: that was my idea of hell. Water is life: without it, we and everything on earth just return to dust.

IV: EUROPE

16 The web spreads

Travellers shoved and pushed each other to get their suitcases from the carousels. That was it: I was back with a bang to stress-ridden, impatient Britain. I sighed as I wheeled my trolley through arrivals, but Rob and James stood by the barriers, waving as I walked through. To see the two people whom you most love in the world after three weeks' absence is heart stopping – I was home! Rob and I gave each other a long embrace, and the tears welled up – how I'd missed them.

Dusk was falling as we sped home along the M25. It was delicious to sit on comfortable seats: my back shouted hurrah as we glided along on smooth tarmac, without a pothole in sight. Spring flowers bloomed along the verges and trees were already in bud, as Rob and James related their news about work, school and the pet topic of all British people – the weather.

Rob had made a warming beef casserole for the evening meal, and it was so good to go to the kitchen tap and know I could drink the water without fear of any bugs. Beef, too, had been a luxury during the fasting period of lent in Ethiopia. Afterwards, we sat chatting about my different experiences of Ethiopia, and I went upstairs to rummage in my suitcase to find the photos I'd already had developed.

It was difficult to convey just how different the country was to what I had expected and to the one-dimensional picture painted by the Western media. I explained some of the important highlights, like meeting Marta, the school secretary; the Pankhursts, the WaterAid visit where I'd met Mamali and his family; Hanna and Sentayehu at AGOHELD and the great privilege of meeting the President. What I held in my heart was the Ethiopians' enormous hospitality and their pride in their country. I really had felt like an honoured guest in my travels.

Life returned to its normal routine. Wandering down the local high street, I missed the smiles of Ethiopians most of all. It was amazing how many people looked away when I smiled or said hello even in a small, friendly town like Buckingham. They seemed locked in a prison where strangers were automatically suspicious – the question 'What do you want from me?' seemed to emanate from them.

I felt like a fish out of water away from the African hospitality, so I compensated by calling all my Ethiopian friends and letting them know about the trip's success. I tried to capture the sights and sounds of my travels, and emails were sent to many different parts of Addis Ababa in my bid to stay in contact.

Mulugeta and I met up in April, in Debenhams department store in central London. It was the day before the Ethiopian Easter, which the Ethiopians celebrate three to four weeks after us, in accordance with the Eastern Orthodox Church. Appraising me keenly, he remarked, "So you didn't lose any weight then?"

We laughed and found a free table. The meeting was to be brief. I was on an errand to deliver the pungent spices from Abebech Gobena for Mulugeta's wife to use when making watt - the smells had been permeating not only the study but the whole of the first floor at home. Mulugeta was very happy to receive the gifts which, only two weeks ago, had been drying in the sun before being pummelled into fine powder in one of Abebech's workshops. From Oxford Street, I took the tube to Knightsbridge and sped as fast as I could to the Ethiopian embassy in Prince's Gate. Fisseha, the ambassador, was also pleased with his spices. Mission accomplished, I now needed to continue with the odyssey to track down the seven women: Hiruth, Fanaye, Silva, Celina, Phoebe, Sumitra and Kathy.

There was one connection to be explored: Ghennet Girma, Hiruth's sister, in Paris. Within two hours of leaving a message on her answerphone, she had returned the call. Ghennet's voice was that of a cultured, well-bred Ethiopian. I was curious about why she was unable to return home, but it was too early in our relationship for me to ask right out. "My background is not of interest: this is about Hiruth," she retorted to my probably rude question.

Her parting words to me were, "The book sounds very worthwhile, but I will have to check with my mother in Washington. All the family need to be happy about it." I sent her the synopsis and decided to bide my time.

I had more fruitful contact with Bernd Dreesmann, the German whom Hiruth had worked with at Deutsche WeltHungerhilfe, an NGO that specialises in providing food and disaster relief.

"Of course I will be happy to help you." he told me over the phone. "How much it will aid the story I'm not sure, but I will be delighted to tell you about Hiruth's time with us in Germany. I have already heard from her father that you are preparing a book. When she accepted my invitation to join us as a fund-raising assistant to help ease the '73 famine, her ceaseless efforts soon made her the Face of Ethiopia in the German media. But I'll tell you more when we meet."

Bernd and I discussed possible dates for this. Cologne was his nearest large town, but it was a long way to go for one story. Money was getting tight, so I had to plan my future trips with care.

His helpfulness and Ghennet's conversation with her mother paid off. A few days after my contact with Bernd, Ghennet sent me an email. She'd been looking through her address book and had found Fanaye Saifou's details, including two email addresses. Fanaye lived in Cologne, and Ghennet advised me to try both addresses.

A week later came Fanaye's pleasantly friendly and informative reply.

"Tanasterlign Annette, I am very surprised and pleased to hear from you. Dehna nesh? is how are you? The answer is 'dehna'. You know, out of the 38 classmates, only ten made it to 12th grade. I have their photos in my diploma and that is how I remembered their names. Hiruth had already left us for Bulgaria after the eighth grade. I was surprised to find her in Germany. I had just moved from Bavaria to North Rhine Westfalia, when I met her together with her sisters at an Ethiopian political meeting in Bonn in the 70s. Her sisters recognized me, but not Hiruth. She was suffering from depression. Remember she used to be very quiet and always together with her friend, Azeb Fesseha?

"In 1986 I went to America for the first time and I met Etenesh Tsige. She is in the front row in the middle of the old school photo. We met in an Ethiopian church in Washington, DC. She told me that besides Hiruth, another of our classmates committed suicide: Bisrat Getahun. She's in the front row, first left of our class photo. Etenesh seems to know more about our classmates. She used to live in

Richmond, Virginia, and we exchanged letters until 1990 and then we lost contact.

"You are welcome to come to Cologne any day you want. It is OK with me. Just let me know beforehand, so that I can make plans to stay at home and not sleep on somebody's sofa, doing one of my jobs. Isshi (OK)?"

I was elated: in three months I had found four classmates and a good enough reason for visiting Cologne. Now there were only five more waiting for discovery.

*****

But then reality hit home. The bank balance was getting low and I was feeling very anxious. I wanted no repeat of the 1997 and 1999 house moves, so early one morning, after a lot of remonstrations from Rob, I logged onto a job website. There seemed to be an ideal position in Hertfordshire and I applied on-line. Luck was with me and three weeks later, the contract with a major retailer was confirmed – there would be more than enough to put food on the table again.

I was conscious that it would be the usual full-on role, with people assuming I'd be delivering the goods in two-thirds of the time expected from a normal employee. I used my last two weeks of freedom to complete the research and contacted our local MP, John Bercow, who was also shadow International Development Secretary, to see whether he knew of any trusts who could provide some form of sponsorship. Perhaps the Department for International Development – DFID - might be able to help. His reply was very quick and he suggested some grant-making trusts, but they were for UK-based projects only. He also promised to contact Hilary Benn, International Development Secretary and son of Tony Benn, the famous socialist Labour MP.

Finding the other classmates was now a daily preoccupation. Reading the material about the Emperor's imprisonment, I decided to call Mary Asfaw Wossen to see how she was getting on with the amendments I'd asked her to make to her chapter. The long, one-syllabled ring of Ethiopian phones echoed in my ear as I waited for her to answer.

"Hello Annette, I'm sorry I've taken a while to reply. I've been a bit busy lately, but I promise to let you have it soon. Listen, I have some good news for you. I spoke to another classmate, Mary Nalbandian, to see if she could help track down some of the other Armenians and she has a phone number for Silva in Los Angeles. Why don't you try it?"

I thanked her and scribbled it down. Glancing at the clock, I saw that it would be about 10am in Los Angeles, eight hours behind London. I dialled the number Mary had given me: my heart was in my mouth as I heard the shrill, insistent rings of the phone.

"Hello?" The soft voice was vaguely familiar.

"Hello, is that Silva Derentz?"

"Well, I used to be, but I am Hagopian now. Who are you?"

"You may not remember me, but I'm Annette Allen, the British girl who used to go to school with you in grades five and six at Nazareth School. Silva, I realise it's probably a shock to hear from me after all this time, but I was given your phone number by Mary Asfaw Wossen – Princess Mary, who's in regular contact with Mary Nalbandian in Addis." I tried to speak slowly, hiding my nerves.

"Well, it's a big surprise hearing from you after all these years," she replied hesitantly. "I remember you, you were short with blonde hair and quiet. Where are you living these days?"

"I'm married to Rob and we live in Buckingham, north of London" I said proudly, "and we have a 15-year-old son, James. How about you, do you have children?"

"I'm married to Jack," she explained, "and we have three grown up daughters. I work in real estate. What kind of job do you do?" I smiled, Silva was very inquisitive.

"I used to be in corporate communications, but I'm now working part-time whilst I write a book about the class to raise funds for charity. I would really like to include an Armenian in the story, and I was wondering if you would consider being part of the book, Silva?" I held my breath, as Silva was silent. I continued: "Could I have your email so that I could send you some details and let you think about it?"

"Sure," she said, "why not? I'll get back to you once I've had a chance to read what it's all about."

I took down her details and sent the email later that evening, keeping my fingers crossed for a positive response. I wasn't sure why I'd picked Silva out of the five Armenians in my class, but I knew she was the right one.

*****

I contacted national newspapers and magazines to see if anyone would feature the old school photo. Some journalists did bother responding, to say that they would interview me when the book was out. Others were more cautious: one women's magazine editor commented, "Your story is so unique, I don't see how anyone could possibly relate to it." Refusing to be downhearted, I turned her response on its head and thought that there must, therefore, be very good news value in it.

Our local newspaper *The Buckingham Advertiser* turned up trumps again. They'd printed a short feature the week before my return to Addis, so I decided to email them, to see if asked they'd be interested in featuring the old school photo. I reasoned that local people appeared to be well travelled and as it was a very small world, you never know, someone just might recognise a familiar face. They were

"Buckingham Advertiser" readers' letters page – 11 June 2004

Searching for school friends

I AM a Buckingham author researching a book on the lives of nine women I went to school with in the Ethiopian capital, Addis Ababa, around 40 years ago.

One objective from a recent visit to Ethiopia was to find out the full names of all my school friends from my old school (I only had the Christian names on the back of the old school photo).

In just five months, I've found four of my classmates; three in the last two months.

The school was very helpful and I now have the full names of all my classmates.

I now have five more to find, all the international students who were in my class.

If you could help me track down the following it would be really helpful: front row, sec-

ond from right, Kathy Miller; second row, second from left, Celina Fernandez; Silva Derentz, second row, third from the left; Sumitra Goyal, second row, fourth from the left, and finally Phoebe Khalil, second row, fifth from the left.

Thanks. I can be contacted at the e-mail address below.

Annette Allen
a.allen@netcomuk.co.uk

CLASSMATES: Do you recognise anyone in this photo?

happy to oblige. It appeared in the readers' letters page on 11 June, with a request for readers to contact me should they recognise any of the foreign ladies in the photo. Four days later, I had a reply. Jack Atamian, an Armenian, had been browsing the newspaper and had spotted the photograph. Seeing the Ethiopian faces, he recognised his second cousin, Silva. He and his wife Therese lived just one mile from us! When I got his email I just burst into tears: tears of joy. I gave grateful thanks to God – more proof that this odyssey was meant to be. The circle of connections was now beginning to resemble a giant web, spreading from the UK to Ethiopia, France, Germany and now the US.

I sent Jack the book synopsis and we spoke a week later. His tone was quite bemused and I could hear the smile in his voice as he said:

"Well, you seem to have set yourself quite a challenge there, Annette, but I would like to help you if I could. How about you and your family coming around for a barbeque one Sunday? Would that be OK?" I accepted immediately and we agreed a date. A week later, my letter of thanks to the newspaper appeared on the same page.

*****

Mary Asfaw Wossen had refused to elaborate on how the Emperor had died. I was curious – a lot of rumours claimed he had been buried beneath the toilet that Mengistu and his senior officers had used in the Menelik Palace. I needed to find an independent source, ideally a journalist, who would know more.

I wondered if Odd Inge might be able to help. He and Berit were spending a week in July sailing down a canal with another Norwegian couple, and we were due to meet them in a pub close to the towpath one Friday evening.

Odd Inge introduced us to their friends, Per and Inger Ulleberg. Per was a tall, studious looking man, with thick grey hair and sideburns, and an easy, calming presence. He had studied at the Tavistock Institute in London and Inger was a teacher. She told me about her job and how much she enjoyed teaching teenagers: she was about to move to another college.

"And tell me, Annette, what do you do?"

Removing the school photo from my handbag, I described a bit of the journey and the dream to bring water to Ethiopia. I mentioned my current challenge, to find out how Emperor Haile Selassie had died, as it was still such a painful subject for Mary Asfaw Wossen.

"Yah, so then, I think you should get in touch with Einar Lunde: he's a well known

TV presenter and journalist in Norway and spent a lot of years in Ethiopia. Perhaps he may be able to help you." With that passing remark, I knew I had to contact him.

Further information:

Deutsche Welthungerhilfe: www.welthungerhilfe.de
Buckingham Advertiser: www.buckinghamtoday.co.uk

17 A little blue Volkswagen

Bright sunlight danced up the walls through the pale ivory bedroom curtains. I stretched slowly – it was a Sunday and today Rob and I were going to meet Jack and his wife Therese and two of their three daughters, Lisa and Gabriella. They would be the first Armenians I'd spoken to for 30 years or so. I'd promised Jack that we'd show some of my father's old slides from Ethiopia, so we loaded the car with the projector, screen and slides.

We drove up a steep hill right to the top of Buckingham and turned right into the small close where they lived. Jack radiated good health and bonhomie as he greeted us, his face and arms tanned from the summer sun. Therese was much paler, her weak handshake indicated delicate health, but she too was all smiles as she shook our hands and said: "tanasterlign", as though it was only yesterday she'd left Ethiopia.

Walking through the kitchen to a pleasant back garden with climbing roses and a pergola, I recognised Carol Iles from church. She and I were being confirmed together on 19th October, and we'd already had one meeting with Kevin, our rector, and the other two confirmees, Gillian and Sian. Carol's daughter, Helena, was best friends with Silva, Jack and Therese's eldest daughter, as they'd both gone to school together. Five minutes later Greg turned up, another Ethio-Armenian and a close friend of Jack's.

As Therese poured glasses of cold rosé, Jack looked at the old school photo and began to relate why so many Armenians had been in my class.

"Well" he began in his melodious voice, like the wind brushing through ripe corn "at the time you lived there with your family, there were probably more than 1,500 Armenians in the city. Many of their parents or grandparents had fled the genocide in Ottoman Turkey and decided to settle in Ethiopia.

"You know one of the foundations of Armenian culture is education: as soon as there are more than a hundred Armenians in a town, we generally build a school where the children can learn about our history, the language and customs, and so keep our culture alive. Today, there are more Armenians living outside Armenia than inside, you know!" he added wistfully.

"Have you heard about the genocide?" he glanced at me over his glasses.

"A bit, but tell me more about it," I pretended to know the details, but it was only a vague memory.

"It was a planned and brutal series of massacres of 1.5 million Armenians, and the displacement of many more from their ancient homeland by the Ottoman Turks which began during World War I and continued until 1923. The Ottomans were keen to extend their empire, and keep Turkey for the Turks."

Jack continued to give more background to Armenia. Their history goes back over 4000 years and their homeland was centred around Mount Ararat, where Noah's Ark is reputed to have landed. Ancient, fertile Armenia was at the crossroads of important trade routes, and thus had been invaded many times over the centuries. Armenians are very proud of the fact that theirs was the first Christian nation, adopting Christianity as a state religion in 301 AD. Today, Armenia is a small country, bordered by Turkey to the west, Georgia to the north, Azerbaijan to the east and Iran to the south.

"My parents fled the genocide, along with many others who ended up in Ethiopia, where they'd heard the Emperor was tolerant and there was a need for their skills and education. Although, in fact, our links with the country go back hundreds of years – to the seventh century.

"Was this to do with religion?" I queried. I recalled Abba Bogale mentioning the connections between the Armenian, Syrian and Ethiopian Orthodox churches.

"Yes, there were close ties between the Armenian apostolic church and Ethiopian Coptic church."

Greg interrupted: "Many Armenians were very close to the imperial family, you know. My uncle was the Emperor's tailor and also godfather to the Crown Prince's son. I went to boarding school in Bath with Philip Mekonnen, one of the royal family. Richard Hamilton was there too – he's the son of Dr. Catherine Hamilton, the Australian, who opened the Fistula Hospital in Addis.

"I still remember my father and I driving past the Jubilee Palace when the Emperor was arrested. It was the day after the Jonathan Dimbleby programme had been broadcast, which the Derg had edited to include scenes of great banquets in the Palace. He was bundled into a little pale blue VW beetle and the soldiers were shouting 'leba!, leba!', which means 'thief' in Amharic. They were blaming him for Ethiopia's famine.

Lisa, Jack's youngest daughter, called us inside to eat. The table groaned with food – there were so many dishes, it was difficult to choose where to start. Jack and Therese were generous hosts and their cuisine is a blend of Armenian and Middle Eastern recipes. There were delicious lamb kebabs, chicken, tabouleh, rice, aubergine with tasty herb sauces and accompaniments. Beside the window hung an original oil painting of the Armenian church in Ethiopia, Soorp Kevork – St. George - where Jack and Therese had married in 1973 before leaving the country.

As there were quite a few guests for lunch, we agreed that it would be better to meet up another time to hear more about their history. After the meal, Rob set up the projector in the lounge and we drew the curtains to transport the Armenians back to their childhood. The three girls sat curled up on the carpet as slides of soaring mountains, deep lakes, tribal costumes and high-cheeked, beautiful Ethiopian faces filled the room with the Horn of Africa – it was the first time they'd ever seen colour slides of their parents' birthplace.

*****

"What an exciting project. I am really thrilled," began the email from Einar Lunde, Norwegian TV's main news anchor.

"Funny you should mention Tutu, Michael Buerk and Olav Skjevesland. Tutu and I met the first time during the apartheid era in 1984: I was in his office when the news about him being awarded the Nobel Peace Prize was announced. Michael was supposed to be there but he had been called away urgently the night before, to go to the famine area of Ethiopia for his famous broadcast. Then Bishop Olav, we spent five years together at Kristelig Gymnasium School in Oslo. We still meet occasionally."

I replied immediately, keen to set a date for a meeting. I could combine it with a visit to Arvid and Olga in Kristiansand. Having become much more confident – cheeky even - I asked whether he'd ever interviewed Nelson Mandela.

"I was the very first Norwegian to interview Mandela, only three to four weeks after his release from Robben Island. It was in Stockholm, where Mandela had gone to visit his nearest friend and ANC colleague, Oliver Thambo. I also hosted a great big people's celebration feast in Oslo on 11 December 1993, the day after Mandela received the Nobel Peace Prize there." ①

Inger had been so helpful in mentioning Einar: he was definitely the right man to help me find out the facts behind Selassie's death. I phoned him a fortnight later, and an Oslo rendezvous was scheduled for November. Since I'd begun the journey, the decision to find old classmates and tell their stories had become an obsession. From dawn till midnight. I plotted, schemed, jotted down notes and kept my daily diary. Invisible threads were spanning continents and guides were stepping forward from all backgrounds. I was ecstatic, but humble. I had also learned to be quiet and very, very patient. But I was still curious as to how much longer it would take to find the four remaining women.

Further information:

Armenian genocide: www.armenian-genocide.org
A very well written book on the genocide is by Peter Balkian,
The Burning Tigris, Pimlico Books 2003

Einar Lunde: www.nrk.no is the website for NRK TV and Radio,
where Einar works.

① Nelson Mandela, *A long walk to freedom,* p 734, Abacus, 2003 reprint

---

18 Connecting dreams

"Cheese," snapped the businessman when the air-hostess asked him what kind of sandwich he wanted. The Friday afternoon flight to Cologne in July was full and the aircraft had been delayed: irritation danced around the man who sat beside me.

Despite that, my mood was buoyant: Fanaye had been so eager to meet up right from the word go. It was apparent from her emails that she lived a simple life: there wasn't room in her small apartment so she'd arranged for me to stay with a friend, Evelyn, during the weekend. Two and a half days would be enough time to swap stories and hear all about what had happened to her since 1964, and we could always catch up on email after that.

Cologne airport is small and not often used, now that the German Parliament's HQ has moved from Bonn to Berlin. I wandered out into the main arrivals hall but couldn't see anyone there, except for a small Malaysian woman with short hair and black-rimmed glasses. I realised that, in all the excitement, neither of us had thought to tell each other what we'd be wearing. Within five minutes, all the other passengers had left the arrivals hall. I could see the woman looking a bit crestfallen, but she kept glancing towards me. I slowly walked across.

"Are you Fanaye?"

"Annette!" she replied jovially, in relief.

She felt like a small child as we embraced shyly. She was no taller than when I'd last seen her in July 1964. I was struck by how Malaysian Fanaye looked, with her colourful shirt, short wavy hair, almond eyes and simple cropped white trousers. When I mentioned this she nodded in agreement, telling me that on holiday in the Philippines two years earlier she'd been mistaken for a local islander.

Outside, the late afternoon sun bounced off car bonnets and windows. We soon found the white car Fanaye had managed to borrow for the weekend. She drove through the increasingly busy afternoon traffic to Evelyn's apartment, where we'd be staying. We made small talk about the weather and talked about faith – I had discovered that Fanaye was a very devout woman from her emails over the past two months.

Cologne is most famous for its cathedral, which escaped the onslaught of the Allied bombing campaign of 1944. It still stands on the banks of the Rhine like a magnificent guardian giving hope, like the ruins of Coventry Cathedral's nave, that faith will overcome any attempt to destroy it.

Evelyn's flat was in a pleasant area in south Cologne. Ringing the doorbell, Fanaye smiled as Alexander, Evelyn's son, a tall, handsome German-Ethiopian, opened the door. Fanaye had known him and his younger sister, Vanessa, since they were tiny babies.

Rush-hour traffic rumbled below but the noise was muted by the distance. The lounge's floor to ceiling windows offered views to the south and west of the city. Fanaye showed me to my bedroom, which had turquoise blue gauze drapes shielding it from the late afternoon sun.

After some coffee, Fanaye visibly relaxed. She beamed, "You know in 2000, I told Evelyn that I was praying for someone to write the story of my life. Evelyn was interested in doing a writing course and I was hoping that she would do it."

"Well, Fanaye, somewhere deep down I must have heard your prayer, because here I am." We burst out laughing.

A few minutes later Evelyn, our host, appeared. A tall, striking Austrian woman at 54, she had still had the figure of a woman in her 20s. I could see immediately what had attracted her former husband. She had spent almost all her career at Lufthansa after working as a tour guide at the UN headquarters in New York. There was very little of the world that she hadn't seen, taking full advantage of the discount tickets offered to airline staff. She spoke four languages, and carried an air of quiet confidence that conveyed she knew who she was and how she wanted to live her life.

An Ethiopian restaurant called Fasika, Amharic for Easter, was the choice for dinner. Off one of Cologne's side streets, it seemed very popular with an under-30s crowd, both Ethiopians and Eritreans. This was in direct contrast to Ethiopia, where decades of war between the countries meant the nationalities rarely mixed.

Except for the décor and menu, we could have been anywhere in the world. Everyone wore western clothing but their identity was advertised in the different hairstyles – from bushy Afros to braids, beehives and hair extensions.

Drifting into conversation about Ethiopia, Evelyn mentioned a radio program she'd listened to the previous week, when the country was referred to as the only place where Muslim and Christians still lived peaceably side-by-side. "But the report said this was gradually changing," she explained. "There's been a big campaign to convert people to Islam, which has upset the Christians."

I had a hazy recollection of someone mentioning this to me in Addis. Apparently, Muslims had been converting Christians to their faith by paying them 500 birr, a fortune for local people. This was creating tension and division, an unfortunate consequence.

Service was swift. We chose a selection of watts – the spicy curries - accompanied by some Ethiopian beers. The injera had been rolled into strips, making it easier to tear off a piece and dip it into the watt. I had to remember to use my right hand only: difficult when you're used to knives and forks. The conversation between us continued to flow and we had coffee back at the flat. At midnight, Evelyn excused herself. She was on a two day course, and had to leave early the next morning.

*****

Light and heat interrupted my sleep. It was 5am and it was going to be another very warm day. I tried to get back to sleep, but failed. I'd taken my Bible with me, and read it for some comforting words. I wasn't very good at this, I thought: by now I should have a study guide, as I was being confirmed on 19 October as a member of the Anglican Church – also my 52nd birthday.

I lay there hearing the morning sounds of Evelyn getting ready: the water from the shower, the hair drier, cupboard doors opening and shutting, the kettle humming to life. After the front door shut, I got up and got dressed. I knocked on the lounge door where Fanaye had slept on the sofa. I was soon to learn that she always put others before her own comfort.

Fanaye had decided to tell her story in another friend's house. Almaz's house was a short drive away, in an unpretentious but pleasant neighbourhood. After unlocking the door, Fanaye bustled around as usual, like a sparrow. No wonder she was so thin. She opened all the shutters to the kitchen and lounge windows. Outside was a small garden, overlooking open space between the blocks of flats.

Turning to me, she smiled hesitantly, "OK, ya, now I'm ready to tell you about my life. Where do you want me to start?"

She sat down in a big easy chair, moving from side to side, trying to get comfortable.

"It's OK, Fanaye – we'll do this at your pace." I could sense this was a big ordeal for such a modest woman.

She brightened. "I was born in October 1950 in Addis – the youngest of four. My father was Saifou Debabe and my mother was Asegedech Takele. She worked for many years as a pharmacist at the Lion Pharmacy, in Addis."

Fanaye went on to relate their shared patriotism and love for their country. Her maternal grandfather, Takele Wolde-Hawariat, was a well-known republican and resistance leader during the Italian invasion. He was a childhood companion of the Emperor and supporter of the regent. But later, they became enemies when the Emperor went into exile between 1936 and 1941. As a patriot, her grandfather could hardly believe that the Emperor, a defender of his country, had decided to leave his people behind to die at the hands of the Italians.

"See, here I have some details about him." She thrust some photocopied pages into my hands. There wasn't time to look at it now, I'd have to have a browse later. "Do carry on, Fanaye," I urged.

"When the Emperor returned from exile in Britain, my grandfather often opposed and openly challenged him. Takele had become popular among the patriots and survived several attempts to kill him. The Emperor retaliated by imprisoning him in various provincial prisons, far from his family and friends.

"My father totally supported my grandfather. When I was born they were both in prison, far from Addis. My mother was not on good terms with my grandfather's second wife. It may well be that my mother had suffered post-natal depression after giving birth to me, as I was one month premature." By this time, a pained look haunted her eyes.

Fanaye had had an inauspicious start to life, not just because of strained family relationships. She had been born with breathing difficulties and a shrivelled left arm, and was kept in hospital for six months before being transferred to a specialist in Harer, east of Addis. Her mother left her in the care of a nanny and returned to work. After a year the nanny lost contact with the family and took Fanaye, then known as Mamitu (little one), to an orphanage run by Carmelite nuns. She was just about to be adopted by Ethiopians in the US when fate intervened.

"My grandfather had been released from prison and sent Samuel, my older brother, to find me and bring me home. From then on, I was brought up by my grandparents. "

"And what about your mother, Fanaye, where was she all this time?" I asked, shocked by what I heard and beginning to understand how she had empathised with my sadness all those years ago at school.

Her soft, rasping voice got lower, her lip trembling: "I saw her only twice. The first time was when I was nine, having a leg operation. She came to visit me in hospital and brought a Hungarian doll complete with national costume: I still have that doll today. The last time was at her deathbed. She was dying from kidney disease – she was only in her late 30s." Her shoulders slumped: she sat with her hands tucked beneath her legs.

"So, it was a difficult childhood. At the orphanage I'd been treated the same as everyone else. At my grandparent's, it was the complete opposite. They cared for other grandchildren whose parents and relatives visited them frequently. Not us - at weekends, the four of us had to stay home, whilst they went out to different places. We were ignored: they didn't even celebrate our birthdays. My brothers were very angry about the way we were treated and rebelled."

Fanaye frowned at these memories: there were traces of tears and defiance in her eyes. I was surprised that she was so calm about it, perhaps that's where her resilience had started to grow.

"So, you can see, life at home was like being imprisoned. No TV, radio nor friends allowed to visit." She almost spat out the words. "There was too much discipline and no love. As a consequence, I loved school and dreaded the holidays. I only got to know my father and his family after I graduated from school."

The harsh tone softened as Fanaye continued: "You know Annette, out of our class of 38 in 1964, only ten graduated in 1969: one was Silva Derentz and another Celina Fernandes – I have the graduation photo at home, I'll show you later.

"My grades were good enough to begin studying medicine at the University of Addis Ababa. But during my first year, another student revolt broke out in December 1969. None of us could attend lectures or take examinations: they were all cancelled. I didn't want to get involved, I wasn't even a member of the movement. I had my own problems: my grandfather had died just before the revolt broke out.

"He had been with some young men who were agitating to remove Emperor Haile Selassie: there had been an attempted assassination when the Emperor was visiting a school for the blind. Spies had named my grandfather as the ringleader. The police came to arrest him, but by then he was 74 and had had enough of imprisonment. They cornered him, but he shot himself before they could put the handcuffs on."

In those volatile times, that would have meant that anyone with his surname would be under suspicion, making it very hard for all the family. "Listen, let me get you another coffee." Fanaye broke the mood and disappeared into the kitchen for a fresh brew. I glanced outside, where two little girls who looked Vietnamese, played catch in the field between apartment blocks.

"Here you are, you don't take sugar, do you?" said Fanaye, placing the cup in front of me.

"You were talking about your grandfather's suicide," I reminded her. "What happened next?"

"I returned to university, wearing a black armband in his memory. As I mentioned, a student revolt against the Emperor had begun – I remember the day very well." Her eyes were distant as the memories played themselves out in her mind. "I was sitting on the grass near the library with three other students. Suddenly, we heard shots and saw students running towards us. They were shouting 'get away, otherwise the soldiers will shoot you'. We ran towards Menen School on the other side of the library, with some others. In the panic, some tripped over and fell. We couldn't stop to help them, we were running for our lives.

"Some boys helped us clamber over the wall very quickly by pushing us over. I don't know what happened to them – by helping us, they may have been shot. We fell to the other side and ran inside the school buildings, cowering underneath desks when we heard the gunshots. Fortunately, none of the soldiers thought to enter the school.

"I heard later that some of my student friends had been imprisoned and others killed. Despite neck and leg injuries, I got home that evening. The next day I had to be hospitalised. My father was very worried and told me that I couldn't return to university. He knew that the police had a list of names and that, with my famously defiant grandfather, I would be a target. With the other freshmen, I was dismissed from the university. This became known as the 'Christmas Graduation of 1969.'"

"What did you decide to do?" Fanaye's story had been pitiful, abandoned by her parents at a very young age, and then placed under suspicion because of her radical grandfather.

Fanaye rolled her eyes mournfully: "Since the police were searching for me and because of my poor health, my father sent me overseas. I already had a cousin living in Bavaria, so Germany was to be my new home."

Fanaye arrived in Munich in November 1970 to start a new life. "It wasn't what I wanted: my aim had been to settle in the US or another English-speaking country. But it was complicated: I had no choice but to stay and learn a completely new language."

Two hours had elapsed. I looked at my watch. "12.45: Fanaye, we had better get going. We need to meet Bernd." Bernd was joining us for lunch in a local restaurant. 'He will tell you about Hiruth,' the President's voice echoed in my head.

We parked the car by Fanaye's nondescript apartment block in the commercial centre of Cologne. Rubbish lay around the parking area, and rows of windows stared gloomily down at the barren courtyard. It was typical of the kind of transitory place that people rented when they first arrived in the country or earned low wages.

We hurried to the restaurant, as I wanted to ensure that we were there before Bernd. I was feeling very nervous: Bernd was a well-read and well-travelled charity director, but he'd been sympathetic and helpful on the phone and interested enough to give up a couple of hours for a lunch.

I was relieved to see that "Das Rhoendorfer Hof" was a good choice: typically German, with locals sitting at the bar enjoying their litres of beer. No allowances for tourists: everything was in German. I could translate a little of the menu in my schoolgirl German – wiener schnitzel, grilled pork chop, smoked sausage. I suddenly felt hungry: the crispbread from breakfast seemed a long time ago.

I saw Bernd before he saw us. His jacket seemed a little formal in the mid-July heat, but I thought it showed a nice deference to our meeting. He had a firm handshake, and when I introduced Fanaye they exchanged a polite greeting in German.

"Well, it's good to meet you, Annette," he said in impeccable English. He glanced at the menu: the waitress came across and took our food order.

"I have been in touch with President Girma and told him I would do what I could to help you with Hiruth's story in Germany. You know," he said, pouring a glass of water, "at the time of the big Ethiopian famine in '73, it was not easy to raise funds for Ethiopia. The Imperial Government denied flatly for quite a time that there were any problems regarding the food situation in the country. Haile Selassie was respected very much by the Germans, because he had been the first head of state to visit Germany after World War II. It then took a lot of courage to do so."

Bernd's confidence told me he was used to being listened to. The flow of conversation had begun straight away. It turned out that Bernd was a lawyer and economist by profession. He belonged to the JFK generation, which took the young president's words, "Don't ask what your country can do for you, rather what you can do for your country," to heart. Bernd wanted to use his skills to make a difference, and in 1969 he left his safe job as legal advisor to the Director General of the German Foundation for Developing Countries to follow a call from the German Federal President to get the Deutsche Welthungerhilfe established. He was elected as its first Secretary-General, where he remained for 22 years.

"It was all new at the time, the idea of NGOs and charities helping people overseas. Germany had no substantial colonial past and no great experience with the situations in Africa, Asia or Latin America. We had to find our way step by step, setting up contacts, creating working relationships. When we heard rumours about the famine in Ethiopia, it was difficult to get the facts. The German Foreign Office and the Ethiopian Embassy in Bonn took a 'there's no problem' position.

"Then Thomas Hoeppner, a well-known photographer, called me on a Sunday afternoon in mid November '73, advising me about a drastic famine he'd come across in Ethiopia. I rushed to Munich to see the photos: they showed the terrible situation of starving people. The next morning we flew to Hamburg and met with Henri Nannen, the editor of *Der Stern* magazine, one of the two most influential weeklies in Germany. Sir Henri, as he was called, got the message and stopped his printing press. Two days later, on 21 November, the publication came out with the true story of the Ethiopian famine – a great shock for the Germans."

"How did Germans react to the pictures, Bernd?" Bernd's memory was good, he seemed to have come prepared for the meeting.

"With great generosity, after we and Oxfam issued a joint press release giving the facts about the starving nation. The British and German people quickly understood the existing misery and funds started to pour in from both sides of the Channel. The Foreign Offices in London and Bonn were dismayed about the publicity, but the NGOs had taught their governments the facts!"

Around this time, Haile Selassie was making a state visit to Germany. As a result of the famine and growing unrest in the country, his reputation had worsened and the Federal Government did not want to welcome him in Bonn. So the provincial authorities in Stuttgart agreed to host the Emperor instead.

"During one of the public events, we had arranged for two Ethiopian children to ask the Emperor to make a donation for the suffering people in Ethiopia. The old gentleman looked very shocked: he seemed completely unaware of what was happening in his country. I think he was a victim of his own court and the government people around him."

Pausing, Bernd took a few bites of food. I felt we were getting off the point a little and gently reminded him: "What about Hiruth's role in the fund-raising campaign?"

"Yes, of course," he apologised. "I met her and her friend on a chilly day in Bonn's flower-market, begging for money for her people at home. I suggested to them that they could do much better if they would join Deutsche Welthungerhilfe in our nationwide aid activities. The next morning, Hiruth showed up in our office and agreed to join us as a fund-raising assistant.

"She was absolutely the right person for the job. She knew Ethiopia and its people and showed a strong patriotic drive. She travelled up and down the country for press conferences and to accept donations from Chief Ministers, mayors and club presidents, all of whom wanted to help the suffering people. Everyone was eager to appear with this stunning young nurse on TV, in magazines and newspapers. In a couple of weeks, her beauty made her a media star - much in demand. The Ethiopian ambassador showed clear signs of jealousy!"

Bernd's tone darkened as he described Hiruth's changing behaviour. Her beauty and caring nature had masked a horrible secret. She was severely depressed and had begun the descent into schizophrenia.

"One day she could be so charming, the darling of the office, but the next day she would be shouting at her colleagues, accusing them of being racist. It became a difficult time for her and other staff members. Around that time I met her father in Ethiopia and he asked me, with considerable anxiety, how her mood was. I told him and he was very concerned to hear the news.

"I think the events in Ethiopia had upset Hiruth a great deal and affected her state of health in a negative way. But at the same time, I heard she met a young African diplomat and followed him to the US, where her sister lived. I was very sad to hear about her death three years later. She had worked so hard during her year with Deutsche Welthungerhilfe for her people in Ethiopia. She, for sure, deserves a lasting, grateful memory."

As he spoke about him, it was evident that Bernd still had great respect for Hiruth's father, President Girma, whom he'd met on several occasions. In 1992, when he visited Ethiopia, he and 'Ato' (Mr) Girma as he called him, had visited Hiruth's grave in Addis.

"For both of us it was once more a sad moment, and I tried to comfort him by saying that his daughter had already fulfilled a very important role for her country in her young years. Destiny is generous with the Girma family, offering its members unique chances to serve Ethiopia."

Another question was on my lips: my meal sat untouched, by now it was stone cold. "Bernd, do you know how Emperor Haile Selassie died?"

"As far as I know, he was smothered in his sleep and his body was buried underneath Mengistu's desk. Thanks be to God, his remains have recently been transferred to a church in Addis Ababa. May he rest in peace. In his younger years he was a freedom fighter against the Italian colonialists. He was also the first African head of state who insisted that girls had to be admitted to education in schools."

He shook his head and was silent a moment, remembering his unpleasant ending.

"Well," Bernd said, pushing his plate away, "I have some work to do this afternoon,

Fanaye Saifou and Bernd Dreesmann in Cologne

and my wife and I are going out to dinner tonight." He stood up to leave.

"Wait!" I almost panicked as I remembered, "I have to take a photo of you and Fanaye!"

We hurried out of the restaurant and they stood beside an oak tree, Bernd smiling slightly and Fanaye grinning broadly. Then with a cheerful goodbye, Bernd departed.

*****

Fanaye and I returned to our table and ordered another coffee. She put her head closer to mine, speaking softly: "Annette, remember I told you that I wanted to share with you my dream that is so similar to the one you had this February? Well, I'd like to tell you about it now."

"Go on," I urged.

"It was February 2002. In the dream I was in an apartment on the ground floor, and I saw hordes of men and women running – running for their lives. I opened the window and called out to them, 'What are you running from: what should I do?' But no one answered.

"The next thing I saw was a European woman walking by with children, and I called her over, asking 'Tell me, what should I do, should I go or should I stay?'

"The woman looked at me and came over, saying reassuringly, 'Don't worry, you are safe, you already have a ticket.'

'A ticket for what?' I demanded.

'A ticket for the boat: look, here is the ticket.'

"She handed me a fine oval-shaped porcelain plate on which was printed an old black and white photo of young women: I stood in the midst of them. Beside me stood my daughter (in reality, Fanaye has never married nor had children). Her name was Haimanot – in Amharic, this means faith.

"I was very puzzled by this dream and the next day, I asked a friend what this meant, and she told me: "Fanaye, this is a very good omen: you will be involved in something which will do a lot of good in the world.'"

At this, the now-familiar shudders of intuition flowed from my head to my feet. I was silent. Another scene from five months earlier played out in my head. I was explaining the dream I'd had the previous night to Abba Bogale. His faith and sense of humour made it easy to talk about such things.

"Tell me about it," he had encouraged.

"In my dream I was with all seven classmates from Nazareth School. We were on a small boat heading towards an old Italian port. In the distance, I saw blue, pink and white houses clinging to the hillside above the harbour, like small pieces of Lego. I was so happy I'd managed to find them all - they were the same age as I had last seen them, dreaming of their future – boyfriends, marriage and fulfilment. As we docked, they left the boat.

"But what I couldn't understand was why I was left on board. There was only one other person there – the captain and steward, a young man with such a loving, kind face, long fair hair and a beard. We sailed out to sea, and the blue sky changed to deep grey. As thunder roared, 40 foot waves crashed over the deck and tossed the boat like a thimble.

I felt dreadfully seasick and pleaded with the steward: 'Are we going to drown? I can't die now after all the work I've done tracking down my classmates and what about the water for Ethiopia?'

'Don't worry, Annette, we'll soon be safe. You'll meet your classmates again,' he replied, touching my forearm reassuringly.

Then the huge waves subsided, the sun shone once more and we made it into port, where the ladies were waiting. As I got off, I thanked the man, and once more saw the face of Christ smiling at me."

"That was a tremendous dream", Abba Bogale responded. "This is indeed a great blessing before your trip to Addis Ababa."

Fanaye sat waiting patiently for a response. I put down my cup as tears fell: we were both crying. It was clear that our destinies were intertwined. Another unmistakable sign of the odyssey's magic.

*****

Later on, back at her apartment, Fanaye showed me the paper where she'd written down her dream, with the date: 5 February 2002 – almost two years before mine. She then took out the graduation photo: "I found this for you last night."

I gazed at it. As Fanaye had intimated, only ten had graduated. Celina and Silva looked very grown up: Celina with her lovely thick hair piled on top of her head and Silva with shoulder-length hair and flick ups. So, Phoebe, Sumitra and Kathy had left school, and possibly the country, before then. I wondered how I'd find them: how different would they look now: were they still alive?

Emotions were roaring through my body and I needed a break, as did Fanaye. This was no simple undertaking, reliving the pain with someone you'd not seen for so long. Fanaye was very brave. We set off for central Cologne for some sightseeing: it was such a lovely summer's day. Cologne was full of tourists and locals shopping and browsing. We meandered along the cobbled streets and peered into shops before visiting Cologne Cathedral. Close up, it was even more impressive.

Inside were more than a hundred tourists filling the pews: talking, taking photos and gesticulating to each other. I had wanted to pray but it didn't feel right: too many people were present. I was too new in my faith to switch off everything that was going on around me: somehow worshipping in front of hordes of tourists seemed sacrilegious. I noticed a beautiful shrine of pure gold in the distance, by the altar, but was unable to get close to it to see what it was, or what it contained.

Fanaye continued her tale over dinner in a Greek restaurant overlooking the Rhine and the great cathedral. My respect for her had grown a hundredfold for putting up with such cruelty at home and then fleeing to a new life abroad with little prospect of returning. Her mood was lighter now, perhaps in telling her story, she had faced some demons.

"I graduated in chemical engineering from the University of Muenster in North Rhine Westfalia," she continued, "and worked for five years in a research agricultural institute. It was a happy time, but the chemicals affected my already weak health and I had to stop. I retrained in business and informatics (IT), but I had to finish working altogether in 1994, because of heart and back problems. My doctor advised me to avoid stress as much as possible."

Fanaye now does voluntary work for government institutions. From time to time she earns some money translating documents for lawyers and courts. This helps her pay for the school fees of her nieces and nephews, whose father, Fanaye's eldest brother Samuel, died in mysterious circumstances in 1980 during Mengistu's regime. It was Fanaye's chance to repay her brother for his diligence in finding her at the orphanage in Harer.

"Have you been back since 1970, Fanaye?" I was interested in her opinion of the country.

"I went back home twice, in '74 and '92. Both times there was a change of government. Most of the people I knew, relatives and friends, had died, leaving behind many children but no money. Some went to America as refugees, where I have visited them.

"I didn't like the changes I saw," she said emphatically. "I remember Ethiopians being kind to each other and helping one another, especially in hard times when they shared food and clothing. But now those good deeds have been replaced with fear and greed. My people have become indifferent to the needs of their fellow men. I saw elderly people begging for food, people who used to be rich.
"I, too, have changed. I don't belong in Ethiopia anymore. I have lived here many years and I can voice my opinions freely. It's this freedom and democracy I value, most of all. But I couldn't settle: deep down inside me was always the wish to go back home and do my share. I felt restless: waiting for something.

"How did you overcome that?" Single, living in a small bedsit, relying on benefits – life must have been very hard.

"I prayed to God to guide me and show me the ways to help. And God heard my prayer. I didn't need to go to them: they were sent to me, they are here! Over the years, many Ethiopians and Eritreans have come to Germany: the young and old, the sick and the healthy. The newcomers need people like me who know the laws, the language, the culture. And I found out that it is not difficult to help, support or relieve my countrymen of their problems. Only my good will is needed.

"In whatever situation they are in, or whatever problem they have, I do my best to help. I put myself in their place and try to feel their problems so that I can solve them or ease their pain. And I know that I have God on my side. With God, all things are possible. That is, so long as I am doing it not for myself but for others. So I am glad to say that with his grace I was able to help over the past ten years." She looked at me cheerfully. "I am satisfied. I find that helping my fellow men is a real blessing."

The following day, we waved goodbye to each other as I walked through the departure gates. Little did I appreciate that the city's connections with Ethiopia extended much further back than Fanaye and others of the Ethiopian diaspora, right to the Middle Ages, as I was to discover that Christmas.

19 Explicit order

Rain had been the souvenir of our camping holiday near Sarlat, in France's Dordogne region. Despite the weather, the surroundings were beautiful. We were in the middle of an oak forest, about 60 feet up from the forest floor, which provided shade during the day and some shelter from the deluges. We'd pitched the tent so it looked onto more trees and I marvelled at the way the sun set, the rays bouncing off the wide trunks, spiralling out beyond them and exploding through the air around us.

Camping was about the simple life, and that French summer was captured for me in the silhouette of a father and son who had stopped close by, their figures lit by the setting sun. The young lad took an ice cream from his father. It was a moment of tenderness and closeness, and although the father may have forgotten it, I'm sure the boy remembers the magic still.

Now that I was away from work, my inspiring dreams had the freedom to return once more. One night I dreamed of my mother in spirit form. She was doing a lot in the hereafter to help with the book's progress. She gave me a lovely hug and was also lifting me up: a good omen for the future. I still missed her a great deal, even though it had been 11 years since she passed on.

Four days later, a little turtle-dove appeared one afternoon, walking towards me across the dry grass and curled oak leaves, completely unafraid. She came within a few feet and looked at me quizzically, her head on one side. After a few minutes, she flew off.

This was one of the small, constant signs that I was on a different journey to before

– the same ring-collared dove had been turning up in many of the places I'd visited since 2003, beginning with a weekend near Fayence, Provence in southern France. We hadn't booked a hotel and found that the one where we'd wanted to stay was full. We drove a couple of miles down the road to a small auberge, where the owner had welcomed us with open arms.

Opening the door to our family room the next morning, I noticed the dove sitting there in the tall oak tree opposite, cooing the three syllabled call 'u-ni-ted, u-ni-ted, u-ni-ted'. I felt honoured that a bird of peace had chosen to always accompany me, like a feathered guide.

*****

Late one morning we went for a long, circuitous walk heading west from the campsite, through fields filled with butterflies, grasses, oak and walnut trees. We were careful where we walked as there were rumoured to be snakes in the area. In the dry heat we passed ancient barns falling to rack and ruin, disturbing blackbirds and starlings which flew, startled, through the trees. I spotted a jay, the increasingly rare cousin of the ordinary crow, with its blue, red and grey colouring.

Chancing upon some houses, we quickly walked through their back gardens to get back on the road to the local bar and then home. It was almost noon and our pace quickened as we headed towards the village's small bar and some cold beer.

Suddenly, out of nowhere, a small Asian woman appeared, strolling towards the post box at the bottom of the drive. Hearing our voices, she called, "Are you English?"

"Yes, are you here on holiday too?" replied Rob.

"No, we live here, we bought this house to convert it to a B&B. Would you like to come up for a drink?" What a bit of luck! I looked at Rob, and we replied in unison, "We'd love to!"

The drive curved round to an attractive two-storey white house with shutters, built in the 1930s. Therese introduced us to her husband, James, who had retired from the Foreign Office. They pulled up chairs for us and we enjoyed some local wine together.

"Where did you live in the UK?" I inquired, as usual being nosier and less polite than Rob.

"Winslow, Buckinghamshire," replied Therese. "Do you know it?"

"Know it! We lived just two miles from you in Granborough. Imagine, what a small world!" We all started laughing as we realised the connection.

We learnt they had lived in Winslow for 19 years in all. Therese still visited southern India, where she had been born. I felt tempted to tell her about my search for my Indian classmate Sumitra, but decided it wasn't appropriate.

Although Rob and James were generally supportive, I'd seen their embarrassed looks when I talked about the dream, especially if I said I believed it was God's will. The UK is such a secular country, where belief in a divine God is something to be hidden, almost to be ashamed of. I had noticed this particularly amongst some Christians. It appeared that revealing our faith was taboo, for fear of causing offence, or being labelled a "Bible puncher." This saddened me a great deal – for me, faith is a reason for joy and hope.

*****

I was looking forward to the annual WaterAid supporters meeting, to which I'd been invited. I hoped that I could mention my book to a few people without over-doing it, but I didn't know what opportunities awaited – if any. Later that morning at work, I bumped into Alex Myers – a lovely young Jewish woman with Botticelli curls, translucent skin and pink apples on her cheeks. We hadn't seen each other for a while, but we had something in common, having joined the company on the same day.

She smiled, "How are things, busy as ever?"

"Yes, loads to do!" Trying not to sound too weary, I rattled on, "There are the head office briefings to finalise, another magazine to write and the audit to finish this month."

"Do you work full time?"

"No, I'm here doing interim work until the end of January." I explained about my book and the journey.

"That's really interesting!" she bubbled enthusiastically. "I think I might be able to help: my boyfriend's aunt is a real expert on the Ethiopian Jews. Shalva Weill is her name. Would you like me to put you in touch with her?"

"I'd love to. I'm so pleased I spoke to you, Alex. This is wonderful news!"

Two days later I was in touch with Shalva via Benjy, Alex's fiancé, and Elroy Dimson, Shalva's brother. Shalva lectured at the Hebrew University in Jerusalem and knew Ethiopia well.

She emailed me: 'I read with great fascination the book synopsis, all the more so since my very first trip to Ethiopia in 1972 was at the invitation of the Emperor Haile Selassie's granddaughter. She was studying at University College, London, and had been married to Colonel Desta, also the middle name of my youngest son, born in 1991. The circle closes as I prepare now to leave for Addis Ababa, where I am organizing a conference on Ethiopian Jewry to be opened by Ethiopia's Foreign Minister. I would love to chat to you about Ethiopia - I have been there many times, and may even know some of your classmates. Good luck with your book. Is there any way I can be of help?'

Shalva was my first real connection to Jerusalem, six months after I'd been shown the Mount of Olives in Lalibela. I could begin to plan a trip there next year – perhaps I might find some details about my father's stay in Palestine. I kept an open mind to the possibilities.

This seemingly random event just confirmed again that there was no need to have a detailed plan, no need to push at all. All that was required was a clear purpose, constant prayer and the courage to be open with people about that purpose.

Whatever was necessary for the next step would appear when the time was right. But that depended on three things: you had to have passed a test, which demonstrated that you were giving up another poor way of thinking and reacting (normally based on the way your ego or logical mind saw the world): you had to be open to what happened next and ready to act immediately to make the most of that opportunity. At its most fundamental, it was the careful use of free will, the greatest gift we are given at birth.

That conversation with Alex precipitated a number of encounters with Jewish people later that day, like a pack of cards tumbling down. I met three women from Tel Aviv on the train to London and two Canadian ladies who ran a shelter for battered women in Jaffa. I had stopped, quite by chance, offering to take a photograph of them together with the Houses of Parliament in the background.

The shorter of the two, Diana, remarked: "You're a believer, aren't you?" When I nodded, they quoted some verses from Isaiah and I left them with yet another book synopsis, my calling card for the foreseeable future.

There was more excitement to come the following Sunday evening, when I got the phone call I'd been hoping for. It was Einar Lunde, the Norwegian broadcaster. He asked me about progress, and I bubbled over with news. But then I hesitated for a moment: he was a very busy, important man: he wouldn't want to hear all the details and ways I was trying to track down my friends. But he was in the mood for reminiscing.

"I know your old school well – I've been there many times, visiting some of the girls whom I sponsored after their parents had been killed during the Derg's time. I felt I owed it to their parents, to continue the children's education.

"But for you, I think you should get in touch with Jonathan Dimbleby. He'll have memories of the famine in '73 that encouraged your classmate to raise funds. I had lunch ten days ago with another man you've already contacted. Desmond Tutu was in Oslo for a few days: we always catch up whenever he's in Norway." We agreed to meet at the end of November, after his holiday in the Canaries.

So Einar had set me another challenge. Jonathan was important because he'd reported widely from Ethiopia - the '73 famine has long since been forgotten here in the west. Jonathan was also linked to Mary Asfaw Wossen and the Emperor's death because of the way that Mengistu had doctored the tape to contrast Haile Selassie's opulent lifestyle with the starving masses.

In addition, there was also a very tenuous link to my past. On my last day at Coundon Court School in Coventry I'd read a tribute I'd written about his father, Richard, the most renowned British broadcaster at the time.

Further information:

Jonathan Dimbleby:
http://www.bbc.co.uk/radio4/presenters/jonathan_dimbleby.shtml
Coundon Court School & Community College:
www.coundoncourt.coventry.sch.uk

20 Women of faith

Clattering along on the Metro towards central Paris, I had plenty of time to kill before the business appointment in late September. The company I worked for had their head office in Paris and every quarter, the communications people met up. I decided on the spur of the moment to contact Ghennet, Hiruth's sister, who lived in the city. It had been four months since we'd last spoken: we'd already planned to meet in October 2004, so I could learn more about Hiruth.

Even as I picked up the mobile to dial her number, old anxieties and doubts knotted my stomach. I was concerned that I wouldn't be sensitive enough about her eldest sister's death. I dialled her number.

Her husband answered the phone. "Yes, Ghennet is here. Wait a moment." He shuffled papers as he passed over the phone.

"Hi, Ghennet, I'm here in Paris for the day. The meeting's over by three. I was wondering if we could meet for coffee somewhere. Do you have some free time?" I held my breath, hoping she did.

"Yes, I think I have some time available," Ghennet replied.

"Where's good for you, that I can find easily? It's been years since I was last in Paris."

"How about Gare St Lazaire? There are lots of cafes on the first floor. I'll meet you outside."

"How will I know you?" I didn't want a repeat of the recent encounter with Fanaye.

"I'm short with lots of grey hair and tight curls, you won't miss me." The appointment was booked, leaving me no time to worry. It was always more stimulating doing things so spontaneously – life had become an adventure once more.

It was just after 8.30 and I had two hours to kill. Perusing the Metro map, I decided to enjoy the September sunshine and visit Notre Dame Cathedral. Walking towards its enormous doors, I suddenly realised it was over fifteen years since I was last here, on honeymoon with Rob, before James was born. Then it had been a cold March day, with leaden grey skies. Now the sky was a clear blue, with just a slight nip of autumn.

Tourists were already pouring into the entrance of France's great cathedral. Just like Cologne, only three people were actually worshipping, but this time I ignored the snappers, made a sign of the cross and curtseyed before the alter. Bowing my head, I said some prayers in deep gratitude for the impromptu meeting with Ghennet and asked for guidance for the next steps on the journey. I glanced to my left and saw that one of the worshippers was a poor, middle-aged man in a grubby coat. The smell of stale breath and cheap alcohol drifted over. Stubble covered his chin and he tipped over to his right, looking as if he was about to fall asleep: perhaps he spent last night on a park bench. But all were welcome here: it isn't our appearance that I think God worries about, but our faith.

Before leaving Notre Dame, I stopped briefly at the shop to buy a simple blue glass cross with a gold stick-like figure painted on it, to denote Jesus. I would put it in the study window, where it would serve as a reminder of enormous sacrifice for the greater good and God's love for us all.

I appreciated enjoying a 'petit dejeuner' in a small café on the Left Bank, by the Ile de France. Glancing up as I buttered a fresh baguette, I recognised the same poor, devout man hurrying past. It was now obvious that he hadn't washed for days, and he stared hungrily at my breakfast. I would have offered him some if I'd been outside: how often did he get a decent meal?

*****

Later on that afternoon, I ran up the Metro steps to Gare St Lazaire's main station, checking my watch – I was late. I hunted along the station to find the steps for the first floor. There were three to choose from – aargh, which was the right one? Lots of building work was going on in the concourse, which involved replacing the higgledy-piggledy flooring. Finally, I turned a corner and saw a short woman, all in black with grey hair and ringlets sitting outside a brasserie, stirring a coffee. I strode up, breathless, hand extended.

"Tanasterlign. You must be Ghennet?" She had her father's broad face and stocky build: we murmured 'tanasterlign' three times as we hugged each other. Ghennet got straight to the point, as time was short.

"What would you like to drink?"

"A Coke please." As the waiter passed our table, she caught his eye: "Garcon, un Coca, s'il vous plait."

"So, how's the book going then? You seem to be making a lot of progress."

"It's just marvellous" I enthused. "It was good to meet Bernd in July, he was very helpful and told me what he could about Hiruth. He still seems to have a lot of contacts in Africa. And it was good to catch up with Fanaye – she seemed to know where a few of the classmates are to be found, but her main contact was Etenesh in Washington, whom she's not seen since 1990."

"Well, Annette," Ghennet swiftly changed the subject "I'm sorry, but our meeting next month will have to be in London." Originally we had agreed to meet in Paris on 20th October, the day after my confirmation. But there had been a change of plan as Ghennet was attending the World Social Forum in London.

"It'll be more convenient for me", I acquiesced. "I have my confirmation at my church the night before, and at least I can have a lie-in!"

Travellers came and went as we sat chatting about Hiruth and Nazareth School, where Ghennet had also been a pupil. The clock's big hands showed 4.30 and I needed to get to Charles de Gaulle airport and Ghennet wanted to avoid the evening rush hour. As we bade each other goodbye, I pushed a note with my home phone number into her hand. Ghennet would call me once she'd arrived in London.

The order of worship for the confirmation came through on email. I was feeling anxious about it: would I be spiritually ready? The insights I'd personally experienced was that faith was about living a life that centred around peace and love, patience, acceptance, being non-judgemental and ensuring that every action was grounded in these principles. It should also mean fun, though – the old ways of self-sacrifice weren't appealing to today's societies.

The evening before, I asked James and Rob if they would be coming along to support me. Neither attended church – and I didn't push religion on them. That would have been too much! Faith was their decision, and it had to be a wholehearted one. James wasn't at all interested, which disappointed me. Rob was uncertain. Seeing the crestfallen look on my face, he agreed to be there. It would mean wearing a suit, something neither of us did these days, but it was important to look smart. There wasn't time to eat before the service. Sitting in the pub and having a drink for Dutch courage, I looked at my watch and realised that the ceremony was to start in ten minutes time. "I think we'd better go now, I have a feeling we should have been there earlier."

My confirmation by the Bishop of Buckingham, Alan Wilson

As I took my seat beside Carol, Sian and Gillian, with whom I was being confirmed, Kevin whispered that he'd almost ordered a guy made in my image to be burnt on Bonfire night. We'd got there by the skin of our teeth! Despite the rush, the service was very moving. We all wore symbols of our faith on us – whether a cross or something in red, which represented the blood of Christ and confirmation of his faith. The Bishop made a point of telling us that God had chosen us to be his faithful servants, rather than us choosing him.

Afterwards, there were congratulations and hugs from regular members of the congregation who'd attended to show their support. I was very touched by the present from Kevin and Alyson, the book "A Weaving of Peace" written by Susan Hardwick. Rob had clearly been very moved by the confirmation: so much so that he'd been in tears. As I walked past to have the sign of the cross made on my forehead, I saw the red rims of his eyes. That was good - he so often told me that religion didn't work: he believed too many millions had been killed as a result of their faith.

As part of the special arrangements, we each had some time with the Bishop of Buckingham, Alan Wilson. I told him about my dream and my journey.

"That's very unusual," he remarked. "Most people who had a dream like that would either have had another drink or turned over and gone back to sleep. It's good that you are pursuing the message you received in your dream. Do save a signed copy for me, please!"

*****

Stepping onto the escalator at Angel underground station, I glanced up at the people in front of me. Most were students, young mothers or tourists with maps in their hands. The morning rush hour was over and travellers were more relaxed. Passing my ticket through the barriers, I looked around for Ghennet. She was nowhere to be seen. I stood outside for a few minutes, and then she came walking over with a wide smile, having just got off a bus.

We meandered along Upper Street looking in restaurant and café windows to see if we could find somewhere suitable for coffee and lunch. We found the 'mediterranean kitchen', a small restaurant with Italian and French food and settled into a table at the back, overlooking the alleyway that ran between the multitude of antique shops which the area is famous for.

I laid out the old photos of Hiruth on the table. I imagined that Ghennet hadn't seen them for some years and she confirmed that this was indeed the case. She told me about the World Social Forum she'd just attended, opened by London's Mayor, Ken Livingstone. The Greater London Authority had given all attendees a free three day bus and tube pass, and ample provision had been made for people to camp at Alexandra Palace where it had been held. She showed me the card and said it would make a great souvenir.

Ghennet Girma, Hiruth's sister

After ordering a coffee, Ghennet began to tell the story of her eldest sister's short life.

"We are five children in our family. Hiruth was the eldest born in 1949, then Manna, me, Solomon and finally, there's Samson, the baby of the family, born in 1966: we were all born in Addis. After each confinement, my mother was looked after by her mother. It's the custom for new mothers to remain in the home for a month, where they have a special kind of porridge to rebuild her strength after everything the pregnancy and birth has taken out of them.

"Hiruth was really my father's favourite, both because she was the first born and also she was a real beauty and highly intelligent. Reading and painting were her favourite hobbies, I remember. Even from the time she was young, she was also very religious," Ghennet sounded surprised as she said this. "We are Ethiopian Orthodox, but when Hiruth went to Nazareth School, she began to attend the Catholic services the Sisters held in the chapel, with her best friend, Azeb Fesseha."

"Hiruth found school work easy and applied herself. In 1967, she had fantastic results in grade 8, achieving the top marks in all subjects amongst all students in Addis Ababa. That was a great achievement and my parents were very proud."

Ethiopia had been developing close relationships with several eastern-bloc countries in the 1960s, and the one with Bulgaria was particularly fruitful. A Soviet cultural centre had been established in Addis and Radio Moscow used to broadcast a regular Amharic programme. Many Russian books were translated into Amharic. At that time Hiruth's father was President of the Ethiopian Parliament, travelling extensively. He made visits to Bulgaria, Spain, Sweden and Canada to encourage trade and investment in the country. The Russians provided funding for Ethiopian students to study in the Soviet bloc, and after some enquiries, Hiruth won an art scholarship to Sofia, Bulgaria, where she was to study fine art.

Hiruth Girma at 16, a real beauty

"How did Hiruth get on in a communist country, Ghennet?"

She rubbed her nose, as she stared into the restaurant "I think Hiruth may well have found it difficult - organised religion was banned under the communist regime. But, she continued to wear her cross, even though it was frowned on, and she made visits to the Bulgarian countryside, meeting ordinary hard working country folk.

Ghennet picked up the photo of Hiruth taken when she was 16, a real beauty. "After just two years of study, Hiruth was restless and decided that she wanted to follow a career which helped others. She left Sofia in 1969 to go to Venusberg near Bonn, where she was to train as a nurse before she studied to become a doctor. Naturally, she had first to learn German.

"From what I can remember from her letters and my parents' comments, everything seemed to be going OK. But things were changing in our country: students were demonstrating for democracy and land reform. You've heard that already from Bernd and Fanaye, I imagine?" she looked at me quizzically.

"Yes, and Mary Asfaw Wossen also. There were tough times ahead for your country." "Naturally," she retorted, "the increase in oil and grain prices meant that many farmers could no longer afford the staples – tef, wheat flour, maize and oil - and so famine began creeping through the provinces in north and eastern Ethiopia.

"Hiruth saw some photographs in *Der Stern* magazine of the enormous famine which had begun back home. She was horrified to see the stick thin figures of the starving, especially the mothers with young babies and their distended bellies. So she talked to one of her friends, and they decided to go out onto the streets of Bonn and collect money to help the poor. It was there that she met Bernd Dreesmann. Shortly afterwards, she left nursing to work for him. In all, I think it lasted about a year."

A waitress approached with a menu: the restaurant was already beginning to fill up with lunchtime customers. Ghennet ignored the menu – the memories were coming thick and fast now.

"I became involved too. I was studying in Switzerland at the time. I got together with other students and we went fundraising on the streets during the Christmas of 1973 – it was such a cold Christmas, but we were committed to raising as much as we could. We worked in shifts and all in all, I was there for a week.

"And what about Hiruth's depression?" I asked gently. I wondered how her depression descended into schizophrenia.

Ghennet's voice and demeanour changed: she sighed as she went on: "My father went over to visit Hiruth in 1974: it was clear that she was becoming increasingly depressed and he was worried about her. By then, she had joined the Jehovah's Witnesses, and was knocking on doors to drum up more members. She was too vulnerable, though, and I think that the religion, coupled with her depression, contributed to her going into hospital."

From the pensive look on her face, I could see this was difficult for Ghennet to talk about her eldest sister, whom she'd looked up to. She sat up in her seat, her voice becoming softer: "Once she was better, she had to decide whether to return home or join other members of the family in the US. In 1975, she moved to Albany, New York, where Manna was at university. But sadly, Hiruth's mental state deteriorated still further, and she was in and out of hospital. In November 1978, she'd had enough of life and committed suicide.

"How, Ghennet?" My heart was in my mouth, how could Ghennet be feeling having to relate this story once more.

"She hung herself. Manna discovered Hiruth's body, with a noose around her neck, in the basement of the apartment where they lived. My parents were absolutely devastated and arranged for her body to be transported back home for the funeral."

Today, Hiruth is buried in St. Joseph's Church near Akaki, south of Addis. Her mother moved to the US in 1991, to live in Washington DC with her sisters. She still commemorates her eldest daughter's death every year.

There was a natural pause in the conversation. I thought how traumatic it was for any parents to have to bury their child, let alone the great guilt that comes with suicide - and to know that Hiruth would never realise her early potential.

A waitress came back to take our order and this time we studied the pages: it was a relief to consider the ordinary after such a tragic tale. Over lunch, we talked about our lives today. Ghennet had lived in France since the mid 1980s, where she heads up the Ethiopian People's Revolutionary Party in exile. The EPRP go back a long time to the early 1970's when they were formed to campaign for democracy in Ethiopia. Her husband earns his living from writing novels about Ethiopia and East Africa. The market appeared to be mostly fellow Africans who enjoy intrigue and figuring out who the fictional characters are in real life. Her daughter was at university.

She seemed to have accepted that she could no longer return to Ethiopia. In 1991, she'd been imprisoned for two months as she is outspoken in her defence of democracy and better rights for women in the country. Africa is a last staging post for misogynists, where men rule the roost. Yet women are essential to the local economy, often working far harder to find water and items to sell at market, whether produce, traditional crafts or firewood. In addition, they cook all the meals and care for the children – it is humbling. And still, some of them are beaten regularly if they haven't done their husband's exact bidding. I, too, felt very angry that they'd not managed to take their rightful places in society.

I had really enjoyed Ghennet's company. I now understood why President Girma had nominated her to be the storyteller and custodian of her sister's memory.

Ghennet had asked me to bring along the list of classmates' names, and over coffee she asked to look at it. She studied it for a while, and then started rattling off more information about where some of the friends were.

"I'm sure that Azeb, Hiruth's best friend at school, now works for the UN in New York," she explained.

That was another lead for me to follow, the more I found out, the greater the chance of recreating the old school photograph with those of us who were left. It now seemed a realistic target.

Before we left, Ghennet brought me up to date with news about her family. She often visits Washington to stay with the family, and that is where all her brothers and sisters now live. Manna is a teacher, Solomon is in the aircraft procurement business and Samson is an IT engineer. Her father was appointed President Girma in 2001 and continues to serve his country at the age of 80.

I called the waitress over and settled the bill. It was past three. As we hugged each other once more, Hiruth's gentle brown eyes stared back at me as Ghennet smiled goodbye. We walked out of the restaurant: Ghennet to catch her bus back to Stoke Newington, whilst I wandered towards the Angel tube station, puzzling over what Hiruth would have looked like if she'd still been alive today.

21 Turning the corner

Rich red wine sauce coated the pot I was stirring. Jack and Therese were coming to lunch. They were such a friendly couple: kind, generous and wise. A good advertisement for their nationality. Apart from my classmates in Ethiopia, I'd not encountered many Armenians – the last was Armen, an IT consultant who'd been married to a Polish friend, Marta, for a short time.

Over several hours, we chatted about local people we knew in common, including how they had met, work and children. Jack and Therese had both attended the Armenian school in Addis Ababa, but went on to different secondary schools after grade 6: Jack to St. Joseph's and Therese to the French Lycee. The Armenians, along with the Greeks, were very important to Ethiopia's economy and government and quite a few had close ties to the imperial family. In addition to the jewellers, master craftsmen and merchants, the Armenians ran two pharmacies and cinemas, and numerous businesses. They were very hard working and successful.

After coffee, Jack began to talk about his upbringing: "Therese and I met at the Armenian 'Ararat' club," he explained. There was a pop group called The Dynamics who used to play there the first Saturday of every month. There were always lots of parties in our community. Then, we didn't see each other for a while when I left the country in 1968 to study in the UK. Initially, I joined my aunt in Derby, and then moved to London to study electrical engineering.

"After graduating with a degree in 1973, I returned to Addis, where Therese and I married the same year. We left for our new life in the UK – Addis was getting too risky, many Armenians and Greeks felt unsafe there."

"How many left the country, Jack?"

"Most of the Armenian community, especially after the Emperor was deposed in 1974. Many went to the USA, Canada and Australia, whilst England, Germany, France, Italy and other European countries attracted smaller numbers."

After living in central London for three years, Jack and Therese moved to Yardley Gobion, Northamptonshire, when his employer moved out of London. In 1976, they were granted British citizenship.

"We enjoyed it there – it was a small community and people made us feel welcome. As the family grew, we needed a bigger house, so we moved to Buckingham. I left the company in 1990 to join the British Standards Institute as a global programme manager."

I cut in, "I don't believe it, that's where my mother worked for 12 years!"

"Ah well, Annette, it's a small world, as you're discovering," Jack grinned wryly. "I worked for BSI for seven years and I've been an independent consultant ever since." It turned out that we had even more in common, as Jack visits Oslo very regularly, working for two major Scandinavian companies there.

I was puzzled about his identity. "Given your background, do you feel more Armenian or Ethiopian?"

"Well, that's an interesting question." He stroked his cheek thoughtfully. "I am an Armenian by ethnicity, but born and raised in Ethiopia. I lived there until I was 18, so most of my early memories were formed in Ethiopia and the lively Armenian community. In 2001, there was a reunion of the Ethiopian Armenians in Los Angeles. Our 35 years' separation from the country became insignificant as we recounted old stories and enjoyed the food and music. The children were so amazed by it all. That's the last time I saw Shake, Silva's sister, and another of your classmates: Shake married my best friend's oldest brother. Unfortunately, Silva couldn't make the event."

I had to smile – everyone in the Ethio-Armenian community was interlinked, and Jack seemed to have particularly strong connections. I considered asking for Shake's details, but decided against it. For now, I had enough on my plate – the priority was to find Celina Fernandes, my Indo-Portuguese school friend.

Conhece Celina Fernandez?

Procuro Celina Fernandez, de origem portuguesa e indiana, formada na Escola Nazareth, em Addis Ababa, Etiópia, no ano de 1969.

Gostaria de incluir a sua história no meu livro Uma Odisseia Etiopiana sobre a viagem que realizei para encontrar nove colegas de turma que vi, pela última vez, em 1964.

O livro nasceu de um sonho, em Abril do ano de 2000, e o seu objectivo consiste em ajudar a angariar fundos para a WaterAid, de modo a possibilitar o abastecimento permanente de água potável para as comunidades pobres da Etiópia.

Se puder ajudar, por favor envie um e-mail para: **a.allen@netcomuk.co.uk**

Please reply in English. – Por favor, responda em inglês.

I'd chosen to advertise for her in Portugal's *Expresso* newspaper. Two agencies, MediaVision and DPP Publicity, had helped book the advertisement and translate it into Portuguese. I'd been fortunate – the translation was free, because the story had touched them.

But I recognised that it was also a shot in the dark: there was no guarantee she lived there. However, perhaps someone in Lisbon might have heard of Celina, or knew where she now lived. All the evidence from my journey so far was just how interconnected the world was.

There were times when I felt very frightened about what I'd embarked on, especially my writing skills. In one of those random moments, which I now recognised as planned from a space beyond our normal consciousness, in 2002 I'd ripped out some details about writing courses in a women's magazine. 'Write your life story' had sounded ideal, and now was the time to book myself on it. It was being held at Meerhay Manor in a sleepy village in south Dorset. It sounded very old and grand and I was really looking forward to meeting new people and developing my craft.

During the Friday evening rush hour on a wet September evening, cars crawled along the M25 motorway, besides extensive roadworks stretching into the distance.

It was stop-start for five miles. Heading west, away from the congested south east of England, I had a new notebook for the course, my Bible and Susan Hardwick's "A Weaving of Peace" to read.①

Dusk folded around me and the sky turned inky blue: trees stood in shadow, bare branches catching the wind. Bouts of rain hit the windscreen and smeared the horizon. The road dipped up and down the Wiltshire hills as I passed Stonehenge, that important place of worship for the Druids and their ancestors. Today the whole site is roped off, in order to preserve the ancient stones, sentinels of a holy place, before man replaced gods, the moon and sun with God and formal places of worship.

Turning off the main road, I drove down a steep hill into the country town of Beaminster in Dorset. I called Bob, the 'lord' of the manor, and he directed me to the house. I drove in to an immaculately landscaped garden that framed a long, T-shaped old house. I climbed out and stretched my aching back and legs. As I followed Bob along the gravelled drive, lights glinted at us from leaded windows, the hallmark of an Elizabethan property. Walking quickly along slabs of grey stone, I found the manor's huge door behind which a bark sounded. Bob shushed at the old collie and the growls changed into a bowed head and wagging tail.

Inside, the flagstoned hall was magnificent, with rooms opening off each side. The manor house was a really well preserved Elizabethan gem, dating from 1610. Six other would-be authors were in the midst of slowly getting to know each other over a glass of wine. Antiques were tastefully arranged around the room and wall lights gave a cosy glow – it wasn't hard to imagine the lord and lady of the manor entertaining guests here 300 years ago.

There was only one man present, and we spontaneously threw our arms around each other. I didn't know why at the time, but he reminded me so much of someone. The face and name would return to me 36 hours later. This made the other women turn and smile – I could see them wondering whether this was something they should know about.

Our tutor was an experienced author with ten books to her name, a very warm, spiritual woman. Over dinner I learned that I would be staying up the road with Jeremy Hammick, an artist, and his wife Melanie. Their youngest son Tom had had a bad asthma attack so Melanie was staying in the local hospital with him while

Patsy Thompson, her mother, would look after us.

After the evening meal at Meerhay, I drove up the steeply sloping track with Anne, another student, to the farmhouse. Jeremy and Patsy welcomed us with a glass of wine, but after a long day, we were keen to get to bed. To lull myself to sleep, I continued reading about Susan Hardwick's experiences and emotions when visiting Auschwitz. My eyes struggled to stay open: five minutes after closing them, I was asleep.

Morning came early – at 8am there was a knock at the door, and Patsy appeared with a steaming cup of tea. I quickly showered and looked out of the bedroom window onto the view before me. Below lay the front garden and green fields stretched into the distance. To the left was the track which we'd driven up last night, leading up to hills full of trees in all their vivid, rich autumn hues. What beautiful scenery to live amongst - people here appreciated nature as something to be cherished and loved, not ignored, nor spoilt.

After breakfast, we all gathered by the sitting room fire as sun shone through the windows, specks of dust dancing in the light as it poured onto the heavy mahogany coffee table. On it, our tutor had laid some inspirational tools of her trade – a beautiful feather with beading presented to her by north American Indians, a smiling Buddha, a jade pendant, and a carved stone sculpture of men with their arms around each other looking down at fire – in this case, a large candle. We were invited to include our own mementoes – I added my Lalibela cross.

Over the next 24 hours, my mouth dried up and my hand stiffened. I was terrified. I couldn't write out my emotions and childhood demons in the way the others seemed easily able to do. I didn't have the courage. They were polite, but I sensed they struggled to connect with my words. One woman had a beautiful bell-like voice and spoke very hauntingly about her terrible childhood. Another had an acidic wit and tears of laughter rolled down our faces as we listened to her. I think she surprised herself, but it was pathos rather than humour that was the driver – her mother thought she'd never been a good enough daughter.

After lunch we had three hours break, and I went back to change and freshen up at the farmhouse. I joined Patsy in the kitchen for some tea. She sat back relaxing, bare feet on the table, chipped red nail polish decorating her toes as she stroked Poppy, the dog. Patsy asked me how the course was going and whether I'd already started writing a book. I told her about my journey and she almost spluttered: "My sister-in-law Audrey used to go to school with Emperor Haile Selassie's daughter!" I burst out laughing. Wherever I went these days, someone connected to the Ethiopian royal family seemed to make an entrance!

Despite the simplicity of the writing exercises, my gloom intensified. It felt like I was a lone tree standing firm in a clearing while all around others bent to the howling wind, creaking, flexing and straining their branches.

Over dinner we were joined by Diana and Bob's neighbour, the author Lynne Reid Banks. Two of her novels had been made into films: "The L-Shaped Room", a seminal book about London in the late 1950s that had sold ten million copies, and "The Indian in the Cupboard", about a child whose toys come to life to teach him some important lessons. Lynne had a very kind, expressive face and she introduced us to her husband Chaim Stephenson, a well-known Israeli sculptor.

She spent time with each guest, asking about their writing, and I told her about the odyssey and my Garden of Peace project. Lynne seemed intrigued and offered to see what she could do to help me: although they had left Israel many years ago, she still had friends in the country.

Even after that good news, my heart was heavy as I went to bed. I became immersed in Susan Hardwick's feelings on her visits to Israel's holy sites, trying to blot out the inevitable decision. Should I leave the following morning and give up the book completely, or choose to reach something deeper inside myself, which sat curled up like a frightened child in the pit of my stomach?

The following morning, we took it in turns to tell each other what we had learned so far and whether it was helping. I was the last: they turned to me expectantly. I blurted out, "I came here wanting to improve my writing skills, because I so want my book to touch people and sell well, but I don't know if I can do it. I may not be brave enough. I saw your expressions and listened to your comments when I read my work. I know I didn't touch you, and I feel so frustrated about it."

As I sat hunched over, the little girl inside me moved and stood up. I decided to let them know how they had touched me with their stories and the connections between us: it was the only honest way. I tried to stifle my sobs as I turned to each in turn.

One woman had lived in Coventry and another had faced the struggle to escape corporate life and her husband had Alzheimer's – now I knew how my second cousin felt when his mother suffered from it. Another writer's father had refused to talk about the death of his first wife - her mother - just as my father had refused to talk about Doreen all those years ago. Such a devastating thing to wipe out her life for my two half sisters.

I continued, turning to the man opposite, "I hugged you on Friday night because your face reminded me of so much of Sam Wanamaker, the actor I met in 1980, who had made it his life's work to rebuild Shakespeare's Globe Theatre."

Finally, I turned to Allegra: "You told us yesterday that your grandfather had died in Auschwitz, which I was reading about on Friday night in a wonderful book "A Weaving of Peace". In Norway, my mother's house was occupied by German troops during World War II, and there was a prisoner of war camp down the road. I've often wondered how many from there were sent to the final concentration camps."

Something magical happened then – the weight began to lift from my heart and I saw sparks of recognition and glints of tears in their eyes. If I could write like that, perhaps it would be good enough. So it proved later that day when the heart burst into my words. It was no longer an academic exercise to see how many words I could write or lines I could fill.

Further information:

Meerhay Manor: www.meerhay.co.uk

① Susan Hardwick, *A Weaving of Peace,* Kevin Mayhew, 1996
Lynne Reid Banks: www.lynnereidbanks.com

22   Shrines of peace and a Saint

Early in November, both Mulugeta and Abba Bogale phoned. They wanted me to meet an Ethiopian who was in London to receive a special environmental award for the work he'd done cleaning up Addis and planting trees. I agreed to rendezvous with Abba Bogale the following week, something to look forward to and good news for my friends. The email updates now went to over 100 people in ten different countries.

We were spending Bonfire Night, 5 November, with Barry and Rose, good friends who lived in St Austell, Cornwall. Bonfire Night commemorates the safety of King James I after Guy Fawkes' attempt to blow up the houses of Parliament in 1605. Rain had followed us the entire length of the journey and it was still drizzling as we parked the car at Barry and Rose's house. But it gradually fizzled out and later, at a seaside pub, we enjoyed the crackle and roar of a giant bonfire on the beach, while children ran around with sparklers.

Then Eden called. We wanted to see how the Eden Project, just a few miles from St Austell, had developed since we'd last visited three years ago. Winding down the steep roads towards it, I could see the two plastic biomes – tropical and temperate climates - shimmering in the watery sunshine. It was early, and we almost had the place to ourselves. The site had become one of the most popular of the Millennium Commission projects paid for by National Lottery money.

The planting, which in 2001 had looked bare and meagre, was now mature, spreading across the thick bark and brushing onto paths, or trained into shapes, winding up poles. Parts of the Project were roped off, in preparation for their winter activities and the tenth anniversary celebrations of the National Lottery that evening. In the temperate zone, there was a new addition – shrines of peace. These were dotted around the biome, in the manner of wayside shrines you'd find along roadsides in devout countries. They were highly decorative and made with colours and materials redolent of particular countries and cultures. One looked distinctly African – perhaps South African. On the inscription below was the artist's name: Charmaine Warrior.

The shrine, dedicated to GAMA, created by Charmaine Warrior

I called to Rob, "Hang on a minute, I want to find out more about one of these shrines." I ran to the special Bedouin tent to discover more about it from a magazine published to coincide with the event. It turned out that it was the first day of a three-month exhibition called "Cultivating Community: Gardens that Grow Peace and Hope." Through a charity, Transforming Violence, Eden had commissioned artists to make shrines that would celebrate projects that used plants, gardens and earth stewardship to heal divided communities in some of the most troubled places in the world.

Scanning the pages, I saw a photo of the shrine that had drawn my eye. It wasn't South African, it was Ethiopian! It recognised the work of the Gashe Abere Molle Association (GAMA) that had been established by a well-known Ethiopian musician, Sileshi Demissie, to clear up Addis when he'd returned after 23 years abroad. As I read the piece, I looked for Charmaine's name and wondered whether she was Ethiopian: she didn't sound it.

I was almost ecstatic as I ran up to Rob and exclaimed, "Hang on, I've got to take a photograph, the shrine's Ethiopian!" He rolled his eyes and sat down to wait by one of the plants.

The discovery was a topic of conversation over a leisurely dinner that night. It would be a while before we saw Rose and Barry again – they were moving house to be closer to their shop, the Lavender Pillow in Mevagissey, which was going from strength to strength.

*****

Abba Bogale waited in his usual spot, by the fountains in the Whiteley's department store complex in Bayswater. He still wore open-toed sandals, even in England's cold winter. His friend, well over six foot tall with a basketball player's lean frame, wore grey combat trousers and jacket. A third man was much shorter and stood there, casually leaning his chin on the handle of his umbrella, looking at me smiling.

Abba Bogale greeted me, "Tanasterlign, Annette, I would like you to meet Sileshi Dimessie and Tekahun Basha, project manager and project co-ordinator of GAMA in Addis."

I began to laugh, groping in my handbag for the magazine which I then waved at him . "But Sileshi, I was reading about you two days ago at the Eden Project. I saw the shrine!"

Smiling slightly, as though this happened to him all the time, he said: "Ah, yes, I know about the Eden Project. Let's go and have a coffee, so we can talk. We don't have much time, I'm sorry, we are meeting a friend for dinner, as it's our last evening in London."

We strolled up the road together. Sileshi and Tekahun had flown over to receive the International Green Apple Award at the House of Commons. We went into a local coffee bar and after ordering, Sileshi started recounting some of the background to their work.

"I was invited back to Ethiopia by the US Embassy in Addis and was really shocked at the state of the city. It was dirty and full of rubbish: there were areas that were really run down, where kids were living on the streets. Also, there were very few gardens or green spaces for people to gather. People need all the trees they can get for both shade and also environmental purposes, but many had been cut down to use as firewood and no replanting had taken place. After the concert, I went back to the States and started to think what I could do about it. I decided to return home for good and make it my mission to create a green, clean and healthy Ethiopia, using all my resources."

Sileshi explained how through music, poetry and drama, he had gone into schools to start energising young people and street kids to clean up Addis. "Mobilising the teenagers and unemployed made sense. I used music, theatre, and discussion groups to get things started. I went to talk to 26 schools and ended up with 13,000 on the team! We established the charity with funding from local banks, some embassies and a Swedish organisation."

These young men and women cleared away waste and made sure it was properly treated or recycled. They have created many small gardens that passers-by can enjoy, using all kinds of materials along with the plants, rocks and lots of aluminium that has been carefully sculpted into different shapes. GAMA has also provided work for poor people, and one of the facilities is a mobile toilet and shop - an amazing combination.

"I'm pleased to say we've been recognised with a number of awards, including the UN Development Programme Volunteer Award in 2000 and now the International Green Apple Awards. Today our projects extend outside Addis to other large towns like Baha Dar and Dire Dawa, and we are working closely with the city on waste management, as well as planting new trees."

"But," Sileshi added, "I don't have much money. We were only able to come here through Helen at WaterAid. I've come to the conclusion that money is not the determining factor for change."

I pondered on this – the return to Ethiopia had been the inspiration for a totally new life for him and worrying about money was no longer a priority. What a free way to live!

Puzzling over how GAMA had inspired the shrine's artist, Charmaine Warrior, I decided to try and contact her. Karen Payne, who runs the Transforming Violence charity with her partner David. put me in touch with Charmaine at her shop, 'Restless Native' in Penzance, Cornwall. When I rang her, I was amazed to learn that she'd not met Sileshi before she created the shrine! Charmaine had used her skills as an artist and decided on red, white and black recycled products for the shrine. The flowers had captivated me – they were the flowers which the GAMA team planted in place of rubbish.

"I did get to meet Sileshi eventually," Charmaine told me, "at the Eden Project's 6th November celebrations and firework display. We spoke for a few minutes, but he was captivated by the fireworks and wandered off later."

*****

Logging on to my computer the day after the advertisement for Celina appeared, a new email popped up. It was from a Portuguese man, Rui Santos, who had spotted the ad and was obviously intrigued. He explained that Fernandes is a common Indo-Portuguese surname and that many people could be or know my classmate. He had obviously made a thorough search on the internet, as he sent me very detailed information.

"In Cascais county, Portugal, there are about 1,000 people called Fernandes and 15 called Fernandez: in Oeiras county, about 640 Fernandes and four Fernandez: and in Lisboa (Lisbon) there are about 2,000 Fernandes and 31 Fernandez."

He narrowed these down to one entry in the Lisbon phone directory for Celia Fernandes, and gave me her address also. I was bowled over by his willingness to help a complete stranger.

I rang the number the following evening. A woman picked up the phone: I asked right away whether she was Celina Fernandes. "Yes, that's my name."

"I'm calling from the UK, and I used to go to school in Addis Ababa, Ethiopia. I was wondering if you were there too?"

"Sorry, I don't speak English," came the terse reply as plates and glasses clinked in the background. "Wait, wait – here is my niece." She handed the phone to her niece, who spoke good English, and I explained that I used to go to school with

Celina in Ethiopia.

It got increasingly difficult – the language barrier didn't ease things and the woman struggled with the word Ethiopia. She batted questions backwards and forwards between me and her aunt. I was shocked when I realised her aunt had never told her she'd lived in Africa: how strange. But somehow, she managed to confirm that Celina was 54 and had graduated from Nazareth School in Addis Ababa.

I could hear her aunt becoming more and more upset by the phone call, as she shouted at her niece, who translated, "That is all in the past now." Look," her niece concluded, "she doesn't want to speak to you, so don't call us again. Goodbye," before hanging up.

My heart was in my mouth and my hands were shaking as I put down the phone. I hadn't expected to have found Celina so quickly, and I was also taken aback to get that kind of negative reaction.

I contacted Rui once more: he was happy to translate a letter into Portuguese for me for free, which was the good news I needed. In my letter, I asked for a response by mid-January: this was something that had to come from her heart. I couldn't and wouldn't push it. Two weeks after the phone call, the letter was sent by registered airmail to Lisbon, along with the old school photo. I kept my fingers crossed for a reply.

Rui turned out to have been a former soldier, fighting the war in Angola. As a result, he had a particular interest in Africa and had become a pacifist. He told me that his full name meant 'saints and angels' in English. He certainly proved to be that for me.

Further information:

Gashe Abera Molla PO Box 33145, Addis Ababa, Ethiopia.
Eden Project: www.edenproject.com
Transforming Violence: www.transformingviolence.org
Restless Native: www.restlessnative.co.uk
The Green Apple Awards are run by the Green Organisation:
www.thegreenorganisation/info

23   A lion beneath his feet

Hot water gushed over me. I was staying at Odd Inge's house in Oslo, and was due to meet up with Einar Lunde to find out just how Emperor Haile Selassie had died. I was also interested to learn more about living and working in Addis during the time of the Marxist Derg (Committee) when so many of my classmates appeared to have escaped the unfolding horrors.

In the background was the shrill ring of a phone. Grabbing a towel, I warmed my feet on the underfloor heating, a luxurious relief in Norway's cold winters. Outside it was -10°C and thick blankets of snow carpeted the city. As I was drying myself, Odd Inge knocked on the door.

"That was Einar - he wants to meet you at NRK's (Norwegian Broadcasting Company) offices at 11am. Breakfast will be ready in 15 minutes."

I dressed carefully, wanting to look smart for this well-known man. I had prepared some questions, but we'd see how the conversation would go: it was good of him to see me, just hours after his return from holiday. It had been four months since our initial contact.

NRK's offices were just out of the city centre, with three large buildings in a U-shape surrounding a cul-de-sac. A few minutes after I arrived, Einar strode out to greet me with a broad smile: "Welcome, Annette, good to meet you."

He was very tall with a natural charisma. Despite thinning hair, he was still an attractive man and his skin glowed after the fortnight's sun he'd just enjoyed with his family. His ID card was slung casually around his neck and dangled down his thick yellow sweatshirt. We walked into his office, a cramped room that he shared with six other journalists on different shifts: PC boxes, files and notes lay all around. Glasses were stacked up in the corner, and the central heating hummed above us. Metal-framed windows looked out onto snow and more offices. The PC sat flickering in the corner as we talked.

Einar leaned against the chair's high back and peered at me over his glasses. "Well, I don't know where you wish to start – I could give you enough for five books if you wanted. I've been through so much in Ethiopia."

As he spoke, light shone on his gold and onyx ring with the lion of Judah on it, just like the one my father had received as a parting gift from Ethiopian Airlines forty years earlier. Einar turned his profile to me and gazed back into his past.

"Ethiopia is my adopted home. I arrived there in July 1973 as a young journalist with my wife and two children, to join Radio Voice of the Gospel (RVOG). My brief was to produce a special series of news and feature programmes about Southern Africa, to counteract the propaganda put out by the state broadcasting stations in South Africa and Rhodesia. Along with the BBC World Service, RVOG was the most credible radio station in Africa. Addis was the right place to be based in, as it was home to the Organisation for African Unity – now the African Union - and the UN.

"I soon learned about the famine in northern Ethiopia, in Wollo and Tigraye provinces, but we weren't allowed to cover it. The government had censored coverage, and it was impossible to get a permit to travel there. I must have met every single government Minister, but still no success. The first witnesses were skinny beggars on the streets of Addis, full of stories of how their families and neighbours were dying. That was until a British journalist, Jonathan Dimbleby, managed to fly straight there somehow. His documentary, "The Unknown Famine", showed the horror of it all and went on to win many awards the following year.

"By November 1973 we had got permission, as the famine was beyond the government's control and they needed international help. I've never seen so many people dying, it was unimaginable. I held dead children in my arms while 400 miles away, my three- and five-year-olds were safe at home with my wife." His eyes had filled with tears as he spoke, and his voice cracked.

"I think it was this that led to the revolution. The government, led by Selassie was just so out of touch with the peasants. In February 1974 the airport was closed, but with all the media coverage, the aid agencies managed to open it again, to allow medical and food aid to arrive.

"The next hint of change was a letter published in August 1974 in *The Ethiopian Herald,* questioning Selassie's authority. Then the army revolutionaries, led by Colonel Mengistu Haile Mariam, managed to get hold of Jonathan Dimbleby's documentary and edited it to include some lavish banquets at the palace. We were watching TV at the radio station on 11 September when they broadcast it. There was an immediate uproar and the soldiers guarding us began harshly shouting, 'Kill the Emperor, kill the Emperor, kill the Emperor.'

"Later that evening, I went to the Jubilee Palace and drove around it for two hours to see what was going on. I returned home that night – nothing had happened. It was the following morning that the inevitable occurred. Selassie was arrested and a friend of mine saw the Emperor being bundled into a pale blue Volkswagen and driven off. The Derg, led by Mengistu, announced that Selassie had been imprisoned and that they were now in power. General Aman Andom was appointed head of state, chairman of the Council of Ministers and Minister of Defence."

Andom was an Eritrean and a well-known, popular commander and hero of the war against Somalia in 1966. He was a Lutheran Christian and a humanitarian. He opposed the size of the Derg (120 members had been appointed to rule the country), and the death penalty for former government and military officials who had been arrested, and recommended reconciliation with the Eritrean insurgents. During this time, Einar hosted with a radio show with Hanna, Andom's daughter, at RVOG.

By mid-November, as charges mounted against him, Andom was opposed by the majority of the Derg: he appealed unsuccessfully to the army for support. Realising that the end was near, he retreated to his home with two bodyguards.

Einar continued, "We knew that something was going on. A Swedish colleague, Carl Gustav, and I lay watching Andom's house from the neighbouring hospital garden. From there, we saw two tanks training their guns on it, and soldiers surrounding the compound. They opened fire on the house and there was a fierce battle, then all was quiet. I went back to the hospital reception as I didn't want to be caught: Carl hesitated and he was seized. I was worried and returned to find him, where I saw him being beaten up. I, too, was captured and we were both arrested on suspicion of being CIA spies. Guns were pressed into our ribs and, as we were bundled into a car, we heard a series of loud gunshots from the Menelik Palace and then everything was quiet again.

"We were taken to a large police station in Addis where they had a number of cells. A captain shouted at the guards, 'I wanted two dead prisoners, not two living ones.' The cells were so full we couldn't be locked up, and so we squatted outside with other political prisoners, playing games to try and keep up our morale."

The noise Einar and Carl Gustav had heard on 23 November became known as Bloody Saturday. Fifty-nine political prisoners were executed, including Mulugeta's father and military officers such as Colonel Alem Zewd and General Abiye Abebe (the emperor's son-in-law and defence minister), three former prime ministers and two Derg members who had supported Aman. Mengistu emerged as the leading force in the Derg and took steps to protect and enlarge his power base. Hanna, her father murdered, had to flee the country.

The radio station was very concerned about the two journalists' disappearance, and began searching all the prisons and hospitals. Einar noticed a man dancing outside the walls next day - he was relieved to see he was the janitor from work. Einar's wife and Carl's mother brought them food, as prisoners didn't get any, which the pair shared with others. They could hear screaming as captives were whipped and tortured. As more police and soldiers entered the prison yard, there was a fierce debate about what to do with the two foreigners. 'Kill them,' some shouted, convinced they were spies.

Eventually they were taken to Menelik Palace and then after a short return to prison, to the Security Police HQ – a place that very few left without being tortured. There, they were stripped to their underwear and Carl was interrogated first. He told the soldiers of Einar's friendship with General Andom, through Hanna. Einar feared the worst: there was no telling what would happen when you were close friends with someone who'd just been murdered.

But fate intervened: after Einar had been questioned for two hours, the Swedish consul came to see them. There were no diplomatic relations with Norway, so Sweden had responsibility for Norwegians in Ethiopia. He left and returned to pay bail for their release. They departed through the prison gates in the Swedish ambassador's car, flag fluttering on the bonnet. Einar and Carl arrived at the Swedish ambassador's residence, where the diplomat cried as he embraced them,

"You don't know how close you came to death."

The journalists returned to the station, where an impromptu party was held to celebrate their safe release. Both were forbidden to leave Addis for six months, and Einar became adept at avoiding the secret police shadowing him much of the time.

*****

On 12 August 1975, Haile Selassie was killed and secretly buried. In 1987, Einar interviewed Negash Tesfatsion, a former member of the Derg's inner circle, about the facts surrounding Selassie's death. After defecting in 1976, Negash had fled to Eritrea.

"There had been a meeting, where all the Derg members were asked to show hands as to whether they should kill Selassie in jail, or leave him to die of natural causes - he was 83 at the time. The majority voted for murder, because they were so scared of his semi-god status in the country. Selassie was smothered in his sleep and his body buried beneath Mengistu's desk in the Menelik Palace."

Ten years before the meeting with Negash, Einar had interviewed Mengistu Haile Mariam in his office on 1 May 1977, where the Derg leader admitted cryptically that "the Ethiopian revolution is built on the remains of the old imperial regime." With the Derg's overthrow in 1991 by Zenawi's Ethiopian People's Revolutionary Democratic Front, the hunt for Selassie's remains began. In 1993, Selassie's corpse was found at that very spot, underneath Mengistu's desk. By this time, Mengistu was in exile in Zimbabwe. Emperor Haile Selassie's remains were exhumed, and he had a full state funeral on 5 November 2000 at Holy Trinity Cathedral in Addis Ababa, where Sylvia Pankhurst is also buried.

Einar continued to cover news in Ethiopia until 1988, when he was once again arrested, during a private visit to see the children he sponsored. He was eventually declared a person non grata, expelled for the rest of his life and put on the first flight out of the country.

With the overthrow of the Derg, he returned to the country ten years later and was allowed to visit the same prison where he was incarcerated in 1988. He still continues his love affair with the country, having sponsored 20 children whose families all suffered during the Derg regime. His help has enabled the sons and daughters to complete their education and go on to live full, productive lives.

Einar Lunde, NRK TV's main news anchor

Later, after lunch, I returned to Odd Inge's house and relished the chance to be on my own, lazing in front of the warm fire. After a while, I switched off the lights to sit in darkness, absorbing the cityscape below. On the horizon, Oslo's fjord lapped into the North Sea, and big ferries entered and left its cold waters. Lights shimmered from advertising hoardings and office blocks, while buses and cars drove through the quiet streets. It was like a picture postcard of Christmas, with the giant fir trees in the foreground, branches drooping, weighed down by snow. All was at peace with the world, and tomorrow I was to see Olga and Arvid, my aunt and uncle, once more in Kristiansand.

Waking up, I was puzzled about why I'd dreamt about someone called Trygve. I didn't know anyone of that name and later that morning, over coffee, I asked Odd Inge if he recognised the name.

"Trygve is my dad's cousin, the father to Olav Skjevesland, the bishop. Trygve Bull was a famous Norwegian historian who died in the late 1990s: he was the inspiration for the book I'm completing about Norway's independence from Sweden."

So now I knew why I'd dreamt about someone called Trygve! I hoped to meet Olav, Bishop of Southern Norway and my second cousin, whilst I was in Kristiansand. I'd written to him about the book, but he hadn't replied.

Over breakfast, Berit told me about the trip she'd made to Israel in October. Her company, Kirkelig Kulturverksted (KKV), produce many compilation CDs with Scandinavian and foreign artists. In 2003, they had released a disk called "Lullabies from the Axis of Evil", a play on words from Bush's State of the Union address in 2002 before he invaded Iraq. It was a beautiful CD, with singers from Palestine, Iraq, Afghanistan, Iran, Syria and North Korea singing lullabies.

Berit's face squeezed in concern as she told me about the teenage soldiers with their machine guns guarding crocodile snakes of Jewish school children. She commented on the injustice of Palestinians being imprisoned for having a gun and how some were incarcerated for years with no reason. But groups like Neve Shalom – the Peace Desert - where Palestinians and Israelis lived side by side and the Rabbis for Peace gave her hope. Berit was the guest of Rim Banna, one of the Palestinian singers on the CD.

The flight to Kjervik, Kristiansand's airport, was swift: the snow was smudged from mountaintops as we flew further south to warmer temperatures. Arvid collected me, proudly showing off his new automatic car, and over dinner Olga and Arvid asked about all the travelling and whom I'd met since I'd last seen them in 2003. We spent several minutes looking at my photos.

"Arvid", I asked. "You know, I wrote to the Bishop, Bishop Olav, to ask for support on my journey, and I've not heard from him. Do you think we could call him tomorrow?" Arvid looked perplexed then smiled slightly: "Ya, sure, we can call him."

"It would be good to meet this famous relative, Arvid," I replied brightly. "It's not every family who has a Bishop!"

He kept his word and rang Olav's office the next morning, before handing the phone to me. I introduced myself, asking Olav if he'd received my letter and the photograph. "Yes, I did actually. I had put it to one side, I wasn't quite sure what to do with it, or how to reply. Are you sponsored by a church?"

"No, I fund everything myself. Would it be possible for us to meet today?"

"When do you leave for Oslo?"

"At noon. Do you have time to meet this morning?"

"Yes" he paused. "Yes, let's do that. Let me think where we could meet – perhaps the Gartneri (garden centre) on the Vennesla Road?"

Arvid agreed to the venue, and I was delighted with the news. They seemed a little nonplussed that the Bishop would come out so quickly for a distant relative, but it was good that we could all meet up. We arrived early, and I could tell Arvid and Olga were a little nervous. When Olav arrived I knew him immediately – he was a younger version of my grandfather, whom I'd last seen in 1975!

We shook each other's hands warmly and he introduced his wife, Anne Katrine. They were off to the Cameroon on a church visit on 12 December. I told him about my dreams and he wished me success. Like some religious people, he also looked a little puzzled, someone doing such a project because of one dream.

Afterwards, Arvid drove me along winding country roads north of Kristiansand past the red, blue, yellow and white clapboard houses, back to Kjervik. As we bade each other farewell my mind skipped ahead to the next challenge - getting help from people in the US to track down my former classmates. By now, I'd learnt that over half of them lived in the land of the free.

*****

Things were really hectic at work, and it was hard to concentrate on the book and my family. This was my old life: work, work, work. My soul chafed at this: it felt so wrong, like being imprisoned, despite the cheerful people around me. I went in search of solace in the local WH Smith's newsagents in Rickmansworth High Street. There, I found the veteran BBC broadcaster, Michael Buerk's new book, "The Road Taken."

Reading it the following evening, I leafed through to the chapter about his time in Ethiopia covering the famine. I read one paragraph, then had to re-read it as my body shuddered in recognition: "Two mounds of rags with legs sticking out, cramped up against a mud wall. A woman's face with braided hair fluffed out behind her ears caught in a scream we could not hear. This was the centre of Korem, northern Ethiopia, in the early hours of 19 October 1984." ①

These were the images broadcast to the world later that day - twenty years to the day of my confirmation into the Anglican Church, when I affirmed my intention to live a life of responsible and committed discipleship.

Further information:

KKV: www.kkv.no

① Michael Buerk, *The Road Taken,* page 282, Hutchinson London, 2004

24 A pharaoh replies

"Celina's been found, perhaps leave Phoebe until the next year." That was the gist of the email from Allen Scott, who'd helped me with the advertisement for Celina. I disagreed: I was fired up with success and the bank balance was healthy once more with full-time work. I asked MediaVision to quote me for advertising in Egypt's main newspapers, both in Arabic and English. They came through a week later, but looking at the cost, I realised I'd have to delay until January. To have the best chance of reaching Phoebe or one of her relatives, I needed to advertise in *Al-Ahram*, read by over 1.3 million Egyptians. It was expensive - almost double the price of the *Expresso's* advertising rate. But there was no other way to find Phoebe.

The quest seemed to be getter closer to its conclusion though, and I'd made far greater progress than I'd ever dared hope or imagine. Through Shalva, I had a great contact in Jerusalem and the opportunity of meeting some Ethiopian Jews there. Silva had agreed a date to meet up in Los Angeles; I was waiting to hear back from Celina and now I had the opportunity of finding Phoebe in the New Year. That would leave only Sumitra, the Indian, and Kathy, the American. In eighteen short months I'd found six of my classmates: Marta, Hiruth, Mary, Fanaye, Celina and Silva. This was an overwhelming achievement, thanks to my faith, determination and kind-hearted people all over the world.

I'd already booked the flights to the US – 12 days in February 2005. I'd be spending four days each in Washington, Los Angeles and New York. Arrangements had now been confirmed with Silva in LA. But, I had no idea where I'd be staying in Washington or NY, but my unending faith in the odyssey and strong intuition made me feel confident that I'd find the right people to help before I departed.

I knew that there were a lot of Ethiopians in Washington and I was hoping that somehow I'd find Azeb's contact details in NY. I just had to work out where to spin the next parts of the web. This was how the journey worked: my heart telling me what to do and then my mind putting it into action through emails and phone calls, and relying on people who were already friends and part of the web. A magnificent web that now spread across three continents: Africa, Europe and soon, the USA.

I deeply believed that God directed all of this, his deep and true wisdom made the sparks and connections happen. Another important aspect of my progress was to listen deeply to others – often in their criticism (which my mind would previously blank out, because of all the hurtful comments from my dad when I was little), there would be the gem of a good idea. They often didn't realise they were giving out pearls along with the barbs.

Reaching out to Americans was really vital. I had heard from many Americans and travellers that the country had changed immeasurably since 9/11, yet it was also apparent that they realised their actions did have an impact on other countries. During the 2004 Presidential campaign, a great deal of anger had been expressed by liberals, idealists and young people about the Iraq war, especially after the appalling abuse of prisoners at the Abu Ghraib prison outside Baghdad. We judge a country by the behaviour of its citizens: no one is above the law or beyond the reach of the UN Declaration of Human Rights.

Living in a country where oil, money, physical perfection and status were gods was beginning to seem a hollow victory. Some people in the US are almost as poor as those in Africa. They are often excluded from the system, unable to get jobs, forced into petty crime, living in areas torn apart and wrecked by rival gangs where the only king is the gun. I had visited the States twice in the 1980s. In Chicago, I was staggered at the gap between rich and poor. Hobos and beggars crouched underneath railway arches, huddling beneath blankets, trying to keep warm. Many were black – they'd escaped slavery only to be enslaved by poverty. Even then, they went unnoticed as, apart from the rush hour, most people drove through the city.

It was a form of social apartheid: the rich moved out to their houses with burglar alarms in the suburbs and rural areas, leaving the poor to live in the inner city in public housing, with its much higher crime rates. It was the same here in the UK – we had no right to crow about our wealth when a third of children here live below the poverty line. It's scandalous in our rich economy and leads to helplessness and bitterness about the system that creates this injustice. Through our apathy, we create the conditions that we most fear.

Washington was an important stop, as it's home to many NGOs, the International Monetary Fund and the World Bank, on whose decisions the lives of many millions of the poor hang. The latter two decide whether young children receive an education or not, whether subsistence farmers can sell their surplus for a good price or not, and whether Highly Indebted Poor Countries – HIPC – can drag themselves out of a never-ending spiral of debt created by repayments on vast loans. I often wondered where their repayments go – do they line the pockets of rich bankers? Do they pay welfare cheques for Americans on the poverty line? Do they help write off America's big trade deficit? My curiosity always nullified the fear, from one question to another.

I needed some exposure for the story in the US, which I hoped would bring forth some more former classmates. Acting on a recommendation from Elisabeth Mekonnen - another old girl from Nazareth School – who now lived in LA, I emailed the website www.tadias.com, to see if they'd run the story and class photo. They also published a magazine, promoting Ethiopian culture to much of the diaspora in the US and all over the world.

The tadias feature which appeared in January '05

Unsure as to how I'd find Azeb through the UN, I asked my friends at WaterAid for a contact there. If nothing else, I could interview someone who did a lot to help promote effective and safe water management. Marcia Brewster was the name they gave me, and I contacted her, asking whether she could also help me find Azeb. Marcia was definitely the right water expert. She'd worked in water resources management and sustainable development for the past 25 years, both in UN Headquarters and at the Economic and Social Commission for Asia and the Pacific in Bangkok. In 2003, she was appointed Task Manager of a UN Task Force on Gender and Water. In the developing world, it's a woman's role to collect and carefully use water for the family's daily life.

Marcia replied within 24 hours, agreeing to see me. Her short, friendly email finished with Azeb's email address. I felt ecstatic as I sent Azeb the old school photo later the same day, along with a cheery message of hello.

Her reply the following morning read, "Oh my God, oh my God, oh my God, I don't believe it!"

She was amazed to have received the email, and told me how she laughed when she saw the photo – she'd misplaced her's a long while ago. Azeb was Hiruth's best friend at school and one who could bring her habits to life for me. She told me a bit about her job with the United Nations Development Programme and her family. She also, very generously, agreed to me staying with her while I was in NY. So, all that now remained was to find a friend in Washington.

10th December 2004 turned out to be a wonderful day: I received the news I'd hoped for from tadias. Liben, the editor, had agreed to include my story in the next issue of the magazine and the website, in the diaspora section – just in time for the Orthodox Christmas which is celebrated on 7th January. Great news, and I hoped it would elicit a response and more renewed friendships with former classmates. The timing couldn't be better either: combining this journey of faith with important dates in the Christian calendar was most appropriate.

*****

One man I'd struggled to reach was Jonathan Dimbleby. Following Einar's suggestion, I'd written to the BBC journalist in October, via his BBC Radio 4 programme *"Any Questions?"* There'd been no response at all, although I'd made a phone call to the programme, to see if the letter had reached him. I wanted to find out how the first major famine in 1973 had changed Jonathan's views about life. His programme, "The Unknown Famine" had had a major impact on TV viewers everywhere, and had been a catalyst for the much needed food aid to read the starving.

The answer to his whereabouts came two weeks before Christmas, in the Landmark Hotel, beside London's Marylebone station. I was having a farewell drink with Annabel, the luscious, dark-haired Corporate Communications Manager, with whom I'd worked since July. In six weeks, I'd be leaving corporate life for a while, meeting former classmates and, if all went to plan, finishing the book.

Christmas revellers packed the downstairs bar, whilst a pianist played popular songs. We nibbled on olives and nuts, chatting about our plans for the festivities and 2005. Our conversation was interrupted by a bleary faced, young blonde, weaving unsteadily towards us

"Annabel, fancy seeing you here! How are you? Come on and join us, we've just finished our Christmas lunch!"

Annabel turned to me with an apologetic smile: "What do you think? Do you mind if we join them? I used to work with them at Woolworths."

"Why not, the more the merrier!" I responded. In the corner, I could see one of my regular colleagues, James, so if the rest were too drunk, I could at least chat to him.

We ambled across with our wine glasses and I sat down in a tub chair, besides a small West Indian lady who smiled in welcome. Sharon introduced herself and she turned out to be James's wife. After the usual pleasantries, the inevitable question about work popped up, so I told her about the book. As I did so, she leant forward in interest.

"Tell you what, my sister Marcia would be very interested in it."

"Why's that?"

"Well, she works for the director of Voluntary Services Overseas."

A connection was instantly made. Trying to suppress my mounting excitement,

I asked nonchalantly: "Does she know Jonathan Dimbleby by any chance?" I knew that Jonathan was their President.

"Yes, of course, she speaks to him every week, if not more often."

We then swapped email addresses and I persuaded Sharon to involve Marcia in getting a letter to Jonathan. Marcia was very happy to oblige. So, another apparently random and spontaneous connection had been very auspicious in moving the odyssey forward!

*****

With Christmas fast approaching, my thoughts turned to the Holy Land, and I decided to contact Lynn Reid Banks, to take up her offer of help finding 'peaceniks' in Israel.

"Annette who?" she asked when I called her. "Oh yes, I remember now: the writing weekend. I've just got out of the bath and it's a very busy time for us right now. I'm not sure if I can help."

"I'm sorry to call at a bad time, Lynn," I apologised. "But I was wondering if you could put me in touch with one of your Israeli friends. I plan to go out there next year, and see the need for peace myself."

"Well," her tone softened, "there's one man who I think may help – Dan, Dan Leon. He's edited an Israeli/Palestinian journal for some years and is very pro dialogue between the two nationalities. But you need to be aware that he's not religious at all."

I thanked her for her help and within 24 hours I had Dan's email address.

This was something I frequently found: many people's biggest fear was that I would try to convert them to Christianity. I think God speaks to our hearts in a way appropriate to each of us. It had also become increasingly clear that there were many very good people who didn't go to church. They had consciously decided to find their peace through other ways – prayer, meditation, sitting quietly in a park, going for long walks, running, mountaineering, watching nature unfold, and helping people around them on a daily basis. I feel that all are ways to reach God, because every path finally has to lead to that deep peace within us.

Later that evening, I watched a BBC TV programme about the three wise men. According to the Bible and legend, Balthazar was dark skinned – in the TV broadcast they called him Ethiopian. These holy men had been much revered in their countries and after some centuries, their bones were exhumed and reburied together in Cologne Cathedral. The precious caskets were placed beneath a huge golden shrine.

Shivers of recognition ran up and down my spine, as I realised that was the very spot I'd been looking at when Fanaye and I were there in July 2004. Was this part of the pattern that God was showing to me – Coventry with its cathedral of peace and now Cologne with the three wise men? I emailed Fanaye the following day and she thought that it was miraculous too.

Even on Christmas Day, I couldn't rest, and after a good lunch with my in-laws who were staying with us, I emailed Dan Leon to see if he could help. He was effusive in his reply, telling me that it would be a 'mitzvah', and recommending some books for me to read about the Israeli-Palestinian situation.

*****

Watching the horrific effects of the giant tsunami on our TV was unbelievable – we sat rooted to the screen as the death toll began to rise. Two days previously, I'd seen dark grey, thick, ominous clouds in the sky. They were so oppressive – like wave after huge wave, advancing menacingly. My heart had felt very troubled as I'd stared at them, wondering what horror they predicted. The real waves hadn't discriminated between nationality, rich or poor - everything in their path was obliterated.

Many of us were home for the Christmas holidays, spending time with loved ones, so people's hearts were deeply touched and the response was instantaneous. Newspapers, websites and TV and radio newscasters broadcast the Disaster Emergency Committee's website and phone number. Shortly afterwards, people began to hit the site or ring the numbers to give what they could. Here in Buckingham, we decided to give cash to Oxfam as we couldn't get through on the telephone. James's school also put on some activities to raise funds and £2,500 went to the Disaster Emergency Committee fund.

Perhaps, because of all the focus on helping people who had lost their families and livelihoods, I had a dream in which I met Bob Geldof in Ethiopia. He had done so much to raise the profile of the deep, grinding poverty on that continent and 2005 was to be an important year for him and us, with the publication of the Commission for Africa Report, and the 20th anniversary since LiveAid. I had already arranged to meet Myles Wickstead in January, who'd been appointed head of the secretariat for the Commission, for news about their plans.

*****

The phone rang insistently. Expecting it to be one of James's friends, I grabbed the handset and almost dropped it when a woman with a Portuguese accent said, "Is that London – sorry, Buckingham? I would like to speak to Annette please."

"Yes, speaking." I tried hard not to show my nerves.

"This is Celina's daughter from Lisbon. You wrote to my mother last month. I'm sorry but she is not the Celina you are looking for. Fernandes is her married name and she didn't live in Ethiopia. Would you like us to return your letter and photograph?"

I was dumbstruck and very disappointed. Somehow, my voice returned: "No, no, that's OK, just keep it as a souvenir for when the book is launched in Portugal. Thank you so much for calling to let me know."

Do you know Phoebe Khalil?
هل تعرف فوب خليل؟

أبحث عن فوب خليل المصرية التي تخرجت في مدرسة
نازاريث بأديس أبابا، أثيوبيا عام 1969. إني أريد أن أورد
ذكر قصتها في في كتابي "المغامرة الأثيوبية" حول رحلتي
للبحث عن 9 زملاء فصل لي شاهدتهم آخر مرة عام
1964. بداية الكتاب كانت بمثابة حلم في أبريل من عام
2000، وكان الغرض من كتابته هو المساعدة لزيادة دعم
معونة المياه، من أجل توفير مياه دائمة ونظيفة للقبائل
الأثيوبية الفقيرة.
إن كان بإمكانك المساعدة، أرجو منك أن ترسل لي بريداً
إليكترونياً على العنوان التالي:
a.allen@netcomuk.co.uk

Please reply in English
برجاء الرد باللغة الإنجليزية

At the time, it had seemed too good to be true and at least now I knew that the trail had gone completely cold. Oh well, I'd just have to see what the weekend brought. The advertisement for Phoebe would be appearing in *Al-Ahram* two days later. I was hopeful because I'd now experienced that whenever one door closed, another tended to open almost immediately afterwards.

And so it proved. On Saturday morning, I opened an email from Ramses Khalil, Phoebe's brother. He and his mother, who lived in Cairo, had spotted the advertisement in *Al-Ahram* and responded straight away. In his reply, he told me that Phoebe now lived in Chicago, giving me her email address. His brief message finished with, "Now, who are you exactly?" Hallelujah was the only word I could think of at the time!

Ramses had given me his mobile number so I rang it, just to double check after the disappointment of Celina. The mobile's short ring sounded in my ear and a European-Egyptian voice answered, "Salaam?"

"Is that Ramses Khalil?"

"Yes, who is this?"

"It's Annette, the woman who placed the advertisement in *Al-Ahram.* I'm so pleased you replied so quickly – thank you so much."

As we spoke I could hear the sounds of cars and vans driving by and bursts of Arabic conversations and music. The man named after Egypt's famous pharaoh was indeed the right person and he even remembered Eric, my younger brother, from their schooldays together at St Joseph's in Addis Ababa. It turned out that Phoebe had lived in the States since 1966. She was married to Cliff and had two daughters, one around 20 and the other about 16, and they lived half an hour's drive from Chicago.

In addition to Ramses, I had emails from ten other curious Egyptians, intrigued by the advertisement and fascinated by a foreigner looking for a friend to help provide water for Ethiopia. Each offered to help, no questions asked. It was an interesting comparison to the single response from Portugal two months earlier. But of course, Egypt and Ethiopia are next door neighbours, old trading partners and fellow Africans, and the Nile river runs through both countries.

At 3.30am the following Wednesday, I got up to call Phoebe, to find she'd just been looking at my email. We chatted about family things – Phoebe had lived in the US since she was 16. I was keen to see her, if I could. Keeping my voice low so as not to wake the family, I asked: "Phoebe, I wonder if we could meet when I visit the States next month."

There was a pause: "I'm sorry, but there's a big inspection at the hospital where I work, which means long shifts for me that week, getting everything ready. But, perhaps next time you're over?"

*****

In another piece of synchronicity, I was given an unusual 50p coin the same weekend. I thought it was fake, as it seemed lighter than most and the picture on the reverse was one I hadn't seen before. It was of a suffragette, her wrists tied to a railing with the words 'WSPU - Give women the vote' and the year 1903 underneath. (Women's Social and Political Union). The coin had been cast to celebrate the centenary of the struggle for women's votes in 2003. I smiled as I thought of Helen Pankhurst's grandmother Sylvia, who'd developed the colours and the logo for the Union. I kept it to give to Helen when I next saw her again in Addis.

Further information:

Al-Ahram: www.ahram.org.eg – their weekly online, English language newspaper.

---

25 Two nieces appear

The January winds were bitter as they roared like a slipstream down Victoria Street, which leads to Parliament Square and the seat of British democracy, the Houses of Parliament. Tall office blocks lined both sides of the street – many were government offices, where civil servants toiled to implement and monitor government policies. I wasn't sure where I'd find number 20, an annex of the Department for International Development (DFID), where I was meeting Myles Wickstead to find out about the Commission for Africa (CFA).

I called in to one building, which turned out to be the Office of the Deputy Prime Minister. You could see just what size of budget they had by the size of the reception area – it was vast. Wandering out, I carried on walking and found a friendly traffic warden who said, "Look, it's there on the corner."

DFID's office was the smallest of all I'd seen. Here the reception was the size of the average lounge, with a small seating area placed in front of the United Nations' Millennium Development Goal posters. I signed in, noticing that someone from the Prime Minister's office had arrived earlier to see Myles Wickstead – no name, just 'No. 10' was scrawled in the visitors' book, with the firm flourish of a government mandarin. With just six weeks to go before the CFA Report launch, I imagined that there would be very regular visits between the two offices.

Making myself comfortable, I took in my surroundings. In the corner, an American fidgeted, alternating between reading the *International Herald Tribune* and playing with his Personal Digital Assistant. His clothes gave off Americana, the black shiny brogues, the white shirt and flamboyant tie: the air of impatience all designed to say

'I'm important, I'm somebody'. He became more agitated as the minutes dragged on and went to speak to the security guard, as by now the receptionist had left for the evening. It was just us and the cleaners - black bin bags full of office rubbish were everywhere.

I was pleased with the wait, which allowed me time to collect my thoughts. Gazing at the UN posters, I took a photo of Goal number one, which read 'Halve world poverty by 2015'. I hoped that upstairs I could take a photo of Myles, to represent something he cared about. The door next to reception opened, and Myles stood there grinning: "Annette, how good to see you, sorry to have kept you waiting."

He looked the same as last time at the Ethiopian embassy, a tall man with intelligent, kindly eyes, grey sprinkling his short beard and sideburns. He looked like someone who plays or enjoys cricket: there was just that sense of Britishness about him. 'A thoroughly good sort' is how he would have been described 30 years ago, when we used that kind of language.

Showing me into a small meeting room upstairs, he waved at a seat. Photos were scattered across the table - printers' proofs of the possible front cover for the CFA's Report. All showed grinning African adults and children, eyes full of hope, imploring us to listen to the recommendations inside.

Myles had a long track record of working in Africa, since 1993. From 2000 to 2004 he was based in Addis Ababa as British Ambassador to Ethiopia and Djibouti. His career working in development previously involved positions as Head of the European Community and Food Aid Department at the Overseas Development Administration (1990 -1993) and Coordinator of the 1997 British Government Development White Paper 'Eliminating World Poverty'. He'd also worked in Washington before he got his posting to Ethiopia.

"Where did the Commission begin, Myles?" I asked. "Was it Geldof's idea?"

He pushed the papers to one side and rested his hands on the table. "It probably was. In 2003, he suggested to Tony Blair that the Commission was set up and we launched it in 2004. There are 17 commissioners, of whom nine are African." I wondered if Meles Zenawi, Ethiopia's prime minister, would be mentioned, as he was one.

"How did you ensure that ordinary people were involved in the debate?"

"We split the continent into five regions: it was each region's task to ensure discussions and meetings were held with people of all backgrounds. We also worked closely with the Economic Commission for Africa and the African Union, both of whom are based in Addis Ababa."

"How hopeful are you things will actually improve in the long term?"

"Well, governance is definitely improving. The foundation stone for better living standards is to create stable societies. In those countries where peace exists, we need to improve infrastructure, health and education. Press freedom is slowly increasing, which has a key role to play in better democracy."

"The Report must be very close to publication now. What are the big ideas that have come from the discussions?"

Inhaling deeply, he responded: "As I said before, the vital importance of good governance in creating the foundations for a secure society. Then there's the role that women can play in improving economies. I don't think there's sufficient recognition that micro-businesses are far more successful when they're run by women."

I nodded. Women were often far better at managing money and ensuring the whole family benefited from profits than their husbands. They just needed to be given the chance to prove themselves, with seed funding. Women in Africa were tremendously resourceful as I'd seen from my visit in 2004.

"What about AIDS?"

Myles paused: "It's devastating the continent, no doubt about it. We need to do more to get cheap anti-retroviral drugs to the poor. Then there's education - we shouldn't just be focusing on primary education, but tertiary, including research facilities at universities. If there were better facilities, there wouldn't be such a brain drain overseas."

As he said that, the only brain drain that struck me was the nurses and doctors emigrating to the west, leaving their countries with a triple whammy: lack of medicines, lack of affordable anti HIV/AIDS drugs, and over-stretched medical staff if the patients finally made it to hospital.

"How about plans to increase trade between Africa and the rest of the world?"

"We need to create a level playing field for trade by removing tariffs and non-tariff barriers. For instance, Africa mostly exports raw products, when the greatest profit comes from adding value to it – turning textiles into clothing, or coffee beans into ground coffee. We also need to stop the developed world dumping surplus products in Africa, whether chickens or even tomatoes. That ruins the market for local producers.

"Debt relief is key: I think we can make a lot progress there. The Chancellor announced the government's intention to pay ten per cent of the developing world's foreign debt bill during his African tour earlier this month. We hope that other G8 and European countries will follow suit. The need for long term support is compelling. We have the greatest opportunity we've ever had with Britain holding the EU Presidency and hosting the G8 meeting later this summer."

Clare, Myles's PA, popped her head around the door. His car was waiting to take him home, all the way to Somerset, where he lives with his wife and two children, Edward and Kathryn. Myles told me that the CFA committee would be wound up the end of 2005. I tried hard to hide my shock: I felt the task would only just be starting. Was Africa only ever an initiative for us?

When I asked Myles for a photo, he walked briskly to his desk, returning with the standard shot – man seated at desk: it was far too formal. I requested, "Can I take one of you downstairs, by the posters?"

"Why not? Let's go."

Back in reception, Myles looked at the UN posters and chose to stand by the first – 'Halve world poverty

Myles Wickstead, Head of the Secretariat, Commission for Africa

218

by 2015'. In many ways, it summed up what much of his life had been about so far. Time would tell what the lasting impact of the CFA Report and recommendations would be.

*****

We trooped downstairs to the basement below the Ethiopian Catholic church: Our Lady Queen of Heaven in London's Bayswater. There were about 40 people there, including an elderly English woman and two Malaysian men. Abba Bogale had invited me to tell his congregation something about the book after their Sunday mass. I had taken two copies of the old school photo to help the story come to life, which I hoped would spark a little interest.

Once in the basement, people gathered together chairs and got themselves a soft drink. It was very informal: children were running around shouting and it was difficult to make myself heard. I stood up and cleared my throat and told them about our time in Ethiopia between 1962 and 1964 and the dream in April 2000. The whispered comments stopped as I continued the story, and who I'd found when I returned in March 2004.

Three young women weren't so polite: one had arrived late, and sat whispering and pointing at faces in the photo to her friends. Maybe she recognised one of the young women? But the rest were captivated as I revealed how I found Marta Asrat, still there as school secretary. I included the story about Hiruth Girma, and finally mentioned Mary Asfaw Wossen's name (the Emperor's granddaughter). As I did so, there was a sharp intake of breath from the group. They were hooked!

There were a few questions, but mostly of the 'when is the book out? I want to buy it' variety, which was very encouraging. Abba Bogale remarked, "Annette will be bringing copies of the book here for us to buy, so we can help our poor brothers and sisters back in Ethiopia."

Afterwards, two women approached me. One had a very modern Afro, large gold-rimmed glasses and a wide smile. She told me, "My name is Negisty: I just wanted you to know that Sister Weynemariam, Nazareth School's Head, is my aunt. I was speaking to her recently, and she is looking for some English teachers to go across and join the school, so if you know of anyone…"

Always full of smiles! Abba Bogale Tiruneh and I

The second was the one who'd sat whispering and pointing at the photo. I'd chatted with her earlier: she told me she wasn't usually at the church as she studied in Brighton. She'd come in on the spur of the moment, as it was where her friends worshipped. Earnestly, she informed me: "My aunt is Marta Asrat, your classmate. I thought you should know that." Without another word, she turned on her heel and left with her friends.

I felt that the odds were extremely low of two classmates' nieces being at the same church meeting. One of the hallmarks of these synchronous events was that people were often in places they hadn't planned to be that day, or doing something they rarely did. It was like Jack reading *The Buckingham Advertiser,* the Saturday the photo had appeared. Spontaneity and a change in direction were what brought forward the desired result. Or as John Lennon had remarked: "Life is what happens to you, while you're busy making other plans."

The next day I had an email from Leikun Tefera, an Ethiopian man who had spotted the diaspora feature on www.tadias.com. He had recognised his aunt, Tiruwork Abebe from the photo, standing first left in the back row! He hadn't known that she'd attended Nazareth School and had rung her daughter, Rebecca, to check this. She confirmed that it was true.

Leikun kindly asked how he could help. As he lived in Washington, I asked if he could meet me at the airport when I arrived. He immediately agreed, so now I had my Washington contact. Everything was in place for my US trip, just as I'd prayed for it to be.

Further information:

DIFD: www.difd.gov.uk. This is a very useful website, which provides information on how the Department is helping other countries. It also has a host of reports which can be downloaded.

John Lennon, "Beautiful Boy" www.quotationspage.com/quotes/John_Lennon/

V: USA

26 Fortress America

Lines of people snaked before me. The arrivals hall at Washington Dulles International airport was packed, as travellers and returning Americans queued up to have their ID checked by immigration officials. It was a patient queue, as most knew that after 9/11, security was a lot tighter. Some chatted and laughed, others hunted around for their passports in preparation. Babies cried and toddlers crawled between their parents' legs.

I had been panicking for the last hour as my immigration form was incomplete – I'd forgotten to ask Leikun for his address. Thus the 'address while in the US' section was blank. I wondered if I'd be allowed in the country. Fortunately, I had his home and mobile phone numbers. I tried to call his mobile, but there was absolutely no signal. I had toyed with putting a false address on the form, but what if I was discovered? My palms and forehead were clammy with sweat. I cursed the terrorists who had caused these problems, when the vast majority of us are law-abiding citizens.

Another young British man was in the same dilemma. He seemed to travel to the US quite regularly, as he commented, "I didn't have this hassle when we flew to LA last month." But it was the system now, and there was no way around it. A United Airlines ground hostess asked to check our forms before the immigration booths, she was very helpful and took phone numbers for both of us. Twenty minutes later she returned with Leikun's address – waves of relief washed over me and I shuffled towards the next free booth. As I pressed both index fingers on a little pad, a web camera took an image of my irises.

"Did I smile?" I asked the immigration official, as he looked at the form.

"No, it's better if people are relaxed. Here you go, welcome to America."

I collected my bags and walked out into the arrivals hall. Standing in front were Leikun and his petite wife, Freghenet, Frey for short. Smiles of welcome lit their faces – how wonderful it was to have kind strangers to meet you in a foreign country! Tanasterligns and embraces were exchanged and we walked out to the cold wintry skies. As we made our way through the parking lot, I saw three police by the boot of a car with an Afro-American spread eagled on it while they frisked him for weapons. "Welcome to America," I muttered to myself.

Getting out onto the six-lane freeway was easy, and Frey chatted as we drove. A bunch of Tadias magazines were on the back seat and I flicked through to see the feature and the school photograph. Leikun had mentioned in his last email that Frey, a broadcaster for the public service broadcasting station, Voice of America (VoA), had interviewed Liben from the magazine. She'd had to speak to him twice as, for some unusual reason, the first digital audio file had disappeared.

Second time around, she'd just seen the latest issue and mentioned to Liben that Leikun's aunt had been in the same class. They had laughed about all the connections and here I was a week later, on the way to meet Rebecca, the daughter of my classmate Tiruwork, and some of Leikun's family who lived in the suburbs. Not just that, but Frey was willing to interview me and one or two of my classmates to help publicise the book!

Washington DC's metropolitan area is large, taking in part of Virginia and Maryland, with over four million residents. As well as being home to the US government, it also has the largest Ethiopian diaspora in the world – more than a million live here. Many come to join relatives for a better standard of living, whether they work for NGOs, the government or small businesses which serve the Ethiopian community.

Within half an hour, we had pulled up outside a pleasant suburban house with a bike and tricycle lying on the grass outside. Leikun introduced me to his cousin, Saba, and three generations of the family: her mother and her children. Rebecca, Tiruwork's daughter, was blooming, just two months to go before her baby was born. Although she and her husband now lived in the United Arab Emirates, she wanted her baby to be born in the US to give the little one automatic US citizenship. It was beginning to appear that people only felt really secure if they were US citizens.

Frey (first left) and Leikun (back row, centre) with Leikun's relatives

The strong black coffee helped ease the jetlag. I noticed that the lounge was littered with Ethiopian souvenirs – lampshades and pictures, with naïve images of men and women in traditional dress, posters, and the small wooden three-legged stools, carved from solid pieces of wood. Saba and her mother both wore Ethiopian jewellery and the older woman wore her hair in the traditional style, with a scarf wrapped around her head. They kept their culture alive by speaking Amharic at home and cooking Ethiopian food. I had some of their crumbly bread, dabo, which is good for people who are allergic to sugar, as they don't use it in cooking.

After coffee, we drove to Leikun and Frey's apartment on one of the longest roads in Washington – Kings Street. Their flat was in a modern block with magnificent views over the city from their 22nd floor lounge. It was evidently the domain of two prolific readers, with books and magazines everywhere. Leikun rang around local hotels, while Frey and I chatted over a glass of wine. She showed me their lovely wedding photos, which had been held at the Ethiopian Orthodox Church, followed by a reception at a local hotel. Frey comes from a family of six children, with two brothers and three sisters, all of whom have the classic Ethiopian high cheekbones, clear skin and heart-shaped faces.

We left for a short tour of the city, driving past the Pentagon and Washington Monument, that stark obelisk which reaches some 500 foot into the sky. In the distance, I could see Capitol Hill, the seat of US Government. Leikun and Frey took me to two neighbourhoods where entire streets are filled with Ethiopian cafes, restaurants, video hire, dry cleaning stores and hairdressers, just as Ghennet Girma had pointed out last October! After checking in at the hotel, we had a meal in a local Thai restaurant. I could finally relax, as we sat surrounded by diners of all nationalities.

During the meal, Leikun told me something about his upbringing in Ethiopia. He'd lived through the time of the Red Terror in the late 1970s when teenage members of rival Marxist groups would randomly open fire on other teenagers in the streets. Innocent people were often shot, including some of his classmates from St Joseph's School. Consequently, everyone was terrified, and it was difficult to socialise as it wasn't safe to venture out at night.

Leikun had worked hard at school, and in 1980 won a scholarship to study in Russia. He'd lived in Volgograd for a year, where he studied Russian, then five years in Voronezh, from where he graduated with a Masters of Science in Industrial Engineering in 1986. From there he'd travelled to Germany, and in 1987 had emigrated to the US. Today. he works for the Citizenship and Immigration Services, which is part of the Department of Homeland Security. He travels a great deal for his job and finds his Russian very useful.

Over coffee, we agreed a schedule for the following day and Frey gave me her mobile number so that I could visit her at the Voice of America where she worked for the Horn of Africa team, producing news for their Amharic programme.

*****

It was hard to wake up the following day: my body didn't know what time it was and my head felt dull from the hotel bedroom's central heating. Opening the curtains, I saw that my room looked onto a side street. It was a drab morning, with threatening grey clouds. As I stood there rain began to fall – time for breakfast.

The large, square dining room on the first floor was almost deserted. It was after nine, and even the traffic outside was light. Bland, beige curtains tried to obscure the view from the panoramic windows. A Mexican woman stood muttering in Spanish on the phone as I entered. She glanced at me, and carried on with her conversation. Breakfast was strictly self-service. There was a tired display of sugar-coated cereals, bagels and buns. Alongside the cereals were sliced white bread, jelly, butter and margarine. It all looked completely unappetising. I managed to find the coffee machine and took a bagel, which turned out to be hard, so I left it. After tasting the coffee, I gave up - it had probably been sitting there stewing since six am.

Taking my notebook and camera, I left the hotel, heading up to Leikun's office at 1525 Wilson Boulevard. On the way, I saw Army and Air Force personnel standing by bus stops or walking into buildings, with uniform crewcuts and faces shining like their polished shoes. Some wore the black patent lace-ups I remembered so well from our time in Addis - even small items of clothing can whisk you back to your past.

Beside the Miracle beauty salon, I saw the Oak Street Café and decided to stop and have a cup of tea. Sitting down, I heard the familiar lilt of Amharic from two pleasant-looking young men. Introducing themselves, Berhanu and Manarik were very chatty, telling me that they were both studying IT in the States. Ethiopians were everywhere! I shook their hands as I left, having made more friends along the journey.

Huge, bright dancing figures marked the entrance to Leikun's office. As I entered the foyer, I saw a Peace Corps office, and thought about Kathy Miller. I made a mental note to return, as you never know, it may have been that her parents were Peace Corps volunteers working in Ethiopia when she attended school in Addis.

Leikun came down to collect me at reception, and his office proved to be just as full of paper as his lounge at home – files were stacked on the desk, cabinets and the floor, everywhere. He told me that he'd soon be working in central Washington, as he'd been promoted. I was pleased for him, I could see how hard he worked. He decided to take an early lunch and once outside, showed me where to get good coffee and hot food in a café just yards from his office. I was amazed to see that you could buy hot or cold food by the pound, most of which sold for under $5. No wonder some Americans were so huge when food was so cheap! They liked lots of different fillings in one sandwich – cold meat with cheese seemed very popular, with all kinds of mayonnaise or relishes.

We strolled down the road to a Mexican restaurant that did lots of wraps and salads. Many people were eating with friends and I noticed that, like in London, lunch was a quick affair. By the time we finished our meal, it was raining really hard, so I stopped to buy an umbrella. Leikun was particularly keen for me to see Freedom Park, a concrete space opened in 1996. Looking at the displays, I noticed some connections to my past – a photo of Mandela voting in the first democratic elections in South Africa and a display about the American suffragette movement. There was also an etched glass and steel memorial to more than 1,500 journalists killed while on assignment in war zones.

I wandered back to the hotel, past Rosslyn Metro station, outside which sat a very obese Afro-American. It was bitterly cold but he wouldn't move – it was his 'pitch' where he begged. He probably knew every commuter by sight, as well as the other drifters and people who'd fallen on hard times. Later that evening, I found an Afghan restaurant to eat in. It had seen better times and there was only one other couple in the vast dining room: perhaps trade had dropped off after the invasion of their country? I found a table for two by the food counter and enjoyed a shish kebab, salad and some wine.

Tomorrow, I would be speaking to another classmate – Etenesh Tsige, the one whom Fanaye had mentioned early last year. I'd got her details from her brother, Atamenta, who'd contacted me when he, too, had seen the photo on the tadias website. I had called him to arrange to meet up for dinner and he gave me Etenesh's phone number. After a better night's sleep, I got up and began to gather my papers for the day ahead. I always put off the important things by re-arranging papers or tidying up. My heart wrestled with my ego, telling me to just get on with it, but the fear still stood there, trembling at times. I was still never sure how people would react when I told them my dream. Even now, after all this progress, it still felt a bit tentative at times. But if Atamenta was eager to meet, then I hoped that Etenesh would be pleased to hear from me.

"Hello?"

"Hi, Etenesh, it's Annette. I'm here in Washington. I spoke to Atamenta yesterday, he gave me your number. How are you?"

"Oh gosh, how good to hear from you!" Her voice warmed with delight and then came the laughter. I realised with a pang that it hadn't changed one iota over the years. "How long are you here for, Annette?"

"Just three more days before I go to LA. I'm meeting Silva – do you remember Silva Derentz?"

"Yes, she was full of mischief! But I can't recall her face that well. It's a pity you're not here longer, it would have been great to meet up. So, what have you been doing with yourself since I last saw you?"

I gave her a few brief details of my life, but kept it short. I was far more interested in how she had come to live in the US, like so many of our classmates.

Etenesh had first visited the US in 1967 as a delegate to the World Youth Forum, having won an essay competition sponsored by the *New York Herald Tribune.* The participants were from forty-five countries and she had represented Ethiopia. She had travelled to several states and participated in various programmes, staying with American families. She'd even been on local TV a few times. In all, her stay had lasted four months.

During her visit to Virginia, an American professor, Mina Abady, who taught at a local university, hosted her and the Egyptian delegate. After Etenesh finished high school, Mina had helped her get into Virginia Union University in 1970. She graduated in 1974 with a major in history and government and went on to continue her studies in Political Science at graduate school. After her studies, Etenesh decided to make America her new home, and gradually the rest of her siblings – three sisters and a brother – had followed. Like Fanaye, she had never married, but was aunt to many nieces and nephews. She now worked as a manager for a big retailer in Richmond, Virginia.

*****

The winter sunshine pierced the bedroom curtains: today was definitely a day for sightseeing. I found the café where Leikun had taken me for coffee the previous day and had a fresh ham omelette, which was delicious. I sat by the window, looking out onto the quiet street. Occasionally, someone would spill out of the brass and glass revolving doors opposite, but other than that, only cars nosed their way slowly up the hill. I appreciated this time on my own - part of the scenery and yet not – quietly observing, as I had always done, since I was a toddler.

The hot, fresh coffee burnt my throat and disturbed my reverie. Now it was time to find out if the Peace Corps office could help me find Kathy. Their office at 1525 Wilson Boulevard was surprisingly easy to enter – there were no security gates, just a buzzer and receptionist. All around the walls were posters that explained case studies of Peace Corps work or exhorted people to volunteer.

"How can I help you?" asked the young woman. I explained about my search for a former classmate whose parents may have been former Peace Corps volunteers in Ethiopia.

"What year was that?" she replied doubtfully.

"1962. I left in 1964, and I know Kathy stayed on, but she left the country between 1966 to 1968."

"I'm not sure that we had been a mission there in 1962-63. However, let me give you a phone number for Leslie Rodriguez. She works on our Africa desk at our HQ."

That was good enough for me, and I hurried back to the hotel to call her. Leslie was very helpful and immediately put me in touch with Janet Meeks on the Ethiopia desk. I explained to Janet why I needed to find Kathy Miller. I could tell she was interested and she promised to look into it for me. I took her email address in case I didn't hear from her.

Browsing the Lonely Planet guide to the USA, I made a list of places I could visit in the two hours I had before meeting Fre and her colleagues later that day. Just as I went down the Rosslyn Metro steps, I looked to my right, and sure enough, the homeless man was sitting there on his own patch of despair, staring out into space.

Leaving Farrugat West station, I headed past the huge, pale grey art deco government buildings, up towards the White House. There were two speeds of pedestrians – families and couples strolling, sight-seeing in the capital, and joggers impatient for the lights to change as they did their circuits in the warm sunshine. It was 60°F and feeling balmy, warm enough to unbutton my long, red coat. My attempt to get to the White House railings was a waste of time. I couldn't get anywhere near it: there was a special event later that afternoon and metal barriers guarded the pathway past the building's iron railings. In any event, the White House was far smaller than it looked on TV, and was situated quite some way from where the public could stand and peer in.

Ambling through Constitution Gardens, I headed past the ducks on the lake and through the trees up towards the Lincoln Memorial. I reverently climbed the steps to the chamber in which the great statue of Abraham Lincoln sat, like a great-great-grandfather, surveying his family. I'd seen this image so often, I just wanted to relish being there in person for the first time.

I looked out over the sheet of water and fountains to the Washington Monument, the graceful obelisk pointing its way to the heavens, built in memory of George Washington. I stood close to the spot where one man had roused the world with his dream for equal rights for black Americans on 28 August 1963 – Martin Luther King Jr, one of the lighthouses on my voyage. Later in the souvenir shop, I bought a copy of that famous speech.

Before I left, I closed my eyes and imagined myself standing there, telling thousands of people about my dream to bring water to people in Ethiopia and, if we had the faith to believe it and act on it, peace in Israel. I sent out my dream and prayers for everlasting peace in the world. I felt sure I was one of tens of millions praying for this every day – but so many of us never speak of it, let alone make the required changes to bring about peace. But who knew where dreams could lead?

As I walked towards the Holocaust Memorial Museum, tourists and birds chattered all around me while helicopters flew low, heralding the comings and goings of the important. Stepping onto the sandy soil alongside the sidewalks, I could see how Washington had been created from marshlands three centuries ago: today the air smelled of petrol, damp and rotting vegetation. Even in February, there was a touch of humidity in the air, as buds snapped out of their winter hiding places.

The museum was a large, modern building, with four floors giving testimony to the suffering of the Jews. It was full of visitors - some elderly Jews sat around PC monitors with museum curators, no doubt researching some events they could still recall from their homes in Europe. That year, 2005, marked 60 years since the concentration camps had been liberated by the Allied Forces. And indeed, we must never forget how one man's desire for purity and power destroyed six million lives and affected the outlook of everyone who came after them. Pondering gruesome photos taken in the ghettos and concentration camps, I thought of the camp close to where my mother had lived in Vennesla, southern Norway. Hatred seems to spread and perpetuate far more rapidly than peace ever will. Is this because of the human animal's totally selfish ego, whose fear of extinction dictates that our tribe must be better than, and rule over, other tribes?

*****

Hurrying along Independence Avenue to meet up with Frey at the Voice of America, I kept looking up the hill, towards the Capitol. The government buildings were vast, some taking up entire blocks, with names I'd read about in many newspapers. Washington was frequently referred to as the world's capital, and it felt like it - the place where all the crucial decisions were taken. Having located VoA's offices, finding an entrance I could use at 330 Independence Avenue was difficult: another casualty of life after 9/11. Only one entrance remained open, around the back. After another airport-like security check, Frey came down to meet me, smiling the familiar, "Hi, Annette, how're you doing?"

Briskly walking down long corridors, she told me about the Horn of Africa team and a bit about VoA. I knew I was in the right place when I saw the large map on the wall and a wonderful lion skin and posters from Ethiopia trumpeting the country's tourist motto '13 Months of Sunshine.' Frey introduced me to many of her colleagues. I showed them the old school photograph, and we chatted about life in the US.

Her manager, Negussie Mengesha, remembered Hiruth from his time in Germany. It was a sad memory, she'd locked herself in her flat for several days, and had to be coaxed out. Another colleague, Adanech Fessehaye, knew Ghennet very well. Everywhere circles within circles – how extraordinary, and yet natural, it all was.

Frey had promised a tour of Capitol Hill and a visit to Alexandria, the original city of Washington, dating from the 1700s. We strolled to her car a few blocks further down and drove up towards the Hill. Vigilance against terrorism had almost ruined the view – two yard high concrete blocks obscured the building's lines from the public. Perhaps you could stand within 50 yards of it, but no more. We drove around the back and then down past the Library and other government offices and headed out towards Alexandria and the Potomac River for some fresh air and an evening meal. Walking towards a boardwalk café overlooking the river, Frey remarked on the unusually high number of Ethiopians in the vicinity. I just smiled.

*****

My last full day in Washington dawned. The sun wasn't as warm as the previous day, which had been a blip in the usual cold winter weather. As I sat stirring my coffee, I looked out of the window and thought about President John F Kennedy. Today, I planned to visit his grave at Arlington National Cemetery, where nearly 300,000 soldiers are buried, including recent casualties from the Iraq War. I wanted to walk among the gravestones and pay my respects to some of them – people I'd never known, who had given their lives for freedom and their ideals. Sometimes, I didn't agree with their ideals, particularly the Iraq war, but I had to admire their courage.

Standing up and being counted for what you believe in is becoming increasingly rare in our societies, as we strive to fit in with what is acceptable and acquire the things and status which count for 'success' today. So many of us have consequently lost our way, living lives of quiet desperation and disconnection with who we really are, deep down inside. The only place many can be themselves is with their family: sometimes not even there, sometimes just in their hearts, and so they put on masks pretending to be someone they're not. Therein lies madness, because true sanity comes from feeling, thinking, saying and behaving in ways that reflect our soul.

At the Arlington National Cemetery, JFK was on all the visitors' minds. Soft rain fell on us, and slim white headstones fanned out as far as the eye could see, like ice lolly sticks. Jack Kennedy's gravestone lay beside his wife Jacqueline's, an eternal flame burning between them. On one long slender piece of concrete had been carved his famous words, 'Ask not what your country can do for you....'

A few yards away was Bobby Kennedy's memorial, with an excerpt from the speech he had given in apartheid South Africa in 1966, the same year we had arrived there. On 06/06/66, he had included a vision of courage in his speech at the University of Cape Town: "It is from numberless diverse acts of courage and belief that human history is shaped. Each time a man stands up for an ideal, or acts to improve the lot of others, or strikes out against injustice, he sends forth a tiny ripple of hope, and crossing each other from a million different centres of energy and daring, those ripples build a current which can sweep down the mightiest walls of oppression and resistance."

The voice of our Latin teacher, Mrs. Rock, came floating back to me as she stood in front of standard 6A in the prefab class at Kempton Park High. "You will remember this day for many years to come – 6th June 1966. We don't get many dates like this."

Africa, was the continent that connected me to the Kennedys – hearing about Jack's death in Ethiopia and Bobby's in South Africa. Despite Africa's reputation for megalomaniac rulers who clung on to power long after they should have relinquished it, ordinary people wanted freedom and democracy, and they revered individuals who stood for the rights of the man in the street.

Before I left the cemetery, I strolled by some fresh graves where bare red earth surrounded the sparkling white headstones. Funeral cars drove to and from the special chapel fifty yards away. I gazed at the newest stone, marking the death of a young US Navy sailor, who was just 21 when he died on 15 December 2004. I wondered about those he'd left behind – perhaps he already had his own young family and it wasn't just his parents who were grieving.

Atamenta Tsige, brother of my classmate, Etenesh

It was eight o'clock when Atamenta Tsige, Etenesh's brother, strolled into the hotel lobby. Tall with wavy hair, I could see the family likeness. He had arranged to take me to a popular beef and rib restaurant. It was crowded, but a waiter managed to find us a quiet table against the wall. Opposite us sat a real GI Joe, the usual short crew cut: a hulk of a man. He was with his father, whose grey shoulders stooped with age, his belly resting by the edge of the table.

Atamenta was eager to talk about his father, whose name had rarely been mentioned in the failed coup d'etat against Haile Selassie in 1960.

"My father, General Tsige Dibou, was one of the young officers who had accompanied the Emperor home from the Sudan after the defeat of the Italians, and the end of World War II. He was a well-educated man, and had travelled – he'd seen how democracy could work in Europe, and wanted to help bring about change in Ethiopia. He belonged to the Gideon Force and, once the Emperor entered the capital and re-established his rule in 1941, was one of the pioneers sent to stabilise and consolidate the volatile parts of the country. One such post was a desolate, far away place in Negelle Borena in Oromia, southern Ethiopia. Beginning as a Major, my father rose to the rank of Colonel while he was there.

"He cared about his men, and wanted to create a self-sufficient and settled community, so he dug three wells to provide sufficient water for the unit's needs. He also built the Church of St Mary (Kidane Meheret) there. By the late 1950s, he had been appointed Police Commissioner, and reported to the Emperor himself. My father was an honest, no-nonsense man, qualities that the Emperor valued."

As Atamenta leaned towards me, talking proudly about his father, I thought back to my conversation with Mary Asfaw Wossen eleven months earlier. She and her young cousins had been hiding in the cellar beneath their house as events unfolded.

"1960 was a year of significant change: the coup's aim was to improve the economic, social, and political position of the general population. My father's part in the coup d'etat has never been well documented, at least to the extent that he lost his life at the Guenet Leul (Princely Heaven) Palace. The ring-leaders were Mengestu Neway, head of the Honour Guard (the Emperor's bodyguard); his brother Germame Neway, Governor of Jijiga; my father, by then General Dibou, the Police Commissioner, and Colonel Workeneh Gebeyehu, head of National Security. My father and Mengestu were already firm friends: they met again when my father was transferred to Addis Ababa in 1954.

"It was on that fateful day of December 12, 1960, while the Emperor was in Brazil, that the coup was hastily declared because the four had learnt of a possible leak. Mengestu was confident that the army, where my father had risen through the ranks, would support them. But my father had misgivings – the army were generally loyal to the Emperor. His insistence that the army wouldn't support the coup may have damaged his friendship with Mengestu. I think Mengestu's grave miscalculation probably doomed events from the start.

Atamenta's tone became wistful. "The coup was initially successful, as they seized the Crown Prince and more than 20 cabinet ministers and other government leaders and took over the palace. Through Gebeyehu, they had the support of the Imperial Bodyguard. However, as my father suspected, the Army and Air Force remained loyal to the Emperor. On hearing about the coup, the Emperor returned to Asmara, from where he ordered the reprisal. The American ambassador tried to negotiate between both parties, but the Army was closing in. The ambassador left and Mengestu managed to escape. My father, an honourable man, decided to stay, fighting for his life from the Emperor's bedroom, where he was gunned down.

"The army took my father's body, tied it up and dragged it behind a rubbish lorry before laying it out on the Addis – Djibouti railway line, to be decapitated. At home, our house was surrounded by about 200 soldiers, and we were placed under house arrest. I was only three at the time. Etenesh and my older sisters asked to go out to get food and managed to escape. My mother was so upset and distraught at the news of my father's death, that she fainted while escaping. My aunt managed to find us a safe house, where we spent two months in hiding. The Emperor heard how hard it was for us, and he summoned us to the Palace where he pardoned us. Nonetheless, all our property was confiscated, and we were placed under constant surveillance. "

Atamenta went on tell how, as his memories of that fateful day faded, life began to improve. Like so many of my classmates' brothers and friends, Atamenta attended St Joseph's School before coming to the US in 1995. His mother died in Addis Ababa a year later.

In another twist of fate, Atamenta told me that the wells his father had built in 1945 were the scenes of the first rebellions against Haile Selassie in January 1974, as they had become contaminated. This, along with other grievances about their living conditions, caused an uprising in the Fourth Brigade army unit. It became a contributing factor in the eventual downfall of the Emperor later that year. ① Atamenta's tale reinforced for me water's everlasting power: to give life and take it.

The waiter brought our coffee. As I stirred it, thinking about this amazing cast of interconnected characters from the past and present, the crew-cut hulk I'd seen at an adjoining table lumbered over towards me. I shrank back in my seat.

"Can you take a photo of us?" he asked, handing me a digital camera, which looked like a silver card in his large hands. "It's not often I see my father." There was no please, no thank you, just an assumption. He hadn't glanced to the right or left, but I had been one of the few white people sitting close to them. Was that why he'd asked me?

Further information:

Peace Corps: www.peacecorps.gov
Voice of America: www.voanews.com
Arlington National Cemetery: www.arlingtoncemetery.org

① Edmond J Keller, *Revolutionary Ethiopia* p.l73, Indiana University Press, 1988

27 Fit for a queen

Sheets of rain bounced off the tarmac, while strong winds lashed the date palms' fronds, outside the baggage hall windows at Los Angeles airport,

"Hi Silva, I've arrived."

"Welcome to LA, Annette," the familiar low chuckle escaped as she spoke. "I see you've brought the British weather with you! Just take the bus to Van Nuys and then I'll pick you up from there. We're looking forward to seeing you."

The small bus crawled along in the LA rush hour. There were five lanes of cars on one side of us and six going the other way. Headlights cut through the heavy downpour. I chatted with a pleasant couple, Thelma and Dwayne, who'd returned from a holiday visiting relatives in New York. Thelma was a small, neat woman, very beautifully dressed. Dwayne wore a thick, expensive leather jacket and a tweed cap. You could tell life had treated them well.

Hearing my English accent, Thelma told me how she enjoyed their trips to the UK, where their son was in the military at Lakenheath. She asked what I was doing in LA.

"I'm here to meet a former classmate whom I last saw in Addis Ababa, Ethiopia, almost 41 years ago. Silva is Armenian, and I'm interviewing her about her life since then."

"That's funny," she said, sounding puzzled. "Dwayne is half-French, half-Ethiopian."

I grinned. "Well, it seems Ethiopians are just everywhere I go these days!"

Thelma continued chatting, pointing out the new Getty museum on the hillside. There was no glimpse of the sea through the deluge, just an ocean of cars. We passed one sprawling suburb after another before the bus turned into the depot. I was the last to disembark.

A young woman with beautiful dark hair approached shyly: "Are you Annette?" She introduced herself as Aida, Silva's eldest daughter. The bump beneath her coat announced her first pregnancy. She led me to the gold 4x4 where Silva sat in the driver's seat. Initially, I thought she was hunched over, but she was just short, not much taller than she'd been in 1964. Her skin was unlined: just a faint trace of small veins on her cheeks.

We kissed and exchanged greetings, and made our way through the traffic to Northridge, a pleasant suburb to the north of LA. Silva parked outside their spacious house, where she and Jack had lived for 28 years, since they emigrated from Ethiopia to the US.

Jack was at the door to greet us. He shook my hand, and wheeled the heavy case to the bedroom. He stood a good head taller than Silva and although his shoulders were stooped with age, his gait was quick and strong. Deep creases furrowed his forehead and the corners of his eyes, but his calm, quiet manner told me they were more about laughter than anxiety. He had the strong, patrician nose of an eastern European.

"Come, Annette, let's have some coffee," Silva invited. "Make yourself at home please – you can sit here in the kitchen with me, or on the sofa, wherever you prefer."

Everything was immaculate. Two lounges led onto a large kitchen, where the family ate most of their meals. At the back of the house was a patio, pergola and a garden full of tropical plants and trees which bent under the weight of the cold rain. Max, the family's golden labrador, looked mournfully at us from the other side of the patio doors. He was too naughty to be allowed in.

Shortly afterwards, Diana, the middle daughter, returned from work and Taline, the youngest, from college. Then Naji, Aida's husband, arrived. He and Aida ran a candle making business that, by all accounts, was doing well. We sat companionably around the kitchen table as Silva served up generous portions of spaghetti bolognaise, with lots of salad and bread. Only Jack and I had some wine, the rest drank water or juice. It was family time, and for Armenians everywhere, cooking and serving good food was all-important, as that is how bonds of love are formed and developed.

Like me, Silva had grown wider with age, and I noticed she walked with a limp, the result of hip problems. But her hair was still her crowning glory, thick and lustrous, and the girls had all inherited it. Working as a realtor meant that she could work from home most of the time, but I noticed her mobile was rarely switched off. Many of her busy customers could only chase up news of properties or visits after work.

Glancing around the kitchen, I noticed that Silva had pinned the old black and white photo of grade 6A, taken in November 1963, on the large silver fridge. It was far more pristine than the one I'd kept, along with other mementoes, after we'd left Ethiopia. Silva's daughters had been laughing at the fashions, and we agreed that young women today have far more choice and flattering styles than back in the 60s. Our hairstyles caused the most hilarity, all that backcombing to create the beehives so popular at the time.

After dinner, the girls went their separate ways, while Jack, Silva and I had fresh coffee. "We've been looking for some photos for you, for your book," Silva announced. "Jack, where have you put them?"

Jack disappeared into their bedroom to collect several large envelopes and when he returned, they tipped each one out in turn, deciding which was suitable. They bickered about which ones to show me, like couples who'd spent a lifetime together. Jack stood behind Silva as she peered at each one before handing them to me.

"I'd like one of you receiving your school diploma from the Emperor, Silva, if you have it?"

"Sure, here it is." The 18-year-old Silva bowed in her mini dress, wearing a pair of smart white patent shoes with silver buckles. The small Emperor perched on his large throne, with a regal air, handing out the diploma, his favourite chihuahua by his feet. There weren't many countries where you could receive a diploma from an Emperor.

Silva receiving her graduation diploma from Emperor Haile Selassie

"Will this do for your book?" Jack said quizzically, handing me a small, hand coloured photo of a beautiful crown.

"This is magnificent, Jack, how did you come to have it?"

Tears began to glisten in his eyes "This is a crown that Emperor Haile Selassie gave to your Queen, Queen Elizabeth, some time in the 50's. My father, Avak, was his crown jeweller and he made it for him. Sadly, a year after he'd created it, he died from the precious metals he used in his craft."

"I'm so sorry, Jack. How old was he?"

"Just 45. He left behind my mother, my sister Aschen and I," he replied. I wanted to find out more about this skilled jeweller: "So young – and how had he come to be living in Ethiopia?"

The crown which Avak Hagopian created for Queen Elizabeth II in 1954

Jack pulled up a chair and sat down to explain: "My father, Avak, was one of the many hundreds of thousands of Armenian children orphaned in the genocide in 1915 by the Ottoman Turks. He'd been born in Van, the capital of Van Province. His mother and father were killed, along with his younger sister, Aschen. Only he and my uncle, Yervant, survived, they were just four and six years old. They joined other refugees, and somehow made it through the Syrian desert to old Jerusalem, where they were cared for by other Armenians.

As I listened to him, I wanted to weep in pity for Aschen and Avak's parents and for Avak, who had survived that desert crossing, only to die 40 years later. Yet, it was extraordinary – Avak was my third link to Jerusalem, in just five months. I vowed, then and there, to find out where he'd been looked after in the old city.

Jack stared intently at me: "Tell me, Annette, did you hear about the 40 orphans?"

"Yes, Jack mentioned something about it – Haile Selassie had adopted them."

"Well," he smiled ruefully, "Avak was the youngest to be adopted. Selassie, or Ras (Prince) Tafari as he was then known, wanted to create an imperial court band. During a visit to Jerusalem, he heard the Armenian brass band playing at the Armenian Orthodox Cathedral. And now, well, you know the rest."

Gazing at the hand-coloured photo of the magnificent crown that Avak had created for one divine ruler to give another, blood roared in my ears and the now familiar shockwaves of intuition sped through my body. The walls of the comfortable Los Angeles kitchen seemed to disappear as I looked in tears at him and Silva.

Breaking the spell, Jack added: "So, will you be able to use it?"

"Of course I will, Jack. It would be an honour to do that for your father's memory."

We looked at more photos of the house in Addis Ababa where they'd lived after their marriage, and I told Silva news of Jack, her second cousin in Buckingham. It had been a momentous evening and I needed to sleep on the facts. Tomorrow, I would hear more about Silva's time in Ethiopia and life in LA.

*****

Rain continued to batter the windows: it hadn't let up all night. The papers and TV news stations were full of the unseasonal California floods and the damage – closed valley roads, and houses sliding down hills, walls cracking whilst the foundations became water logged with sand and mud.

The watery light eased through the blinds, doors opened and closed and showers turned on and off. By 8 am, the house was quiet, all the family had gone to work or college. Silva knocked on the door and asked if I was ready for some breakfast. Toasted wholemeal muffins were the order of the day, with more fresh coffee and juice.

"Later today, after you've asked me the questions you have, I'll take you over to meet Seta, my sister, and Arakel, my brother. We can have some lunch and then, if you like, I can take you to the mall if you want to do some shopping?" Silva was a very good host, nothing was too much trouble.

"There's nothing I need, Silva, but I'd like to get a couple of CDs and T-shirts for James, if there are any punk shops around."
"Sure," she demurred, "I'll ask the girls, they'll know where to go."

Silva settled herself down on the low couch in the lounge. The table lamp relieved the gloom of the wet day, and its soft glow glimmered on her hair. Her voice grew pensive and quiet. "Like Jack, my parents were orphans of the genocide. My father, Yervant, had had to walk through the Syrian desert as a seven-year old boy. The men were rounded up and shot: many women were raped, and sometimes all their clothes were taken – this, of course, in front of the young children. The elderly and children were killed by dehydration and starvation. It was truly horrific." She sighed and smoothed down the sleeve of her cardigan.

"My father was lucky, you know, as a kindly Turk saved his life by hiding him on his farm for a while. He ended up in Beirut, Lebanon, and was adopted by a Lebanese couple, where he completed his education. He heard that there were opportunities in Ethiopia for hard-working Armenians and went to Addis when he was 21. There he met my mother, Vartouhi, which means Rose in English. She was another orphan and had been sent to live with an uncle in Addis Ababa.

"How many sisters and brother did you have?"

"I'm the youngest of five, two boys and three girls. My sister Seta is married to another jeweller, Mardig Pogharian, who worked for the Crown Prince – Mary Asfaw Wossen's father, of course!" Silva looked at me, smiling: "I even think he made some gifts for the Crown Prince to present to your Queen. The Crown Princess is godmother to Seta's eldest daughter, Silva. In fact, she visited here last year. I think Seta has some photos."

I recalled the meeting with Crown Princess in Addis in that rather bare sitting room in Mary's house. It had been just a brief conversation, but the confident regal air was still there - she seemed very polite and well educated. Mary had mentioned that her sister Sihin – the princess I used to sit beside - lived in LA. I wondered where she was and whether she was connected to Silva and Seta somehow.

Seta's daughter, Silva, (left) with her godmother, Crown Princess Medfrish Worq, and daughters. The Crown Princess is Mary Asfaw Wossen's mother

"You know, my parents were so strict, I wasn't allowed to attend any parties, I could only go out with the family," Silva continued. "But I was close to my dad and they were good parents. Mum had learnt how to cook Ethiopian food and we had a mix of Ethiopian and Armenian meals at home. Every other Sunday, we went to the Armenian Orthodox Church, Soorp Kevork, where I sang in the choir. We had a weekend house in Beshoftu, south of Addis, and my dad would barbecue most weekends, putting a whole lamb on the rotisserie.

"Christmas was celebrated on 7 January. We'd have a Christmas tree at home and go to the church service, before coming back for a traditional turkey meal followed by baklava. Gifts would be exchanged on New Year's Eve."

If Silva's parents were so strict, it must have been difficult dating young men. "Silva, how were you able to meet Jack, if you couldn't go to parties?" I probed.

"He and I were neighbours," she responded quietly. "We fell in love after he'd returned from studying electrical engineering at UCLA in California. When we dated, I had to be chaperoned. At that time, I had just graduated from Nazareth School and had begun studying Biology at Haile Selassie University, which I graduated from in 1971. We married later that year and enjoyed a month-long honeymoon in Mombasa. For the first time I was free!" Silva stretched and threw back her head, chuckling in the way I remembered from school.

"Aida was born in August 1972. It was a difficult birth, because I was attended by an inexperienced Bulgarian doctor. It's only thanks to my mother's intervention and finding a much more qualified Armenian-American doctor, that I didn't die.

"What made you decide to leave Ethiopia, the country where you'd both been born and brought up?"

"Jack and I noticed that the situation was becoming more tense in Addis: there were lots of street demonstrations, and people who had always been friendly towards us began to ignore us. On one occasion, the car was badly stoned, leaving dents in the bodywork. The rich and middle class were being targeted.

"After the killing of 40 generals in January 1973 by the Army, we decided it was time to leave Ethiopia for good. Jack had been offered residency in Canada, Australia and the US – we chose the latter as my brother was here in LA. We were lucky, we were able to sell our furniture: this was before many foreigners and middle class left in the mid 1970s. But we had to leave the house behind. All we took with us was some cash, our clothes and Jack's qualifications.

"Diana and Taline were born in the US, and all the girls attended the Armenian high school – one of three in LA. Over 100,000 Armenians have settled in the city today, the largest group in America. The girls have done well: Diana and Aida both have degrees. Aida went to live in Lebanon for five years with Naji after they married, but it's good to have her back home with us.

"The only problem we've had here is the earthquakes – the one in '90 was terrible, it was 6.3 on the Richter scale. All the neighbours went onto the streets in their nightwear, we were terrified the houses were going to fall down. I was so worried for us all that, after that night, I insisted we took the bed mattresses and slept in the lounge together every night for three months." Silva's head shook in horror as she recounted the events.

The phone beside her rang. "Hi, Seta, yes, we're just about to leave now, we'll see you in a few minutes."

During the drive to Canoga Park where Seta lived, Silva described her hopes for her daughters' futures. "I want them to have good lives and meet the right men – happiness, I guess. But health is the most important of all. Jack and I are doing our best to pass on our Armenian culture to the girls, which we hope they pass on to their children. We must keep the Armenian flame burning in their hearts, after all our people have been through."

By now we'd arrived at our destination. The road and others surrounding it were full of orange trees, reminders of the groves that once grew here. Seta and Mardig Pogharian's ranch-style house was cosy, and we sat in the kitchen chatting. Arakel, Silva's brother, reminisced about Ethiopia and fishing and how he missed game hunting in the bush. He had been a real ladies' man, and had only settled down in late middle age. He and his wife now have a 16-year-old daughter.

As Silva had mentioned earlier, Mardig confirmed that he had made some pieces for the Crown Prince to give to Queen Elizabeth II. He showed me a photo of one of them, a beautiful silver replica of St George's trapezium church, in Lalibela.

This was the church I'd stood beside, talking to Alan about Ethiopia's image in the west – where Josef had come across and introduced himself. It had been a very special moment, as this was too. It was as if I was living in a dream – a dream that I could never have imagined, but it was all being played out for real on this earth.

Mardig and the replica of St. George's Church

Magnificent, and so moving and humbling. It was all I could do to hold back my tears – all these caring guides, including my classmates and the Armenians: now so special to me, like real angels on earth.

Lunch was a mixture of shuro, a mild vegetable watt, wrapped in injera, like a lasagne. It was delicious. Ethiopia was still present in conversation and on the lunch menu. The four of them had travelled halfway round the world to be where they were, living quietly in a democratic society so that they and their future generations would never again have to experience genocide, the loss of family and their homes. Culture, an incredible spirit and good education were the things that had ensured the survival of the Armenians.

Silva, second left with Arakel, her brother, left and Mardig and Seta Pogharian

The next two days passed in a whirlwind – a trip down to Malibu to see the wonderful beaches, driving along canyon roads cut deep into the hills of LA, and enjoying fresh seafood in a picnic area overlooking the sea, while the wind hissed and slashed at the plastic tarpaulin. We had a respite from the rain, and in the sunshine I appreciated just why people chose to live here. There was space wherever you looked, the light had a luminous quality and, by the ocean, the air was exhilarating. The sea swept in and out from the shoreline like a giant lung. Far from the suburbs, nature reigned.

Hollywood was disappointing - preparations were in place for the Oscars, but apart from the Kodak Theatre it looked grubby and rundown. We went out for a meal at an Ethiopian restaurant in a part of LA now called 'Little Ethiopia.' Jack and Silva slipped back into the Amharic of their youth, chatting amiably with the waitress. Taline, her boyfriend Pablo and his brother joined us. Ethiopians arrived for a small child's birthday party. Now only the older women wore the shamas and netallahs of home: the others were dressed in the latest western fashions, although Ethiopian jewellery seemed popular. The music was all modern Amharic pop - wailing voices, organ, drum and flute accompanying the singer. We mix and match culture according to our moods and needs these days.

I chatted with some of Taline's friends, immigrants from many different countries. They all worked hard. Living in LA meant joining the motorway at 6am in order to beat the rush, so one young man of 24 spent half of his weekend sleeping to catch up. I was amazed that with all that technology, there wasn't some way he could work from home two days a week, so he'd have more energy and help save the planet through less petrol consumption. As he'd remarked, when he saw a tramp swaying across a street in front of us, "Hollyweird, man."

*****

The rain had returned on Monday morning: it was time to leave. Silva and I were deep in thought on the journey to Van Nuys. I was thinking about everything I'd learned and experienced. Silva's parting gift had been a copy of an Ethiopian magazine, printed in 1966, which had included details of high achieving students. There were photos of her, Azeb, Hiruth and Celina. Celina had been joint first in English in the eighth grade, along with Azeb; Silva first in Science and Hiruth first in all exams in the eighth grade. It was also a souvenir to pass on to Azeb when I met her in New York that evening.

Silva parked the car and came in with me to the bus station. We stood awkwardly, not really knowing what to say. Friends from so along ago, and already saying goodbye again after such a short time. We hugged and I and noticed tears in her eyes. I promised her that I would do the best I could to honour Avak's memory.

Silva and Jack Hagopian

28 The peace cranes flutter

Fresh snow lay piled up on the pavements, and cabs slithered along in the wet at JFK airport in New York. It was 40 degrees colder than LA. Warm breath frosted the air as the taxi queue shuffled up one by one. Beside us, a man walked up and down shouting, "Anyone want a cab for the Bronx? Anyone for Queens?" I'd been warned by Azeb to only use yellow cabs. She'd also told me that I'd have to pay a toll for crossing the Triborough Bridge. I had memorised her address and the instructions for the last half mile or so.

Traffic was thinning as we drove into Manhattan. Lights from the skyscrapers beamed into the evening sky, like rows of gold nuggets sparkling on dark velvet, as the Hudson glided silently out to the Atlantic Ocean beneath us. There were few boats to be seen. We turned down Madison Avenue and eventually to 129th Street, full of brownstone houses, some of which were immaculate and others boarded up, the last of the tenants gone forever. This part of south Harlem had been gentrified in the past five years.

When the taxi stopped slowly on the sleet-covered road by a well-kept house, a tall, slender young man stepped out of the shadows and said, "Hi, let me help you with your bags." I recoiled, a bit bewildered at first, having heard all sorts of stories about New York. He must have read my thoughts and, extending his hand apologetically, said, "I'm Jonathan, Azeb's nephew."

He gamely took the heavy suitcase up the ten steps to the front door, from which yellow light illuminated the thick snow that blanketed everything. Looking up, I could see Azeb standing in the doorway. Although her hairstyle was very different, time had treated her kindly, like Silva. "Annette, hi, how good to see you at long last! How was your flight? Here, come on in, let's get out of the cold."

We stepped into a stylish New York Ethiopian home. At the windows, Azeb had used thick, striped cotton material from Addis. The light shades were decorated with similar naïve images to Saba's house in Washington and Ethiopian fabric decorated the cushions that brightened up the two black leather couches. Wooden Lalibela crosses adorned the wall at the foot of the stairs. The polished dark mahogany floor led the way into a large kitchen diner, at the back of the house.

She introduced me to her niece, Serki. The three of us sat in the brightly lit kitchen, chatting about old times and family. It was late and there was a lot of history to explore with one another, but that was for tomorrow. I also wanted to hear how much she could remember about Hiruth. The plan was to accompany her to work the following day. I was really looking forward to meeting Marcia Brewster from the Division for Economic and Social Affairs, and planning my sightseeing, although in my heart there was just one place I wanted to visit: Ground Zero.

*****

The alarm shattered the silence. The heating was on, but even so the room felt cold. I put on my thick dressing gown, walking sleepily to the bedroom window and looked out onto snowdrifts in the back garden – I'd have to wrap up warm. I cursed myself for not bringing boots, but there'd been no room in the case. After dressing, I went upstairs to have coffee with Azeb. There was just time for a slice of toast and juice before we had to grab our things, and head out for the subway.

In the daylight, I could take a proper look at the neighbourhood. A man walked his dog on the other side of the street - all three of us were wrapped up against the icy cold. The cars were mostly second-hand – people around here must invest their money in property or just rely on public transport. We turned right onto Madison Avenue: buildings had sprung up in the last century or so and were mostly low rise, as the Americans would say. One householder swept the pavement outside his house. I caught his eye and said good morning, and he cheerily replied with the same greeting.

Walking along 125th street to the subway, every fifth building was a fast food place of some description. Chicken was really popular and prices were very low, so for some families there was no point cooking, I guessed. The city was already alive: people either heading off for work, selling newspapers or snacks or trying to do some kind of deal with their neighbours. An irate pedestrian banged on a car roof when the driver had jumped an amber light. Looking around, mine was the only white face among 100 or so people. I didn't feel uncomfortable though – perhaps from the years in Africa and the 18 months when Rob and I had lived in Brixton, south London: another melting pot.

The accents were a melody of Africa, the Caribbean and native New Yorkers. There were a few drunks, or people high on drugs, shouting good-naturedly even at that time of the morning. I wondered if they could make out our faces: were we just a blur they called to? Everyone ignored them. I recognised Ethiopian cheekbones and saw every hue of brown skin, from pale latte to the inky blue black of west African, the colour which always glowed, no matter how pale the light.

Reaching the station, Azeb pointed to signs and told me to always head downtown when going to central Manhattan or uptown when heading back home. We trotted quickly down two flights of steps and took the first train that arrived. Like London, no one spoke to each other on the trains: passengers either read, stared into space or listened to their iPods.

We left the subway at Grand Central Station, a childhood dream of mine since I'd read the book: 'By Grand Central station, I sat down and wept', heading for the United Nations (UN) Plaza. I felt really privileged to be visiting the UN headquarters. I'd come so far on this journey, never dreaming that three of my classmates would be working for the UN – two in the field and Azeb at the HQ. And Evelyn, too, Fanaye's good friend, had worked here at the start of her career.

Security at the UNDP building was a lot more relaxed than in Washington, something I experienced in most of New York. After signing me in, we took the lift to the 24th floor where Azeb worked in the Africa section. Here they used dolls, tapestries, carvings and posters to symbolise the countries they represented. Azeb pointed to a huge silk scarf pinned to the panel by her desk – an exact replica of the mosaic in the African Union HQ in Addis Ababa that had been opened in 1963.

I was able to use an office to collect my thoughts for the meeting with Marcia Brewster, the woman who'd given me Azeb's details two months previously. Opposite was the UN HQ, dominating the north bank of the East River, with the

Azeb in the United Nations Development Programme offices

Roosevelt Island in the middle of its pale brown waters. Flags lined the UN concourse, representing its members. I thought of the historic speeches made here, all the resolutions, the politics and infighting, the effort to get your country's voice heard. The UN's reputation was faltering, with the investigations into the oil for food programme. And only two weeks before, UN soldiers had been accused of raping women in the Congo – refugees they were supposed to be guarding. Where in the world was safety, if we couldn't even trust representatives of the UN? But I marshalled my thoughts – I was here to hear about water.

Marcia's office was full of books, papers, photographs and touching little children's drawings. She had a firm handshake, and her eyes conveyed a sharp intelligence, borne of her many years at the UN. Like Leikun, her office was stacked full of files. "Hello Marcia, I just wanted to say a big thank you for giving me Azeb's email address last year."

"It was a pleasure," she responded. "Are you having a good time catching up?"

"Yes, but I only got here last night, so over the next few days, we should know a bit more about each other."

"That's good, glad I could help." Her responses were brief, our time together limited.

"Marcia, I'm interested to know what the UN's doing in the area of water management." I hurried on: "I realise you have a big co-ordination role across the world. How does your work link to the UN's Millennium Development Goals?"

"It links to MDG 7 – to ensure environmental sustainability. Our target is to halve the proportion of people who don't have sustainable access to safe drinking water and sanitation by 2015. We also want to link this to Goal 3 on gender equality and women's empowerment. One leads to the other." I recalled the Oromo women of my childhood collecting water from Lake Langano, and the women and children walking for miles whom I'd seen with Berhanu and Tirlaye last year.

"How big is the problem?" I back-tracked, that sounded trite. "I mean, how many lack safe drinking water?"

"1.1 billion. Even more – 2.6 billion – don't have access to sanitation. By that, I mean they don't have a sanitary way to dispose of faeces, not even pit latrines."

The ones I'd used in rural Ethiopia were simple holes dug in the ground, with some kind of step where you could squat, with a structure built over it, for privacy. There was no flushing water, just a large oil can outside filled with water, and if you were polite, you slopped out after yourself. Many didn't bother. But still, at least there was a hole away from dwellings, and it was private. So, almost half of the world doesn't even have that basic facility – that was shocking.

"How does the UN work with non-governmental organisations and governments to improve things?"

"In all, there are 23 United Nations agencies involved in improving water resource management, and access to water and sanitation. Our role is to monitor the situation and provide a range of educational materials and publicity, and host conferences and workshops where people can share best practice. Next month, we're launching the International 'Water for Life' Decade.'

"You know," she added, "although sub-Saharan Africa is one of the worst areas, Ethiopia has the Nile, but only uses ten per cent of the water available from it." She looked at her watch. "Sorry, I've a meeting to prepare for. It was good to meet up, I'm glad I could help you find Azeb. If you know of any senior women involved in water management whom I could invite to join my network, please let me know."

*****

Hurrying to the lift, I decided it was time for a coffee. A small poster by the up/down button caught my eye. On it was the smiling face of Deepak Chopra, the Indian spiritual guru and author. The poster read, 'Book signing today of Deepak Chopra's latest book "Peace is the Way" at 2pm at the UN bookshop.' I decided to buy a copy and ask the great man to sign it.

There was an expectant air in the UN bookshop. People were going over to the till to buy their books, and then joining the line that snaked a third of the way around the store. A cameraman was there, and a small table and chair had been set up by the door. Deepak arrived without any ceremony, sporting glasses with multicoloured frames, probably designer. He sat there, quietly smiling at people, signing and then posing for photos. The cameraman captured everything – he must be part of Deepak's entourage. Another woman opened the book at the required page, before his pen touched it. Every thing had been thought of: it must be nice being a famous author!

In front of me, a UN employee titillated a Chinese woman he was plainly trying to impress, with details of the latest meetings and gossip about the rape scandals in the Congo. It was clear that lots of management time was being devoted to it. I wondered how much energy had been invested in advance, in ensuring that soldiers who wore the blue beret represented everything the UN stood for, especially security and safety. Particularly when ordinary people had endured great devastation, whether through natural or man-made disasters.

After the UN man had told Deepak how many times he'd met him, it was my turn. I blurted out, "I'm writing a book to help fund a Garden of Peace in Jerusalem. It will be published next year." "Ah," he leaned back, pushing his glasses back up his nose. There was the slightest pause, and flicker of his eyebrows. "That's a very good idea," he continued in a professional manner, composure restored. He wrote 'Good luck with your book on peace' and signed it with a flourish.

Later that afternoon, I joined a UN tour, and visited the three main chambers and saw some of the wonderful works of art that different countries had donated to the UN. I was so proud to see that Norway had donated all the furnishings for the Security Council chamber, the 'emergency room' of the United Nations, whose role is to maintain peace and security between nations. Sweden and Denmark had provided funding for two other chambers, the Economic and Social Council and the Trusteeship Council respectively.

It had been a busy and tiring day, as I made my way back to the UNDP reception in time to meet Azeb for the journey home. It was 5pm, and she had been at her desk since 7.30am, a long enough day. At home, after taking off our coats and shoes, we'd watched the news on *BBC America,* a habit of Azeb's, to find out more about what was happening in the world.

*****

After a meal, we sat around the coffee table with a bottle of wine. Azeb was a shy woman: she appeared a little uncertain, unsure where to begin. She curled her legs beneath her as her low voice began, "Hiruth was my best friend. She loved reading so much, she used to get very upset when a book came to an end. Do you know her aunt was the first Ethiopian woman to fly an airplane?"

She continued: "At school I was also friendly with Salome Yilma, whose father was the Finance Minister. The first time I ever went to a party was at her house – my father was so strict! Her family were more cosmopolitan and travelled a great deal." In the old school photo, I could see Salome, cheeky as ever, standing beside Azeb peering at the camera over Celina's shoulders. Salome had been a very confident young woman, and always immaculately dressed. Azeb explained to me that Salome, along with Tsion Gad, another classmate, had spoken English at home, not Amharic. They were very westernised.

Azeb was one of five daughters born to Fesseha and Shetaye in Addis Ababa, and the second youngest. Her father, who was fluent in Italian, French, English and Amharic, had been a liaison officer between the government and Impresit, an Italian construction company. Impresit had built the Koka Dam, the large hydroelectric dam south of Addis Ababa that provided much of the city's water resources. Beside the dam was the hotel where Roy, Eric and I had watched the chef running down the hillside, cleaver in hand, whilst the dead chicken jerked crazily in its death throes. Later that afternoon, we'd swum in the pool overlooking the great expanse of water.

"Necessities were important in our family: I don't particularly remember special festivities, but we were encouraged to work hard at school to get a good education. That would give us choices in later life. I attended Nazareth School from grade one to grade twelve, and I was best friends with Hiruth until she left for Bulgaria. We were together every break and every lunchtime. She was quiet but generally happy and I never noticed any traces of depression. When she won the award for top student in the eighth grade, our friendship sadly came to an end, as she went to Sofia to study Fine Art. She was such a brilliant kid, I still miss her a lot," Azeb sighed wistfully.

After graduating in 1969, Azeb joined her older sister Worke at Kianda College in Nairobi to do secretarial studies for two years. Azeb's parents had agreed to her leaving home, provided that the college was suitable for young African women. Kianda College was established by Opus Dei (Work of God) in 1961 to provide education to women in Kenya. Worke and Azeb remained on the campus most weekends and were joined by Kukusha, their youngest sister, a year later. After finishing her studies, Azeb taught there for a year, before returning to Addis to work for an oil drilling company.

"Finally, I had freedom! Now I'd finished my studies and was working, I could meet young men and go to restaurants and clubs. The developing political situation didn't much interest me, although I can still recall when the 60 bureaucrats and members of the Royal Family were executed in November 1974. My husband to be, Tessema, and I had been out that Saturday night. We'd stayed over at the Ras Hotel. On our way home the following morning, everyone looked very subdued and whispered to one another. Events escalated from there. There were many demonstrations against Selassie and one of the groups had the slogan 'Land to the Peasant.' There were many different factions, and thousands of people were killed. One of my cousins found her two daughters dead beneath a bridge. Through his spies, Mengistu learnt who the opposing ringleaders were, and had them killed."

Tessema and Azeb married in 1974, at the Ethiopian Catholic Church in Addis. The wedding was followed by a cocktail party. Their first daughter Yemeserach, which means 'good news ', was born in 1979, followed by Eskedar, 'boundless', another girl, in 1984.

"The situation was worsening, and I was very concerned for my family's safety. There were food shortages and people dying from the famine up north, and the frequent shoot-outs between rival political parties. I remember teenagers shooting indiscriminately from Peugeot 404s. I was determined to get a job with the United Nations, and in September 1985, I left the family behind to fly to New York. Little Eskedar was only a few months old then. Tessema encouraged me - he had been educated in the US and taken his first degree there. I was offered a job after six months. It was so hard being on my own, I used to cry every day. I really missed the children," she continued, mournfully.

"When they arrived at JFK airport in April 1986, I dropped to the floor and kissed it. People must have thought I was mad – I was so happy to see my family again! Unfortunately, Tessema was unable to find work here, so he couldn't renew his visa and he had to return to Addis. Essentially, I've brought up the children on my own, although we see each other once a year, and he calls our daughters regularly. He often goes to visit my mother and his family in Addis, to ensure they are OK. Today, he runs an advertising and promotions company in Ethiopia. The girls have grown up, Yemeserach is working while Eskedar continues her studies. I speak to them every day – I'm so proud of them."

At that moment the phone rang. Azeb switched between English and Amharic effortlessly. It was Yemeserach making her daily phone call. When they had finished, Azeb paused for a moment. Her eyes lit up: "Wait a moment. You know, I've got an old photograph album that Hiruth sent me from Sofia. Let's see if I can find it," she said, getting up from the couch.

Azeb returned with a small, pale beige leather album. Black and white photos were stuck to the black card, with sheaves of transparent paper between each page. Hiruth had written a special message inside. She pointed out photos of former classmates, including one of 16-year-old Hiruth, already such a beauty, and her cousin Tsehai, another striking young woman. Azeb told me that she had met up with Ghennet and Manna, Hiruth's sisters, at a Nazareth School reunion in Washington DC in 2002.

"Ah ha," she exclaimed, pulling out another old photo. "Look what I have for you – see, this is St. Josemaria Escriva who founded Opus Dei. The head teacher gave

St. Josemaria Escriva
founder of Opus Dei

me this when I was studying at Kianda College." I stared at the image of the kindly man with glasses and Roman Catholic robes as a question flashed into my mind – how were they dealing with all the rucus caused by the 'Da Vinci Code'?

The wind was still bitterly cold the following morning. I allowed myself a lie-in, stretching out under the Ethiopian blankets and covers – they were warm and heavy, meant for the Ethiopian highlands. I turned to the black and white photos that Azeb had given me, scattered on the bedside table. I stared at Hiruth's image: she'd died no more than 100 miles from here in Albany, New York. Yesterday evening, just before we went to bed, Azeb had promised that Salome, she and I could meet up before I left New York.

Today my main aim was to visit Ground Zero, where my intuition told me I would find a link to peace – with something representing a rainbow. I was unsure how the place where almost 3,000 people had died would inspire me, but I believe rainbows represent peace, as well as God's covenant to Moses that the earth would never experience a great flood again. The peace after the storm, the reminder of our multicoloured world, the refraction of light through liquid and the prism of sunlight.

I approached the site from the bottom of West Street, walking alongside Battery Park City. Very few pedestrians were about, and I stood looking at the place where two great towers had stood, protecting the waterfront and proclaiming the might of American commerce and architectural ingenuity to the world. Ken, my former RAC boss, had celebrated his wedding anniversary here in 2001, with dinner and drinks in the restaurant at the top of the Tower.

Now it was a desolate sight, just a ramp leading down to the very core of Ground

Zero. Although the competition to design a replacement had been won by Daniel Libeskind, it looked like work was a long way from starting. The only way I could look onto it was from a walkway surrounded by strong metal railings, wire fencing and barbed wire. It felt like standing behind bars, looking out at a shattered, barren moonscape. America was no longer free. There was such an atmosphere of despair, that I needed to go somewhere to reflect. A small church stood a few yards away. I walked past the graveyard at the rear and round the corner, to the entrance of St Paul's Chapel.

I felt drawn to go in and pray – I was dumbstruck that it hadn't been damaged by the World Trade Centre attacks. Outside was an exhibition telling the story of the little chapel, and its role in providing shelter for all the emergency services who'd sifted through rubble after 9/11, to clear the site twelve hours a day for eight tumultuous, heart-rending months. Built in 1766, St Paul's was very similar to some London churches. I noticed that it was twinned with St Mary le Bow, a small church in Cheapside, in the city of London, almost opposite where I'd worked in the early 1990s.

Inside was an indescribable feeling of peace. Visitors stood by display stands, tears trembling down their cheeks: others sat in the 200-year-old pews and prayed. There were cards, bits of paper, poems and photos of those who'd perished, along with deeply moving personal messages from family members, and well wishers who'd come here to make sense of it all.

As I turned to my right, I saw what my heart had been searching for – a glorious, flamboyant rainbow coloured display. My heart leapt in joy, and I strode quickly towards the different hued streamers which tumbled over a panel. They turned out to be Japanese origami peace cranes, from the cities of Hiroshima and Nagasaki, which had been bombed on 6th and 8th August 1945. The Japanese children had sent a gift of peace to young Americans who had suffered the same life-shattering, instantaneous death from the skies.

I prayed, my heart full of wonder and compassion for all those who'd suffered so needlessly: for the families of the deceased, and those who'd survived 9/11. But most of all, I prayed for the light of love to come into the hearts of all terrorists and would-be terrorists. Violence never works – it's like a tornado whirling around the world, you never know where it will spring up next. There's no warning, just enormous damage and the immediate desire for revenge – like war. We continue our dreams and prayers for peace, yet this odyssey had shown me that we have never

The rainbow peace cranes light up a corner at Saint Paul's Chapel

learned the lessons of history. We seem to find it almost impossible to take the next step – a smile for a stranger, a coffee with someone who's just moved into our town.

Sixty years after World War II, I felt it was time for everlasting peace to be imprinted in all our hearts, words and actions. Before I left, I bought a key ring with a replica of the cross which they'd found at the bottom of Ground Zero, a symbol of hope, just like that of the twisted metal cross at Coventry Cathedral in 1940, after the German bombing raids.

In St. Paul's churchyard, the sycamore tree - which had saved the little chapel from being destroyed by debris from the World Trade Centre attacks - had been removed and a Norwegian spruce planted in its place. Today, there are plans for a sculpture of its roots to be displayed in the churchyard, to remind visitors of the tree that saved St Paul's.

Later on, I wandered down Broadway and into a ceramics gift store and asked Jack, the manager, a lively Jewish man, what it had been like working there on 9/11. "It was just a really crazy time for about a month," he told me. "We were closed all that time, there was so much debris." We spoke about peace, and I mentioned my visit to Jerusalem later in 2005. I told him about my plans to find two important places – the area in Kastina where my father had served, and the monastery in Jerusalem where little Avak Hagopian had been cared for.

Jack was a regular visitor to Israel, and told me about the Ethiopian soldiers serving in the army, and how beautiful he found the Ethiopian women. I bought a small figure of a Kenyan boy tending a lamb. It reminded me so much of Jesus's command to his disciple, Peter, to "feed my sheep."

*****

"Time for some wine! Let's see now, I think we have some more of the Chilean merlot." Azeb reached into the cupboard by the stairs. We were celebrating my last evening in New York, and a fortnight that had really changed my life: the clear and subtle links to peace, Jerusalem, and to water. The hospitality from kind guides – classmates and their relatives – had been overwhelming. In my joy, I also felt very humble – so grateful for their care and belief in my dream.

The evening ended later than usual and tomorrow was my last day in New York. I felt very reflective as I fell asleep and another message came to me in a dream. I was speaking to a lot of people in a large room and prayed that their hearts became open to the 'other' – the stranger in our midst. Whether homeless, hungry, old, refugee, another nationality, heterosexual, homosexual, religious or atheist. Then, the only sound to be heard was that of concrete smashing onto earth, as one by one, each person's heart broke free from their old thinking.

I was hoping to meet Salome, another classmate and Azeb's friend, tomorrow. The meeting would be confirmed in the morning. This meant I would be missing an important sermon at St Paul's Chapel, by a man of peace, Archbishop Desmond Tutu. But like honouring my dreams, promises were promises, and I always kept mine.

Further information:

Tours of the UN headquarters:
http://www.un.org/pubs/cyberschoolbus/untour/index.html
UN Development Programme: www.undp.org
UN Millennium Project – the project to ensure that the Millennium
Development Goals are reached: www.unmillenniumproject.org/reports
St. Paul's Chapel, New York: www.trinitywallstreet.org
St. Mary le Bow Church, London: www.stmarylebow.co.uk

VI: CONCLUSION

29 The Concept of Enough

In the early stages of my journey, I relentlessly asked my heart: 'Tell me, what do I stand for?' I kept forgetting my covenant with God, and needed reminding until the words I'd uttered in the darkness in May 1995 were written into my DNA. That way, every breath, every word and action would synchronise with who I really was.

My heart replied on 12th April 2003, the same day that I saw the face of Jesus on the garden fence, with a manifesto for my life: the "Concept of Enough." At 5am, I hurried to the PC to let the inspiration pour out onto the keyboard. In the way that creativity always begins, it was written when my views on this book's subject matter were still half formed:

"I started writing *The Little Book of Culture* at the beginning of the Iraqi war. Tensions had been escalating during the past three years across the globe – Rwanda, the Congo, Iraq, Zimbabwe, and Sudan as people from different tribes, class structures and religions fought each other for the earth's resources. Whether it was land, oil, gold, water, opium or diamonds.

Wherever I looked, I saw that each army had support from other groups outside the conflict – whether neighbouring countries: religious groups or the US, Europe, Middle East, or Far East. Often these links came about through businesses, as their sales territories and operations moved from local to regional to global. Companies paid highly for good investor relations companies to lobby politicians to bend the rules, in favour of more trade and more money. And of course, someone's misery was another's opportunity!

So, at a time when Microsoft earned $1 billion a day, and I drove past houses with four cars outside on the drive in an ordinary neighbourhood, Enron's directors had stolen $billions from their employees, customers, and shareholders, our wealth in the West still wasn't enough. I visited shopping centres and saw shoppers laden down with bags, whilst outside a beggar sat on dirty blanket with a small paper coffee cup in front of him. Most ignored him: occasionally a young man would stop and put a few coins in, whilst shy children would give him some of their pocket money, as their fathers looked on, embarrassed. More often, a lady, frequently middle aged, would give him a little more.

Wherever I went it was the same – in Europe, the US and South Africa. Is it the same in your country? We are all embarrassed by this, I for secretly watching; the beggars for being reduced to living off the kindness of strangers and the donors, secretly fearing others would laugh at them as they put money in the cup.

I had been reading a great deal, and using my experience of working in corporate communications roles in big companies, to try and find the answer to the questions: "What is enough?" "When do we know when we have enough?": "How can we end poverty, in a simple way, without feeling guilty about it?"

I looked at balance sheets, studied Business in the Community reports here in UK, but it was apparent that in the past ten years, donations to charitable causes had been falling. There were few big companies giving more than one per cent of their profits to charity, but up until 2001, many had benefited from changes to markets and exchange rates. This was at a time when directors' incomes had grown from 15 x the earnings of their lowest paid worker to 30 or even 40 times their salary in the UK.

We helped them by investing our own money in their companies, hoping to make a quick buck, or through our pension schemes, investing for a golden retirement. So that we'd have sufficient when we stopped working, and didn't have to spend our abundance of time worrying about how to get enough money.

From 2001, recession began to bite in various economies, because of over-capacity, and the fact that we just couldn't afford to buy any more. This was because we'd used our credit cards to their maximum limit, and we couldn't afford to top up the mortgage or take out any more loans. At home, our bookcases, cupboards, wardrobes and lofts bulged with yet more and more goods, some of which we hadn't even bothered unwrapping. Our fridges groaned with food, along with our stomachs.

We tried to blame banks and building societies for being too generous in their lending: we tried to sue fast food companies for making us put their food in our mouth: we blamed the government for not improving public transport as we got in our cars for a short ride to the shops. The dot.com bubble burst, because we found that that without content, a mobile phone, TV, or website, is only that – a channel to communicate, not the actual meaningful communication.

The world stopped and paused, shaken to its core on 9/11/01, when two planes flew into the World Trade Centre in New York. So many people dead, so many families suffering and grieving, with just the last recorded message from their loved one on their mobiles or answer machines to console them. We quickly took action to find and root out the perpetrators, and began the witch-hunt for fanatics so angry with us that they had to destroy almost 3,000 people's lives.

In all the media coverage and assessments, only one voice in a thousand dared to ask the question: "What have we done that these people hate us so much?" Only one voice in 100,000 asked the question "How can we begin to heal the rift between the haves and have-nots?" The latter was the biggest question of all, and one I believe many of us have been thinking in our own way for the past 30 years.

This question has never been answered, and is still borne on the wind in the Gaza Strip, the streets of Baghdad, the farms in Zimbabwe, the favellas of Rio de Janeiro, and the slums in Cape Town. It licks at the heels of young girls as they walk five miles at 5am to get water for their family's use during the day. It hangs from the nipple of a starving Ethiopian mother crying as her baby nuzzles uselessly for milk, his belly growing more distended with malnutrition. It rattles from the throat of a young boy in the last throes of AIDs, starving to death because his throat is covered in thrush because his family can't afford the medication costs demanded by the big, multinational pharmaceutical companies.

The question is also in the mind of Iraqis looting their neighbours' homes because they have a TV and fridge, whilst their own small house is bare of electrical appliances. The US and UK stood by and said they'd send in police forces, but how to police, when they didn't know the customs, and don't speak the language? They too would be seen as invaders and infidels, making it the most dangerous post-war policing job in the world.

And so, we decided that everyone was wrong except for you and I, the individual. Yet you and I had acquiesced in the growth of greed and the belief that unless we kept buying, stealing or invading, we'd never have enough. As I contemplated these events, and realised how greed was gradually killing us all inside, I realised that I had to start by not criticising, but by setting an example. As Gandhi said: "Be the change you want to see in the world."

Thus, I began to think about all the things we have in common, and the things I'd experienced as a girl growing up in Norway, Ethiopia, South Africa, and the North, Midlands and South of England. This travelling was all down to my father – an aeronautical engineer – and his itchy feet! At the time I hated the constant moving, but I now realise that he did me an enormous favour.

I remembered the little things that we often talked about in coffee and tea shops, in restaurants, by the water coolers at work, in pubs and bars and over dinner with good friends. As I recalled the thousands of conversations over the years, the stories that we enjoyed, the experiences that we shared, I realised that there was one connection: culture.

What is culture?

Culture is what defines us, in a group as small as a family, or with our partners: in our places of worship and the celebrations and ceremonies we share there: our food and drink – and the recipes we hand down from generation to generation, in our sports clubs, whether local or international like Manchester United Football Club, in our music – in local clubs or concert halls where we gather in our thousands. It's in our dress and jewellery – both contemporary, and signifying our race – the wonderful netallahs in Ethiopia, with their multiplicity of borders; the saris from India.

It's the celebrations and ceremonies we have to welcome babies into the world, engagements, marriages, rites of passage and finally, death. Lastly, and most importantly, nature. Everywhere in the world you will find unique plants, insects, birds, and mammals. It is also, apart from sunshine, the main reason for leisure travel across the globe – because we want to find out about new customs and what interests you. Culture is incredibly attractive, and makes us much larger than we are as individuals, because it's about the shared connections between us.

As you told me about your culture, I saw the look of enjoyment or pain in your eyes, I heard the emotion in your voice, and the laughter from your stories: your body language changed and became more expansive, as you rolled out imaginary pastry, danced round the room showing how one drunk wedding guest behaved at your wedding, or swung an imaginary golf club hitting your first birdie!

It was something so ingrained in you, of which you were so proud, that I realised how it came to be that people would fight to the death to preserve their culture. I heard those words from a smiling West African lady who talked about the community's important customs, and said "I would die for my culture", just two weeks after I wrote this.

I also recognised that globalisation, whilst initially good for the countries where the jobs are being exported to (until their labour costs also got too high) is seen as a tidal wave by many, obliterating all that they'd grown up with, and much of which they hold dear. Globalisation depends on market forces, and ultimately, as Charles Handy so wisely puts it in his book "The Hungry Spirit", the market's master is the need for profit and not to do good. ①

So I decided to write this book, as a celebration of our world and our lives and to donate 50 per cent to charity.

Those donations would be permanent, because I believe the following:

Profit x $^1/2$ given away = Enough

This manifesto was emailed to a few friends to see their reaction. It touched them deeply, and some sent it to friends and relatives in different countries.

*****

Four months after it had been written, I was on a barge trip with some colleagues from work on a beautifully sunny day, sailing down the Thames. Marie, a very bright, feisty Mauritian, turned to me and remarked: "You know that Ravi Shankar's been sent your 'concept of enough'?"

"No, really!" my eyes widened with surprise "how did that happen?"

"Some friends of ours know him."

So, those friends had created a cord of connection between India's famous sitar player, me and one of my dream guides, George Harrison. Ravi Shankar had taught him to play the sitar.

Further information:

①Charles Handy, *The Hungry Spirit,* pages 13-24, Arrow Books, 1998.

30 From fragmented to connected

I'm sitting here in the study once more, going back frame by frame, to half-remembered words, shivering emotions and hazy images. I think it was Matthew who set me on the path, all those years ago. Matthew, the errant houseboy in Addis Ababa, whom dad had dismissed in 1963. He had created a cord of connection and identity for me, as that was when I decided that my parents weren't always right. I began to see with clearer eyes.

During the intervening years to April 2000, painful events and dreams wove together more cords to create the two things I really cared about: peace and water. Thank God I learned to listen to my dreams. As I got older, my life became more fragmented, rather than connected: I was to all intents and purpose a hu-bot – half human, half robot. But then came mum's death and, well, you know the rest. As for the events of Easter 2003 – the awakening – it signified that I could see the world and people differently. After that weekend, everything changed forever.

Following my visit to New York in February 2005, the signs and miracles slowed down for a while. They told me that I had to end this journey there, in St. Paul's Chapel by Ground Zero. So much in the world has changed since then, it is as though we've lost the grail of freedom forever. And yet, I've found people are still so good, so extraordinary and courageous. On my journey, I've been honoured with the help of many men and women, some of whom I've still never met today.

I can't put into words how grateful I am to Marta, Mary, Ghennet, Fanaye, Silva and Azeb for their help. Tragically, Marta died a year after I met her, from kidney disease, which is why the book is dedicated to her, as well as my parents. I am still in regular touch with the rest these days – school friendships restored!

In return, I tried to help answer some of the unanswered questions they had. For Silva and Jack, I contacted the Royal Collection, ① to find out when Emperor Haile Selassie had presented Avak's crown to Her Majesty Queen Elizabeth II: it was during his State Visit to the UK in 1958. I also travelled to Norway to find out for Mary how her grandfather had been killed, from a factual source, the journalist Einar Lunde. My odyssey had become intertwined with my classmates'.

For Azeb, I met Jack Valero, UK spokesman for Opus Dei, on 25 May 2006 at their offices in Orme Court, London to verify that the Latin handwriting on the reverse of the photo was that of St. Josemaria's.

He commented: "You have a great photo here. It was taken in Bond Street, London, in 1959. We used it in the past for his prayer card, but now a different photo is used. The handwriting is definitely his. Let me translate it for you. 'Sancta Maria, filias tuas adiuva' means 'Holy Mary, pray for your daughters. Rome 1970'."

*****

My personal odyssey was one of courage, miracles and a multitude of connections. I had learnt to let my soul go to the edge of the universe and stand there, where the sea touches the sky and thought has not yet formed: just sending out energy waves of peace, love and water. I found that it is a place of complete silence and total love, where illusion, time and space disappear. It is the closest state to the dream in 1997, where I found God's love behind the door. I prayed hard and learnt to patiently see the symbols and energy flows in breathing, conversations, and the way things moved. I listened for the messages and acted on my intuition, the wise compass of my tall ship. My friendships grew from a mere handful, to people all over the world – and shared laughter. So much laughter!

I encountered no enemies on the journey – this was very unusual, as generally, there are always enemies lurking round the corner in most heroic books and films. In the early stages, the biggest enemy turned out to be my ego.

There are people, places and companies mentioned in the book which you may ask 'why haven't you explained more?' I will, I promise, in volume II of the odyssey.

After all, the least I can do for you is reunite the rest of the classmates and recreate the old school photo with us as we are today! I will also explain more of the miraculous connections of my journey to world events which occurred in 2005. Some joyful, some tragic, just as life is.

****

Today, we are standing at a new dawn, the divisions and fears between families, generations, tribes, societies, nations and religions so deep, that we just know the old ways of fear and control will no longer work, will not solve our overwhelming problems, nor sustain our planet.

In the retelling of their lives for this book, many shared their deep pain with me. It was a privilege to listen to their stories and I realised that the suffering their parents and grandparents had endured, stayed with their descendants – places of undeniable pain and horror. People in positions of power: politicians, the military, academics, authors and even some religious leaders and their allies, often do everything possible to eradicate these memories, particularly those concerning genocide. History books are rewritten, ancient places of worship and tombstones obliterated, cultural artefacts plundered or destroyed.

Such actions are folly. Whilst their relatives continue to draw breath, these atrocities are told, and retold, at important family and cultural occasions. When will we ever truly learn to acknowledge and learn from such grave injustices? We have taken the first steps with the Holocaust, but there are other genocides still waiting to be acknowledged by the world, including the Armenian one.

The only way forward in our interconnected world, where many now fear to talk to strangers, is to follow the path of Peace. To achieve this, I think we urgently need to balance the feminine nature of our soul, with the masculine of our ego. The latter has run riot for many centuries, and all our wealth and technology have made it worse and greedier. I would like to see a world where women in every country and community play a much more active role in religion, politics and business – and where men feel that they, too, can show their caring sides and not be ridiculed. The soul's way is more peaceful and co-operative, and that's what the world needs right now, if our grandchildren are to inherit a planet that can sustain their grandchildren into the future which God granted us, when he created the most beautiful place in the universe: Earth.

The power of love and compassion is much greater and quieter than the power of fear. It teaches us remarkable focus and patience, endurance, solitude, faith, and hope. You don't need books or guides to begin your journey – you just need to really listen and open up to your heart, the wisest guide you will ever have in your life. Find somewhere to be still on a daily basis, and listen to its gentle call to freedom and a magnificent life.

Trust, set sail on your odyssey and see how magical it will be! Discover how your illusions will disintegrate, and the scars inside you heal forever. In the doing of this, you will come to appreciate for yourself that Life is sacred and We are each holy.

In the words of Jesus: "Peace I leave with you: my peace I give to you. I do not give to you as the world gives. Do not let your hearts be troubled, and do not let them be afraid." (John 14:27).

Further information:

① The Royal Collection includes gifts given to Her Majesty and previous monarchs over the past 500 years and is on display at the royal palaces and residences, all of which are open to the public.

Following the cataclysmic war between Israel and Hezbollah in the summer of 2006, peace between Israel and Palestine appears almost unimaginable. And so many hundreds of innocent civilians were killed. My dream of a Garden of Peace in Jerusalem is hopelessly naive in the circumstances. As I followed spontaneous connections in 2005 and 2006, one name kept being mentioned: Christian Aid. Thus, we are supporting their Middle East crisis appeal. 10% of the profits from this book will go to help reconstruction and rebuilding hope in Lebanon, Palestine – especially Gaza – and Israel.

http://www.christian-aid.org.uk/middle_east/index.htm

April 2009

The scars had healed. The small Abyssian ass, its tail flicking away flies, raised its head to look curiously at me, a visitor, before continuing to munch on the green grass which now grew in Mamali's kebelleh in Wolle Dagna. I could see the ridges from the jerry cans no longer pitted its' back – the thin ribs, too, had disappeared. In the field alongside, vegetables and herbs had been planted, which could be bartered in the local market.

Children laughed and shouted as they used a sawn-off jerry can to throw water at each other in the heat. There was now enough water for all the kebelleh's needs, and it was a weekly treat to have a water fight for half an hour or so in the afternoon heat. This had been the gift that you and I had brought to the community, and hundreds of others in Ethiopia.

In March 2009, serious peace talks were still continuing between Israel and Palestine. This time, America hadn't set the agenda, it had been courageous, peaceful politicians, business and religious leaders, and civilians. The military and media had finally learnt to be patient. One of the dialogue methods being used was South Africa's Truth & Reconciliation model, so that both sides began to understand the enormous pain and suffering each had caused the other. We Westerners had learnt to listen quietly to the pain of the Palestinians first, and to focus on establishing equality between us, rather than always trying to move on to a solution which suited our egos, as soon as possible. It was in this quiet acknowledgement, that great sorrow and early signs of respect could finally be set free.

Every Middle East country was involved, and Palestine's allies - especially the oil-rich nations - had come to the conclusion that the only way for sustainable peace in the region was to invest in Palestine's future. Women and other pragmatists were also involved in the process: brave individuals who had the necessary stamina and self-discipline during the often chaotic steps towards a peaceful future. The Palestinian diaspora were beginning to have genuine hopes of a return to, and pride in, their homeland.

Our taxes would be used to fund the building of new homes, infrastructure, educational facilities, hospitals and companies in the new state – rather than to buy arms. Israelis, too, were willing to give a percentage of their taxes, called the 'Peace Tax', to help Palestine over the next 60 years, in compensation for the land seized in the formation of the state of Israel.

At last, Palestinians could hold their heads up high, and Israelis could live without the fear of suicide bombers. During the dialogue, which was taking place amongst all levels of society, trained peace negotiators had helped people realise that we all wanted the same thing: peaceful families and communities, jobs we enjoy with enough income to provide a secure future for our children, and pride in our identity.

The Garden of Peace I'd dreamt of, and asked God for in 1995, would one day become gardens – domestic gardens, where Israelis and Palestinians slowly and tentatively began to gather, share stories and meals and begin to build the social friendships and trust which, they acknowledged, was essential for both countries. And I continue to pray that one day Jerusalem will become the world's city of peace: a beacon for all mankind.

Could you help me find Kathy Miller, Sumitra Goyal and Celina Fernandes?

Now this book is complete, I am already writing volume II, with the remaining stories of my classmates and – most importantly – recreating the old school photo with us as we are today!

Largely through tadias.com in the United States, I've found 24 out of the 38 ladies, but I'm still searching for Kathy or Kay Miller (as she was known to some classmates); Sumitra Goyal and Celina Fernandes. I understand that Celina did return to Goa, but I'm not sure where Sumitra or Kathy are now.

In the old school photo, Kathy is in the front row, second right – beside me - wearing glasses and a check cardigan. Celina is second left in the second row, and Sumitra fourth left, with the thick plait and white blouse.

Funds from volume II will be helping peace-making groups around the world. In my travels since April 2005, I've discovered just how poorly-funded these organisations are. I would like your help to correct that, and you will be discovering some more stories about amazing and courageous people in the next book, not just my classmates.

Additional images and stories can be found on: www.anethiopianodyssey.com. Please leave a message on the message board to let others know how you enjoyed the book, or with details of Kathy's, Sumitra's and Celina's whereabouts. The site will grow and develop, as I hope and pray love and compassion for others, especially the poor, will also manifest around the world. I will always give half of the royalties from my books to help those who so richly deserve it.

Every blessing.

Ornelle

A random spark

Change starts with a thought:
A random spark
In the universe.

Then amidst the silence
Comes an explosion
And the cosmos
Is transformed
Forever.

The world sighs
And gathers itself
In readiness
For the next thought.

Index

My former classmates' names are in bold

A

L

M

N

S

T

U

V

W

Y

Yekatit 12 Hospital, Addis Ababa   83-85
Salome Yilma   257, 263. *3rd row, 1st left*

Z

Meles Zenawi   123, 216
Seifu Zewdu   94
Zimbabwe   81, 200

By the age of nine, Annette Allen had been to five different schools, trailing behind her father, an itinerant aeronautical engineer. In Ethiopia, she sat beside princesses at school whilst witnessing heart-breaking poverty; falling in love with the complex people and magnificent scenery. After apartheid South Africa, she returned to middle class life in Britain.

But Annette was not your normal type of girl. For as long as she could remember, vivid dreams predicting the future had disturbed her nights. Juggling motherhood with a successful corporate career, things began to disintegrate from 1996. Something told her that she needed to leave the stress behind, and use these visions as the catalyst to discover her destiny.

The answer appeared in another dream in April 2000, transporting her back to the heat and drought of Ethiopia, glimpsing she was there to help provide water for the very poor. It almost spelt out that she must go back – to be reunited with her old classmates.

Little did she know that the 25,000 mile quest would reveal how interconnected everything was. Travelling reawakened the childlike innocence within her. Compassionate people around the world helped, because they also wanted her dream to come true. Half of the royalties are going to charity – the majority to fund permanent clean water in Ethiopia.

"Thank you for sharing your dream with me. I read about it with great interest and wish you well with 'An Ethiopian Odyssey'."
Desmond Tutu, Anglican Archbishop Emeritus of Cape Town

"I am happy to know that you were in Nazareth School with my daughter, Hiruth. I am sure your book will be a success."
President Girma Wolde-Giorgis, Ethiopia

" I very much admire your determination and commitment to the cause of poverty reduction. I hope that others are inspired by reading about your experiences."
Gordon Brown, British Prime Minister

Please visit:
www.anethiopianodyssey.com

CPSIA information can be obtained
at www.ICGtesting.com
Printed in the USA
FSHW020811131220
76856FS